Churchill's
Secret Invasion

This book is dedicated to

CORPORAL BERNARD GREHAN
17 Platoon, "D" Company,
1st Battalion, Royal Scots Fusiliers

Churchill's Secret Invasion

Britain's First Large-scale Combined Operations Offensive 1942

John Grehan

Pen & Sword
MILITARY

First published in Great Britain in 2013 by
Pen & Sword Military
an imprint of
Pen & Sword Books Ltd
47 Church Street
Barnsley
South Yorkshire
S70 2AS

ISBN 978 1 78159 382 0

Typeset in Ehrhardt by
Mac Style, Driffield, East Yorkshire
Printed and bound in the UK by CPI Group (UK) Ltd, Croydon,
CRO 4YY

Pen & Sword Books Ltd incorporates the Imprints of Pen & Sword
Aviation, Pen & Sword Maritime, Pen & Sword Military, Wharncliffe
Local History, Pen and Sword Select, Pen and Sword Military
Classics, Leo Cooper, The Praetorian Press, Remember When,
Seaforth Publishing and Frontline Publishing.

For a complete list of Pen & Sword titles please contact
PEN & SWORD BOOKS LIMITED
47 Church Street, Barnsley, South Yorkshire, S70 2AS, England
E-mail: enquiries@pen-and-sword.co.uk
Website: www.pen-and-sword.co.uk

Contents

List of Illustrations

1. Churchill (left) watching a landing craft and Valentine tank being released into Loch Fyne during his visit in the summer of 1941. (Imperial War Museum; H11177.)
2. HMS *Ramillies*, flagship of Force F, off Madagascar. (Imperial War Museum; A8858.)
3. The Special Operations Executive vessel M/V *Lindi*. (Imperial War Museum Department of Documents, the Papers of H. Legg.)
4. The crew of the *Lindi* constructing the torch which would guide the assault convoy into Courrier Bay. (Imperial War Museum Department of Documents, the Papers of H. Legg.)
5. Courrier Bay as seen from Windsor Castle, looking towards Basse Point. No.7 Battery is located on the high ground on the right of the photograph. (Author.)
6. The great natural rock monolith of Windsor Castle as viewed in 1942. (Courtesy of A. Lowe.)
7. The infantry post on the summit of Windsor Castle. (Author.)
8. One of the 138mm gun emplacements of No.7 Battery at Courrier Bay. (Author.)
9. Part of the barracks complex at the rear of No.7 Battery at Courrier Bay. (Author.)
10. One of the machine-gun posts above Red Beach that was overrun by No.5 Commando. (Author.)
11. The remains of a Potez 63–11 bomber being inspected by British Officers in the hanger at Arrachart airfield. (Imperial War Museum; A8997.)
12. The French Air Force hanger now sits abandoned at the end of the modern runway at Arrachart airport. (Author.)
13. A view of Antsirane, taken in 1942, looking towards Port Nièvre. (Courtesy of A. Lowe.)
14. A British despatch rider in Antsirane opposite the Malagasy infantry barracks. The motor-bicycle is a Harley Davidson. (Courtesy of A. Lowe.)
15. A damaged gun emplacement of No.6 Coastal Defence Battery. (Author.)
16. The entrance to the dry dock at Port Nièvre. (Author.)
17. The pillboxes, adjacent to the main Antsirane road, which formed the centre of the French defences. (Imperial War Museum; A8888.)
18. The same pillboxes today. (Author.)
19. The central gun emplacement of Fort Caimans as seen today. (Author.)
20. Looking southwards from Fort Caimans, in the direction from which the British attacks were delivered on 5 and 6 May. (Author.)

List of Maps and Plan

Acknowledgements

The assistance and advice provided so unselfishly by Lieutenant-Colonel Nick Weekes, particularly with regards to sources in The National Archive, has been so significant that the completion of this book is nothing less than a tribute to his endeavours. My thanks go also to the following people for the help which they have given me throughout five years of research:

Peter Crocker and David Bownes of the Royal Welch Fusiliers Museum at Caernarvon. Catherine Roundsfell of the Fleet Air Arm Museum in Yeovilton. L. Jooste, Secretary for Defence in Pretoria, South Africa. Yvonne Oliver of the Photograph Archive at the Imperial War Museum, and Jim Jepson of the Combined Operations Association.

To Ernest Butterfield, Arthur Lowe, Jim Howell, and my father Bernard Grehan, for sharing with me their recollections of Madagascar. Miriam Palmer for her translation of Annet's memoirs. Israel Togoh for his persistence in gaining access to the archives at the Château de Vincennes when others had failed and Stéphane Allion of the *Etat-Major, Service Historique de l'Armée de Terre* for his exceptional assistance when everyone else was on holiday!

My gratitude also goes to Sally Spears, Librarian at Magdalene College, Oxford University, for sacrificing her weekend to allow me to inspect the Lush memoir, and to Andrew Gunstone and Ray Cusick for the many hours spent reading my manuscript. Thanks especially to Martin Mace for sharing the dream.

Finally, I must state that my trip to Madagascar would have been far less rewarding in every respect without the knowledge of Hilary Bradt and the assistance of the British Consular Correspondent in Diego Suarez, Bruno Ndriamahafahana, and Saula Floris of the Université du Nord Madagascar – thanks for the memories.

Antsirane

They sailed from home across the sea
To gain a smashing victory
Past Freetown and its lovely bay
Past Durban and its life so gay.
At last to Madagascar's shore
The lads arrive hard times before.

On the sixth of May at break of day
The Seaforth's land in sheltered bay,
They rest awhile then march ahead
No-one could guess where that road led.

Up hill, down dale, twenty weary miles,
Yet march they did with gallant smiles,
From heaven's height that blazing sun
Shone down upon them, everyone.
Each Highlander out here a stranger
March to face their foe and danger.
O'er eighteen miles with scare a stop
The lads trudge on but never drop.
A few hours rest and on they go
To action, danger, against their foe.

At 8 p.m. that lovely day, they met their foe at bay
Machine guns spat, the shells came o'er,
They halted there seconds, no more.
Then Caber Fiedh rang through the air
And on they charge with bayonets bare,
Some fell, never to rise again,
The rest drive on, avenging men,
So soon it's over, the foe have fled
The ground is littered with the dead.
Seaforth and French lay peaceful there
Never again to breathe earth's air.

Danny Cunningham,
6th Battalion Seaforth Highlanders, 1942

Introduction

"A Turning Point in the War"

The combined operation by Allied forces to take and hold Madagascar's principal naval base in 1942 is considered to have been Britain's first successful major amphibious operation of its kind since General Wolfe captured Quebec almost 200 years earlier. Unlike previous hit-and-run raids against enemy-held coasts, Operation *Ironclad* was a "land-and-stay" expedition which led to full military and political control of an entire country.

Yet *Ironclad*, and the series of combined operations to seize control of the rest of Madagascar that followed, has been largely neglected by mainstream historians. Martin Gilbert, for instance, one of the most respected of the Second World War historians, devoted just one paragraph to the campaign in his huge 800-page *History of The Second World War*. Similarly, John Keegan wrote over 600 pages in his book *The Second World War* but found room for just half a sentence on Madagascar. These men are not alone. Many other distinguished historians have failed to register the significance of this operation.

Why the capture of this vast island should be so widely ignored defies explanation. It cannot be due to the length of the campaign. The attack upon Dieppe in the summer of 1942, Britain's first combined operation after *Ironclad*, boasts a catalogue of books, articles and papers devoted to the subject. Yet this was a single-tide, six-hour, raid upon a small French port. The Madagascar campaign lasted six months and involved the occupation of a country greater in size than the whole of continental France.

Nor can it be that the campaign lacked significance either tactically or strategically. As Britain's first large-scale amphibious landing of the war it was the forerunner of the great amphibious assaults upon North Africa, Italy and, of course, Normandy in 1944. Many new tactics, ships and formations were tried for the first time at Madagascar and many lessons were learnt.

Strategically, at a time when British ships could not pass through the Mediterranean, it was even more important. A single Japanese submarine flotilla operating in the waters around Madagascar in the spring and early summer of 1942 damaged one British battleship and sunk twenty-five merchant ships in little more than two months. Allied shipping to Egypt and India had to be re-routed and convoys re-structured. If the Japanese had been able to establish a base in Madagascar, the accumulation of men and material that preceded the El Alamein and Burma offensives would have been seriously delayed with potentially devastating results.

Immediately after the fall of Singapore, the Special Operations Executive's Headquarters considered Madagascar to be "an imminent menace to the Allies".

Churchill believed that if the Japanese established themselves in Madagascar it would be "disastrous", and General de Gaulle saw Madagascar as being "of such high importance" that its occupation by the Japanese would be "so great a disaster to our cause". Admiral Fricke of the German Navy's High Command went even further by stating that "the focal point of the entire war lies today in the western Indian Ocean, as the crushing of the British position in the Near East and the establishment of direct contact [there] with Japan will decide the war".

The British Admiralty shared this view. In the Introduction to Volume III of the official *Naval Staff History, Second World War,* the author states that: "To prevent Germany and Japan from joining hands in Madagascar was recognised as one of the main defensive tasks of the Allies".

The official histories published by the Ministry of Information and HMSO, during and shortly after the war, provide accounts of the Madagascar campaign which are as detailed as other campaigns of similar importance. Churchill, as the man who ordered Operation *Ironclad* and understood its significance more than any other, devoted a complete chapter of his *History of the Second World War* to the actions in Madagascar. But after these early years, the British occupation of Madagascar faded from the pages of the history books so that, by 1989, H.P. Wilmot could publish *The Great Crusade,* which he claims is a new "complete" history of the Second World War, yet makes no mention of the event at all!

Martin Thomas, in an article in *The Historical Journal*, 34, 4 of 1966, states that such omissions are "easily" explained because once Madagascar was garrisoned by Allied troops its strategic importance was diminished. Whilst this is certainly true, the island was not taken by Britain because it offered her a strategic advantage. As Edward Harrison explained in his article "British Subversion in French East Africa, 1941–42", it was not the Allied occupation of Madagascar that was significant; it was its denial to the Japanese which, in his own words, was "to prove a turning-point in the war".

Historians, quite rightly, have to assess and balance events and a consensus appears to have emerged in which the invasion of Madagascar is regarded as lacking in significance relative to other events of that period. That is not how it was seen in 1942. At the time of the British landings in the north of Madagascar the subject was headline news for many days both in the UK and abroad, and it caused a considerable international outcry. Reports from or about Madagascar were featured in thirty editions of the London *Times* throughout 1942 and a secret War Office report of October 1942 (*Notes from Theatres of War* No.9) stated that: "The possession of Madagascar was of paramount importance". According to the report, the potential threat to Allied shipping posed by enemy bases in Madagascar was so great that: "To have remained inactive under such a threat would have been suicidal".

Britain did not remain inactive. Naval reinforcements were called in from the USA and an elaborate cover-plan was put in motion. Other operations were re-prioritized and a huge convoy accompanied by a battleship, cruisers, aircraft carriers, destroyers and minesweepers, steamed over 9,000 miles to undertake the capture of the fourth-largest island in the world. Subsequent operations in Madagascar also included forces from South Africa, Kenya, Uganda, Tanganyika and Rhodesia. Yet, remarkably, the Allied occupation of Madagascar has become little more than a footnote in the history of the Second World War.

In many respects Madagascar has always been, and remains, a remote and forgotten country. Yet for a brief period in 1942, and for the only time in its history, Madagascar held centre stage in world affairs. After its capture Madagascar slipped from the headlines but the island continued, according to official documents in the Imperial War Museum in London, to make a "serious economic contribution" to the Allied war effort. In particular, Madagascar was a major source of high quality graphite of which, because of its use in the munitions industry, there was an acute world shortage.

Large quantities of fine graphite were also used to build the chain-reacting piles at the Los Alamos atomic weapons programme and within forty-eight hours of the capture of the island's capital, and while the opposing forces were still fighting, arrangements were made to ship 8,000 tons of graphite from Madagascar to the USA and the UK.

Little can the Japanese have realized that their failure to capture Madagascar before the Allies could intervene in 1942 would lead to the cataclysmic events at Hiroshima and Nagasaki in 1945 which brought the Second World War to such a violent and dramatic conclusion.

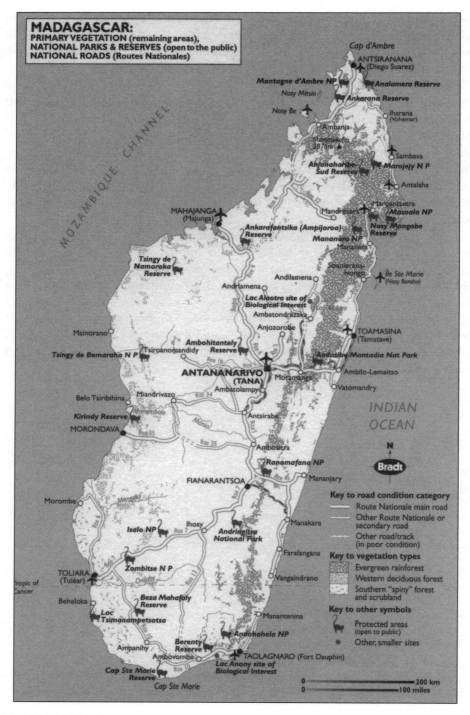

MAP 1: The island of Madagascar with the main towns shown. (Reproduced with the kind permission of Hilary Bradt and the Bradt Travel Guides; www.bradtguides.com)

Chapter 1

"Age-Long Enemies"

It was summer in Scotland and it was raining. The men of the 29th Independent Brigade Group lined both sides of the avenue at No.1 Combined Operations training centre in Inveraray to watch Winston Churchill as he walked through the relentless downpour. Earlier in the day it had been the Prime Minister who had been the spectator when he observed the 29th Brigade take part in an exercise along the nearby coast.

For the previous two months the 29th Brigade had been embarking into, and disembarking from, assault landing craft at sea and had been practising landings upon a hostile shore. More amphibious training was to follow Churchill's visit until this force, along with the Royal Marine Division and the Army Commandos, would be amongst the most highly trained units of their kind in the British Army.

As autumn passed into winter the brigade practised moving over rough country in full fighting order and learnt to operate, both day and night, with tanks and Bren gun carriers. On 12 March 1942, the 29th Brigade Group embarked at Gourock for yet another exercise. It was known that this was a rehearsal for an actual operation, with the 29th Brigade acting as the "enemy" in an amphibious raid by the Royal Marines. But the exercise was suddenly cancelled, the troops were returned to barracks and the entire brigade's mail was held. Then, nine days later, the 29th Brigade moved to Greenock. The men were told that it was just a continuation of their training, but this time it was real. Though their destination would remain a closely guarded secret for many weeks, they were about to attempt the capture of the vast French colony of Madagascar.[1]

Before the outbreak of the Second World War, France had been considered to be one of the mightiest military and colonial powers on earth. But in just six remarkable weeks during the late spring and early summer of 1940, Hitler's armies overran northern France and all but destroyed the French air and ground forces. Britain, as France's principal ally, had sent an Expeditionary Force to assist the French, but the speed of the German advance overwhelmed the Allies. The British Expeditionary Force (BEF) found itself cut off from the French armies in the centre of the country and all but surrounded by the German divisions. Only a desperate retreat to the French coast at Dunkirk saved the British army from complete encirclement. The BEF was rescued from the beaches of Dunkirk and returned to England, but almost all of its weapons and equipment were lost or destroyed. Though the intention was that the British troops would eventually be re-organized and re-equipped before being sent back into France, this did not happen and many Frenchmen felt that, after being dragged by Britain into a war they did not want, they were now being callously abandoned.[2]

Though France was on her knees, her colonies and her fleet – the fourth-largest in the world – remained beyond Germany's grasp. So it was proposed that in order to continue the war against Germany the French Government should evacuate the country and re-form in one of the colonies. The remnants of the army would follow and, combined with the colonial forces and the navy, France would continue the fight against the Germans.

All of the most senior French colonial officials, including Armand Annet in Dahomey (present-day Benin) and Marcel de Coppet, the Governor-General of Madagascar, offered their support for such a measure.[3] But, unlike the authorities in Holland and Norway which had established governments in exile in Britain, Marshal Pétain and his Cabinet refused to abandon France in her hour of need.[4] Though General de Gaulle, the French Under-Secretary of State for War, slipped out of France and escaped to England, most of the leading politicians stayed to share the sufferings and humiliation of their countrymen.

Pétain feared that if France fought until she was completely beaten he would have nothing left to bargain with and Hitler would be free to impose the harshest of surrender terms. The Marshal also believed that with France out of the war Britain would choose to make peace with Germany in a deal which would be disadvantageous to France. It was widely believed in France that Britain, having committed only ten divisions to the Battle of France compared to France's sixty divisions, never intended to take an equal share in the fighting. The withdrawal of the BEF from Dunkirk after losing just 68,000 men against France's 1,870,000 only served to confirm these beliefs.[5] So, with the approval of most Frenchmen, Pétain decided to capitulate immediately, abandon the alliance with Britain, and engage in close collaboration with the Germans.

In the subsequent Armistice negotiations, Hitler therefore allowed the French to retain control of a small part of their country and they established their seat of government at the provincial spa town of Vichy, from which place the regime became known. Meanwhile in Britain, de Gaulle, viewed by Vichy as a British puppet, set up the Free French (later called the Fighting French) movement. De Gaulle, however, was considered by the Vichy authorities to be a deserter (and, of course, a threat to their legitimacy) and was tried as such in his absence. He was found guilty and sentenced to death.[6]

Now that France was no longer in the war, the fate of her overseas empire, second only in size and importance to that of Britain, became the focus of much attention. If the resources and manpower of the French Empire could be employed on behalf of the Allies, and those territories denied to the Axis Powers, the benefits would be immense. It therefore became the British Government's "goal", as the historian Hytier put it, to keep as much of the French navy and as many parts of the French Empire as possible in the war, or, at least, out of enemy hands.[7] Fully aware of the importance of France's imperial possessions, her defence minister, General Weygand, ordered (on 25 June 1940) all the commanders throughout the Empire to observe the Armistice, the very first article of which stated that hostilities would cease "in France, in French possessions, colonies, protectorates and mandated territories".[8]

Britain's first and most immediate concern following Pétain's surrender was with the French fleet. If the French warships were handed over to Hitler, the combined French and German navies would out-gun the British Home Fleet, exposing Britain to the risk of a sea-borne invasion. Consequently, in the first week of July 1940, Operation *Catapult*, which called for the seizure or disablement of the French fleet, was undertaken. French ships (including merchant ships) which had sought sanctuary in British harbours were occupied by British troops and their crews placed in holding camps. This was achieved with little loss of life, but more serious action was to follow. A large French squadron stationed in North Africa was blockaded in the harbour of Mers-el-Kébir by a powerful British naval force. The French squadron was told that if it did not surrender its ships to the Royal Navy it would be bombarded. The French refused to comply and, despite offering assurances that they would scuttle their ships rather than allow them to be taken by the Germans, the British battleships opened fire. Many of the French ships were sunk or disabled and almost 1,300 French sailors were killed. It was France's most costly naval engagement of the war. Other French warships were attacked at Dakar and France's most modern battleship, *Richelieu*, was damaged. Fortunately at Alexandria, where both French and British squadrons were stationed, an agreement was reached and no blood was shed, though in achieving this compromise both admirals disobeyed their respective governments.[9]

In response to Operation *Catapult*, French aircraft bombed Gibraltar, and the Vichy authorities, still angry at being abandoned by Churchill during the Battle of France, broke off diplomatic relations with Britain. There was a real danger that the two former allies would soon be at war, particularly as Britain had already alienated the French by promoting a propaganda campaign in French North Africa, which included dropping leaflets in Morocco, urging the colonies to declare their independence from Vichy.[10]

In mainland France it was not leaflets but bombs which were being dropped by the RAF. Though the raids were limited and the objectives had been mostly German military targets or industrial sites, French property and French people had been hit.[11] The result was that many of the French colonies, the majority of which had at first been against collaboration with the Germans, became supporters of the Vichy regime and, as Churchill was soon to discover, violently anti-British.

Despite being well aware of the anger and the sense of betrayal generated by Operation *Catapult*, Churchill hoped that the French colonies would not resist the occupation of their territories by the Allies. This was first put to the test in September 1940 at Dakar in the French West African state of Senegal. De Gaulle, who had only a small following at that time, led the expedition with 2,400 Free French, supported by 4,270 British troops and 16 warships. De Gaulle hoped to gain credibility amongst his countrymen by basing himself on French soil and establishing "the capital of the Empire in arms" in West Africa.[12]

Churchill was also interested in Dakar being controlled by the Allies. It was a major commercial port and it possessed a well-defended naval base, a large dry dock, an arsenal, a destroyer basin and an international airfield. Dakar was the nearest point in Africa to South America and if handed over to the Germans its use by them as a naval and air base could imperil Britain's vital Atlantic convoys and her communications with South Africa.[13]

The force sailed to Dakar and demanded that the Free French should be allowed to take over the town. The Governor-General refused, and the fighting began. An attempted landing by the Free French was repulsed and two British battleships, *Resolution* and *Barham*, were damaged, the former being torpedoed by a French submarine.[14] The attack upon Dakar was an embarrassing failure for Churchill and de Gaulle, and it further alienated the French colonialists. Only a relaxation of the blockade which the Royal Navy had imposed upon French ports and a promise by Britain not to attack, or let de Gaulle attack, any other French colonies, eased the tension between the two countries.[15]

However, the next conflict between Britain and Vichy occurred just a few months later. In May 1941, the French allowed the *Luftwaffe* to take over airfields in Syria from where German aircraft were used to assist a revolt against British interests in Iraq. Nor was this just passive assistance, as the French serviced the German aircraft and sent weapons and military stores to the rebels.[16]

Britain had been planning to seize Syria – to prevent a move by the Germans through Turkey to capture Egypt and the oilfields of the Persian Gulf – long before the Germans had requested access to the country, and the actions of the *Luftwaffe* provided the perfect pretext for an invasion of the French Mandatory territory.[17] That the Vichy forces in Syria would resist the Allies was clear from the statements of the French High Commissioner, Henri Dentz. To him the Gaullists were "debtors, climbers, depraved and embittered men" and the British were "the age-long enemies who think only of having, when peace comes, France without an army, without a navy, without colonies and without traditions".[18]

Syria was the main French military base in the Middle East. Before the fall of France, the "Army of the Levant" numbered 120,000 men and, in 1941, there were still some 32,000 French and colonial troops under arms with more than 90 tanks, 60 aircraft and 9 batteries of artillery.[19] Consequently a large British and Free French force of all arms was assembled for the invasion of Syria. This was open warfare in all but name.

The result was five weeks of intense fighting before the Vichy forces surrendered. There were more than 10,000 casualties, most of whom were French, and a large amount of Vichy equipment, including three warships, was destroyed.[20] The Vichy regime in Syria was displaced and, after bitter wrangling between the Allies, de Gaulle took over control of the country, though very few of the defeated colonial troops chose to join the Free French.

Understandably, it was Britain, rather than Germany, that was increasingly seen to be the enemy of France. Indeed, many in Vichy continued to believe that it would be in France's interest for Britain to lose the war. Amongst these individuals was Admiral Darlan, who became head of the French Government under Pétain in February 1941. Darlan considered that in any future peace settlement Hitler would only demand Alsace-Lorraine, which the Germans had already occupied, whereas Britain, Darlan suspected, would insist on France handing over control of Dakar and Madagascar.[21]

In July of 1941, the Vichy Government then collaborated with the Japanese in French Indo-China, the consequences of which were calamitous for Britain's armed forces in the Far East. Vichy signed an agreement with Tokyo which allowed the Japanese to establish air and sea bases around Saigon. From these bases the Japanese aircraft could strike directly at Singapore, completely outflanking the fortifications on the Malay Peninsula which formed the basis of Britain's defence of the entire region. The Vichy authorities readily agreed to the take-over of Indo-China because they were in no position to resist if the Japanese were to use force. But publicly they stated that they allowed the Japanese into the colony to prevent it being occupied by Britain and the Free French.[22]

Such, then, was the state of Anglo-French relations when, on Sunday 7 December 1941, Japanese aircraft attacked the US Pacific fleet at Pearl Harbor. The sudden entry of Japan into the war placed another French colony directly in the line of operations – the island of Madagascar, which is situated in the western Indian Ocean, approximately 250 miles off the south-eastern coast of Africa. Madagascar sits astride the shipping lanes that travel round the Cape of Good Hope to the East and was, in the days before mass air transportation, of immense strategic importance. Already, even at this early stage of the war, hundreds of supply ships and more than 250,000 service personnel had travelled these routes. Oil from Iran and Iraq, provisions to Russia via the Persian Gulf, troops and equipment for the defence of Egypt, aid to Australia and New Zealand – all crossed the Indian Ocean.[23]

The anchorage in Diego Suarez Bay, in the north of Madagascar, is one of the finest in the world, being larger than Scapa Flow and considered capable of holding the combined fleets of all the maritime powers. It had ten miles of quays and docks, and the harbour entrance was sheltered behind a great jetty. Money had been spent lavishly over a period of more than ten years on the building of a naval base and it had become the best-equipped French station outside metropolitan France. A dry dock, completed in 1936, could hold a 28,000-ton battleship and its arsenal was capable of repairing the largest of guns.[24] If the Japanese navy was able to establish a strong force at Diego Suarez it would, by Churchill's own admission, "paralyse" Britain's communications with its eastern empire. Such a prospect, the Prime Minister told President Roosevelt, was one of Britain's "greatest dangers".[25]

Just six days before the attack upon Pearl Harbor the Chiefs of Staff had advised the British Cabinet that, in the event of a war with Japan, the Axis Powers were likely to demand access to the island from the Vichy Government, or, if necessary, take it by force.[26] In fact German long-range U-boats, operating out of south-western French ports, had already rounded the Cape and had attacked Allied shipping in the southern Indian Ocean. This had prompted Churchill to toy with the idea of approaching Vichy with a joint Anglo–American request for Madagascar's ports to be placed under British control.[27]

The Chiefs of Staff had considered a military operation to seize the naval base of Antsirane at Diego Suarez as early as December 1940. Whilst acknowledging the importance of Madagascar, their recommendation at that time was that no action should be taken until there was evidence the island was being used by enemy raiders, even though Diego Suarez had been used by Japanese warships during the First World War.[28] However, on 27 November 1941, the Chiefs of Staff asked the Joint Planning Staff (JPS) to re-examine the original 1940 report and to suggest "the quickest and the best method of carrying it out".[29]

The Joint Planners responded by suggesting to the Chiefs of Staff three possible courses of action. The first was for a cruiser, supported by carrier-borne aircraft and a naval bombardment, to storm the entrance to Diego Suarez Bay and land a party of Marines directly upon the quay at Antsirane. The harbour entrance, however, was known to be defended by heavy artillery and the JPS felt that such an assault would only succeed if complete surprise was achieved.

The second course of action proposed by the Joint Planners was again for a warship to force the entrance to the harbour under an air and naval bombardment, but combined with a landing by assault forces to capture the shore batteries.

The third option, and the one which was eventually adopted, was for a powerful infantry force to land on the coast outside the harbour and seize the naval base from the landward side. As with the other two proposals, considerable naval and air support would be required.[30] (There was also an extraordinary proposal put forward in which a Q-ship would enter Diego Suarez harbour late one evening disguised as a Spanish or Portuguese vessel. Early the next morning two more ships, both packed with commandos, would arrive a few miles off shore flying the French flag. These ships would pretend to be under attack from the British and be steaming for the safety of Diego Suarez, making smoke and flying distress signals. Once these vessels were inside the harbour, the Q-ship would throw off its disguise and, together, the three ships would attack the port. The main British assault force, lying over the horizon, would then make its move. Unsurprisingly, the proposal was rejected!)[31]

Further meetings of the Joint Planners and the Chiefs of Staff took place over the next three weeks to finalize the details of which military personnel and naval vessels could be made available for the assault upon Diego Suarez. The operation, which was given the code-name "*Bonus*", would require the deployment of two infantry brigade groups, with accompanying artillery, and a large naval force, including one battleship and two aircraft carriers. To transport the troops, shipping would have to be diverted from other planned expeditions.[32]

Having decided on giving Madagascar priority over other pending operations, on 18 December 1941 the Chief of Staff recommended that the Force Commanders should be appointed and preparations put in hand "at once".[33] The next day, the Chiefs of Staff produced the following statement: "If the Japanese were to get the use of a naval base in Madagascar it would make it very difficult for us to continue convoys to the Middle East and India; therefore it is advisable to make all preparations to carry out operation 'Bonus' as soon as possible."[34]

On 10 December 1941, just three days after Pearl Harbor, General de Gaulle had also suggested to General Alan Brooke, Chief of the Imperial General Staff, that Free French forces should take Madagascar on behalf of the Allies. Claiming that the support for Vichy by the authorities in Madagascar was "opposed to the wishes of the population", de Gaulle then wrote to Churchill offering a joint Anglo–French "plan of action" and stressing that it should be carried out "in the shortest possible time."[35] De Gaulle (who also advocated the occupation of Madagascar's tiny Vichy-held neighbour, Réunion[36]) followed up his suggestion with another letter to the Prime Minister on the 16th: "It is not necessary", he told Churchill, "for me to demonstrate to you the capital strategic importance of Madagascar from the moment when Japan has access to the Indian Ocean and in view of the role that the Cape route plays in the war in the Middle East and as regards Russia. It is obvious that Vichy is absolutely incapable politically, morally and materially of opposing the occupation of Madagascar by the enemy should the latter so decide."[37]

Despite de Gaulle's repeated appeals, neither Churchill nor the Chiefs of Staff wished to include the Free French in any military operations against Madagascar. De Gaulle lacked the resources to mount such an expedition by himself, and after the Dakar fiasco and the protracted Syrian adventure, the Chiefs of Staff did not want to be involved in any further joint operations with the Free French.[38] The authorities in Madagascar were still staunchly pro-Vichy and the handful of Gaullist sympathizers in Madagascar had been arrested and interned.[39] Any military forces landing in the country which included Free French troops would, almost certainly, be fiercely resisted. Yet Churchill still clung to the belief that most Frenchmen did not want to fight the British. Despite the recent blood-letting in Syria, he hoped that if the despised Free French were excluded from the operation the authorities in Madagascar would co-operate with their former allies.

The capture of Madagascar would therefore have to be undertaken solely by British or British Empire troops. But France's defeat was a great humiliation which Britain's continued resistance did nothing to mollify. The prospect of British success after France's embarrassing capitulation was a bitter pill for the defeated French to swallow. Furthermore, both Pétain and de Gaulle were highly suspicious of Britain's motives and Madagascar, strategically so important to Britain now that the Germans and Italians controlled the Mediterranean, must have appeared to the French to have been high on the British Government's list of territories it wished to annex.[40]

Vichy's status, and even survival, depended entirely upon retaining its control over the Empire and the fleet. As the German Foreign Minister made clear in June

1940, there was no need to add detailed clauses to the armistice arrangements because anything in mainland France that Germany wanted it could simply take when it pleased. Not so the Empire. Hitler wanted to avoid driving the colonies into the arms of the Allies and this gave Vichy some leverage in efforts to prise concessions out of the Führer.[41]

It was not only Britain that France had to fear. Others saw in a weakened France the opportunity to acquire territory. Spain had a long-standing claim upon Morocco, Siam (Thailand) was in dispute with France over areas of Indo–China, and Italy wanted Tunis, eastern Algeria, Djibouti and Chad. Hitler also had colonial ambitions of his own, particularly in West Africa where France remained the major colonial Power. France had to demonstrate that it would defend its colonies against any aggressor. If it showed any signs of pusillanimity it would encourage these countries, and France might find its empire dismembered.[42]

It was therefore utterly unrealistic of Churchill to expect Vichy not to oppose an Allied occupation of Madagascar. Without an empire there would be no reason for Hitler to tolerate the Vichy regime and it would quickly disappear under the Fascist jackboot.

With the exclusion of the Free French, several of whom had served in Madagascar, there was little information on the difficulties which might be experienced in the country for the JPS to draw upon.[43] The island had only been attacked once in its history and that was by the French in the nineteenth century. Before that time British and French interests in Madagascar were roughly balanced. The successive rulers of Madagascar played one Power off against the other and successfully maintained the country's independence.[44] The opening of the Suez Canal in 1873 meant that Britain's shipping route to India no longer passed Madagascar. Britain's attention turned instead to protecting its control over Egypt and the Nile, and the French were given a free hand in Madagascar.[45]

Though Britain may have accepted France's position in Madagascar, the Malagasy had not and France had to assert her authority over the island by force of arms. It took some 15,000 soldiers and a large naval force more than nine months to fight their way through the trackless and inhospitable terrain to reach and occupy the capital, Tananarive (now re-named Antananarivo). Though the French had lost just 20 men dead and 100 wounded in battles with the Malagasy, nearly 6,000 (or around 1 in 3 of the total force) died of disease. It was France's most costly colonial campaign.[46]

Conditions and communications in Madagascar had improved a little under French rule, but if the British were to attempt to take control of the whole of the island they could expect to face similar problems if the French were to resist. Everything therefore depended on how the colonists would react to a British landing. If the French were prepared to make a serious defence of their territory, the expedition to Madagascar would require a very considerable deployment of force.

Immediately after the fall of France, the majority of the colonists in Madagascar had opposed the Vichy regime. Yet, as with almost all the colonies, the bombardment of the French fleet caused a significant change of opinion on the island. Coppet, whose loyalty to Pétain was suspect, was replaced as Governor-General by Léon Cayla, who arrived by air from Dakar. Cayla declared Madagascar for Vichy, immediately putting in hand a campaign of anti-British propaganda. He toured the island with his assistant telling the colonialists that Britain had "let France down in her hour of danger".[47] As a result, on 29 July 1940, Britain placed Madagascar under a maritime blockade. It was to prove the single most effective blockade of any Vichy colony and it caused a dramatic collapse in exports and serious food shortages. This embittered the colonialists. To the senior member of Malagasy judiciary Britain had become "this nation, yesterday our friend and our ally, forgetful of the brotherhood of arms, forgetful of the blood shed in common, forgetful of piety, forgetful even of honour".[48] As a demonstration of defiance against the blockade Cayla issued an order forbidding British ships to come within twenty miles of the coast of Madagascar.[49]

Cayla reached retirement age and was superseded by another ardent Pétainist, the 52-year-old Armand Annet, who arrived in Madagascar in April 1941.[50] Annet, who has been described as "a perfect bureaucrat, to whom conformism was a matter of heart and soul",[51] was provided with a small air contingent, which included both fighter and bomber aircraft, and a number of warships and submarines.

Since his arrival in Madagascar, Annet had clearly demonstrated his allegiance to Vichy by using his naval vessels to aid the pro-Vichy forces in the colonial port of Djibouti in French Somaliland. A small Free French force had blockaded the port from the land but the Royal Navy had been unable to maintain a blockade from the sea, and a sloop and submarines from Madagascar had taken supplies in to the defenders.[52]

An intelligence report on Madagascar compiled for the War Office saw Annet as being "incapable of taking the smallest decision without first referring to Vichy, to whom he is completely subservient".[53] Yet Churchill, regardless of all this contrary evidence, expected little opposition from Annet. This view was apparently based on the experience of his wife, Clementine, who had met him "in a train somewhere once" and found him "quite a good chap"![54] There was also a report sent to London from the Anglican Bishop in Madagascar which claimed that the colonists might actually welcome a friendly proposal from Britain. According to the report, the blockade had been ruinous to the island's economy and this prompted the Reverend Vernon to write: "If approached in the right spirit the Madagascar Government might enter into an economic agreement with Britain or South Africa."[55] Information supplied by the Wireless Interception Service in nearby Mauritius, which monitored Madagascar's telecommunications, confirmed Vernon's assessment of the country's perilous domestic situation.[56] But any approach would be certain to alert the Japanese to Britain's interest in Madagascar and that was the last thing that Churchill wanted. Nevertheless, Lord Mountbatten, Chief of Combined Operations, was asked to investigate the possibility of devising a plan "which might lead to success without a shot being fired but which would not prejudice success in the event of it being impossible to avoid active resistance".[57]

How the Malagasy people and the conscripted Malagasy soldiers would react to a British invasion was also uncertain. During the First World War, 46,000 Malagasy soldiers were recruited to fight for France, and over 2,000 were killed. Though a strong independence movement had developed in the 1930s, with the outbreak of war in 1939 the Malagasy showed great support for France. When Marshal Pétain capitulated in the summer of 1940, there were 34,000 Malagasy troops in France with a further 72,000 in Madagascar preparing to join them.[58]

There was also a contingent of Senegalese troops on the island. These had been sent to reinforce French Indo-China in August 1940, but after one of the transport vessels had been intercepted by British warships the two other transports were diverted to Madagascar.[59]

With all these factors having been borne in mind, the Joint Planners chose to limit the operation to the capture of Diego Suarez, with the possibility of secondary operations against the island's principal commercial ports, Majunga and Tamatave. The Force Commanders for *Bonus* were appointed on 23 December 1941. The Naval Commander, and Commander-in-Chief of the operation, was Rear-Admiral T. B. Drew with Major-General 'Bob' Sturges in charge of the land force which was to be the 102nd Royal Marine Brigade, the 36th Brigade, two battalions of Army commandos and a Mobile Naval Base Defence unit. Sturges, a survivor of Britain's last major amphibious operation at Gallipoli in 1915, had already assembled the nucleus of a Force Headquarters, complete with an operational signals section, which had been working together with the Royal Marines and Combined Operations HQ, ready for just such an operation.[60]

Having selected the military forces, the JPS now had to find a suitable landing beach for them near to Diego Suarez. There were possible landing places on both the eastern and western coasts close to Antsirane but the beaches on the east coast are exposed practically all year round to strong on-shore winds. The plan put to Drew and Sturges by the JPS was, therefore, of a landing on the western coast, the establishment of a secure beach-head, followed, on day two or three of the operation, by an advance across country to capture Diego Suarez. The attacks upon Majunga and Tamatave would only follow if considered necessary, and only after Diego Suarez had been secured.[61]

This was rejected by the Force Commanders. They argued that, by not advancing upon Diego Suarez until one or two days after the initial landings, any element of surprise would have gone. Instead they wanted the first brigade ashore to move upon the port as soon as it had landed in the hope of catching the French unprepared.[62] This was a very unorthodox enterprise and ran contrary to the general principles of warfare which dictated that an attacking force would concentrate all its resources before engaging the enemy. If they met strong opposition there was a very real danger that the troops, strung out along the road, would be destroyed piecemeal. Substantial aerial support from the Fleet Air Arm would be essential, as the proposed landing beaches were just twelve air miles from the French air base at Arrachart. All that was to be allocated to the operation, however, was a single squadron of Lysanders.[63]

The plan which de Gaulle had submitted to the Chiefs of Staff was entirely different. In the Free French leader's proposed operation, Diego Suarez would only be blockaded by the Royal Navy. The main landings were to take place at Majunga followed by a rapid advance upon the country's capital, Tananarive.[64] Key bridges on the road from Majunga to Tananarive would be secured by parachutists to prevent them being destroyed by the defending forces. Following the capture of Tananarive, the Free French would then assault Diego Suarez from the interior. For these operations de Gaulle believed that the following land forces would be adequate:

Three battalions of infantry
One scouting and combat company
One artillery battery
One company of parachutists
One signals detachment
One engineers detachment
Some logistics services

Britain's contribution would be limited to the provision of air and naval support to supplement the limited naval units available to the Free French.[65]

This plan had two advantages over the British operation. Firstly, Diego Suarez was Madagascar's largest military base outside the capital and if the French forces chose to resist then a major battle could be expected. Majunga, on the other hand, was a civilian port and would be only lightly defended. Secondly, the capture of Diego Suarez would leave the rest of Madagascar in Vichy hands, whereas the occupation of Tananarive was likely to result in the collapse of Annet's administration.

At this time, however, every available soldier was being shipped out to reinforce the British garrisons throughout the globe. In North Africa, Rommel's panzers were proving more than a match for the British tanks and the threat to Egypt and Suez was as serious as ever. Yet it was the Far East which was causing the most concern where Singapore – the "Gateway of the Pacific" – was now in grave peril. Churchill was acutely aware that Britain could not afford another defeat and the Chiefs of Staff had told the Prime Minister that the capture of Diego Suarez would require a "considerable" force to guarantee success.[66]

Such large numbers of troops, and the ships to transport them, simply could not be spared for what was increasingly being regarded as a secondary operation. Furthermore, General Alan Brooke was not in favour of the operation at all and he believed that it would be "a reasonable gamble" to leave Madagascar in Vichy hands.[67] Though the Chiefs of Staff and the Joint Planners met to discuss Madagascar at least once a week throughout December and early January, Operation *Bonus* was officially "dismounted" at the end of January 1942.[68]

De Gaulle, meanwhile, continued to press for action against Madagascar, though at an interview on 19 February 1942 in the Foreign Office he was informed that other, more pressing, matters had a prior claim on Britain's limited resources. De Gaulle, nevertheless, insisted that he had sufficient Free French troops and that the necessary shipping could be provided from the French vessels already in British hands. All he required from Britain was air support. According to one Foreign Office official, de Gaulle was "dwelling in a world apart from that which most of us are called upon to inhabit", and his proposal was rejected.[69] For the time being, Madagascar was off the military agenda.

Until the war's centre of gravity shifted eastwards following Pearl Harbor, it had been Germany, not Japan, that had designs upon Madagascar. For a number of years German Nazis, as well as many anti–Semites across Europe (including some in Britain) wanted to rid the Continent of all Jews. Their solution to the "Jewish Question" was the wholesale deportation of European Jews to Madagascar. What became known as "The Madagascar Plan" was first discussed as early as November 1938, a year before the outbreak of war. France's right-wing government, which had already considered deporting 10,000 of its own country's Jews to Madagascar, was expected to cede the island to Germany for this purpose.[70]

The annexation of Poland in 1939 brought yet more Jews under German administration. This led to a revival of The Madagascar Plan and prompted the President of the Academy of German Law – Hans Frank – to suggest that as many as three million Jews should be shipped to Madagascar. This would have meant German occupation of the island and this was certainly discussed in 1940 within days of the fall of France.[71]

Indeed, Franz Rademacher of the German Foreign Office proposed that this should be included in the peace treaty with France. Rademacher drew up firm arrangements for installing the Jews in Madagascar in September 1940, and he planned to visit the island so that he could "map out" the details himself.[72] In Rademacher's scheme Antsirane would become a German naval base and the area around Diego Suarez a separate military zone from which the Jews would be excluded. German air bases would also be constructed at suitable points around the country.

It was intended that the island would be under the authority of Heinrich Himmler though largely administered by the Jews themselves. Though some Jewish groups opposed the scheme – little realizing what the alternative would prove to be – Frank, in a speech in July 1940, was able to claim that Jewish leaders had accepted the Madagascar Plan.[73]

However, the Jews had been deceived if they thought that Madagascar had been chosen as the place for a sustainable Jewish homeland. Madagascar was to be a vast "reservation" in which, because of the poor climatic and agricultural conditions, the Jews would slowly die out.

Some have gone even further and suggested that Madagascar was to be the place where the mass extermination of the Jews – with the gas chambers, ovens and all the associated paraphernalia of the death camps – would take place. Certainly the remoteness of Madagascar would have provided the Germans with the privacy they wanted in conducting such atrocities.[74]

Until well into 1941, the Madagascar Plan was Germany's stated "Final Solution". It was only when such a policy became impractical, and it was Britain's capture of Madagascar and the Royal Navy's mastery of the seas which made the plan impractical, that exportation gave way to extermination. Britain therefore, unwittingly or otherwise, foiled Hitler's plan to deport the Jews from Europe and another, even more terrible, "Final Solution" to the Jewish Problem took its place.[75]

Chapter 2

"A Considerable Gamble"

Within weeks of the Japanese attack on Pearl Harbor, the entire strategic situation in the Far East had changed. The pride of the British fleet, the battleship HMS *Prince of Wales*, and her escort HMS *Repulse*, had been sunk and the rest of the British, Dutch and United States cruisers were then defeated at the Battle of the Java Sea. This left the Japanese in control of the entire southern Pacific and there were no Allied forces left capable of preventing the Japanese from penetrating the Indian Ocean.[1] By 15 February 1942, Hong Kong, the Philippines, the Dutch East Indies, the whole of the Malay Peninsula and the great island naval base and fortress of Singapore were in Japanese hands. The capture of Singapore, in which 70,000 men were taken prisoner, was the worst defeat in British military history. It had only been made possible because the Japanese aircraft based in French Indo-China had been able to control the skies over Malaya.[2]

Just weeks later the Andaman Islands in the Indian Ocean were taken and Colombo, the principle port of Ceylon, was under aerial bombardment. The British army had been driven out of Rangoon and the Japanese were now threatening the borders of India. The speed and extent of the Japanese advance had defied all expectations and it seemed that only the most immediate reinforcement of the Imperial forces in India could halt the aggressors.

Every single convoy from the United Kingdom carrying arms and men destined for India passed through the Indian Ocean but it was impracticable for the Japanese to attack the convoys from their bases in Malaya, as the distances were too great. The great French naval station at Diego Suarez in the north of Madagascar, however, would be ideal for such operations and, with Japanese aircraft and submarines ranging increasingly further west, it appeared inevitable that the island would be one of Japan's next targets.[3] Indeed, the leadership in both Germany and Japan saw quite clearly that control of the Indian Ocean was "essential" to an Axis victory and the Japanese Naval Attaché in Berlin (Vice-Admiral Nomura) had already signed an agreement on spheres of interest in the Indian Ocean which permitted the Japanese to operate as far west as South Africa. Such an arrangement, Nomura told Admiral Groos of the *Oberkommando Wehrmacht*, would allow "a Japanese thrust against Anglo-American sea routes in the western part of the Indian Ocean".[4]

This led the Japanese Naval Staff to consider using Madagascar as an advanced operational base, which prompted Nomura's counterpart in Tokyo to write, on 18 February, that "the take-over of the island in some form or other is already being viewed with very eager eyes".[5] The Japanese position was then explained to Hitler in a report by the German Naval Commander-in-Chief, Admiral Raeder, following a meeting at the Führer's headquarters on 12 March. The report read as follows:

"The Japanese have recognised the great strategic importance of Madagascar for naval warfare. According to reports submitted, they are planning to establish bases on Madagascar in addition to Ceylon, in order to be able to cripple sea traffic in the Indian Ocean and the Arabian Sea. From there they could likewise successfully attack shipping round the Cape. Before establishing these bases, Japan will have to get German consent. For military reasons such consent ought to be granted." [6]

Ten days after this meeting, a message, sent by the Japanese Ambassador in Berlin, was intercepted, which revealed the Germans had actually offered their support for a Japanese attack upon Madagascar. The interception was made using the "Purple" machine which was installed alongside the famous Enigma machine at the Government Code and Cypher School at Bletchley Park. The Purple machine, which was given to Britain by the US in February 1941, was able to decipher Japanese diplomatic messages. The encode of the message, labelled as BJ No.102443, read as follows: "RIBBENTROP enquired whether Japan did not consider it necessary to occupy MADAGASCAR as a base. Japanese ambassador stated he did not know. Ribbentrop said GERMANY would back JAPAN if she wanted to act. He thought JAPAN should present a fait accompli, on the basis that she was only occupying it for the duration of the war."[7]

MI6, Britain's secret intelligence service, also produced a number of intelligence summaries for the War Office between December 1941 and March 1942, documenting reports received concerning Japanese interest in Madagascar. Included in the papers was a report from a highly placed French officer, who stated that France had agreed to place Diego Suarez "at the disposal" of the Japanese for provisioning their naval raiders. Other reports, from various sources, appeared to confirm that the subject of Japanese bases in Madagascar had been discussed at the highest levels in Vichy.[8] A diplomatic source in neutral Lisbon went as far as to claim that German and Japanese officers (the latter named as Captain Hasaki Tugura and Major Hauki Tengo) had actually travelled to the island to identify potential sites for new airfields. "It is reasonable to assume", concluded a secret report submitted on 18 February 1942, "that Japanese attentions are directed towards Madagascar, and the establishment of Japanese forces in the island may well take place in the near future." [9]

Inevitably, the South African defence forces were put into a state of alert amid reports of subversive elements within the country predicting that the Japanese would soon occupy Madagascar and the Mozambique ports. Madagascar was only 900 miles from Durban, well within the reach of long-range bombers. In January the *Cape Times* published an interview with Jules Clermont which was entitled "How Madagascar menaces Union" with the subtitle "Vichy would hand over to Japanese".[10] A month later an article in the same paper bore the title: "If Singapore falls, Madagascar becomes our advance line of defence" and on 16 February the subject was debated in the South African parliament.[11]

South Africa's prime minister, Field Marshal Jan Smuts, was so concerned with the danger which an Axis-occupied Madagascar would pose to his country he implored Churchill to intervene. "I look upon Madagascar as the key to the safety of the Indian Ocean," Smuts told his British counterpart, urging him to take positive action against the Vichy authorities on the island. "All our communications with our various war fronts and the Empire in the east may be involved."[12]

Admiral Somerville, who commanded the Eastern Fleet, agreed. The Japanese battle group had demonstrated that it was superior "in all respects" to Somerville's hastily formed command. If the Japanese chose to push deeper into the Indian Ocean there was little that the Eastern Fleet could do to stop them. The Second World War, Somerville wrote "could not be won in the Indian Ocean, but it might very well be lost there."[13]

On the very same day that the Axis Powers discussed the occupation of Madagascar, 12 March 1942, Churchill wrote to General Ismay asking the Chiefs of Staff Committee to revive the plans for a combined operation to capture the island before the Japanese could intervene. General Brooke, however, was still against the venture, which he saw as "full of complications".[14] Rather than tie up troops and shipping in secondary operations, he wanted to concentrate Britain's resources in the main theatres of war. Lord Mountbatten also now considered that the operation had become "a considerable gamble". Nevertheless, the Chiefs of Staff and the Joint Planners knew that if the Japanese were allowed to gain a foothold in Madagascar it would be very difficult to dislodge them and they recommended that the operation should go ahead, as "a matter of urgency".[15]

Unlike the attacks upon Dakar and Syria, which had been undertaken with the express objective of replacing one French administration with another, this was to be an exclusively British operation. There were potentially grave political consequences associated with such a move. The US in particular had maintained good relationships with France, and Churchill was worried that Roosevelt might object to unilateral British action against a French colony. The US also had other interests in Madagascar. The island exported a variety of minerals including mica and graphite which were of importance to the munitions industry. The US Government, which had recently opened its consulate in Tananarive after being closed for twenty-two years, told Britain that it was considering entering into a trade agreement with Madagascar in order to obtain these minerals. Anthony Eden warned Churchill that any such arrangement between the US and the Vichy authorities would restrict Britain's freedom of action. Churchill agreed: "We should certainly oppose any agreement to maintain the status quo in Madagascar and Réunion. This would tie our hands while leaving the islands defenceless against Japan and liable to be betrayed at any moment."[16] Churchill then wrote to Roosevelt: "I hope nothing will be done to give guarantees for the non-occupation of Madagascar and Réunion. The Japanese might well turn up at the former one of these fine days, and Vichy will offer no more resistance to them there than in French Indo-China. A Japanese Air, Submarine and/or Cruiser base at Diego Suarez would paralyse our whole convoy route both to the Middle and to the Far East." It took the President just four days to send the Prime Minister his assurance that he would not conduct any deals with the Vichy authorities concerning Madagascar.[17] Churchill was free to act as he pleased.

With these political concerns resolved, General Sturges was summoned to the War Office on 14 March 1942. There he learnt that at 23.00 hours the previous evening the Chiefs of Staff had decided to reinstate the operation against Madagascar under the code-name *Ironclad*. The operation would take place during the favourable moon and tide conditions which would exist in the first week of May. Sturges was told that most of the senior officers involved with the planning of Operation *Bonus* would be available for *Ironclad* except that the Combined Commander was now to be Rear-Admiral E.N. Syfret. The Admiral would be in command of the approach to the theatre and the assault. Subsequent military operations would be entirely the responsibility of the General. After the capture of Diego Suarez, Sturges would assume the position, temporarily, of Fortress Commander.[18]

Syfret was currently in charge of the naval forces at Gibraltar and would not be able to meet Sturges until the ships from Britain and those from Gibraltar converged at Freetown.[19] So the meetings that took place over the course of the next few days to discuss the composition of the assault force, the number and type of vehicles that would be required and the allocation of personnel to the available ships, had to be conducted without the involvement of the operation's commanding officer.[20]

A large convoy of troops destined for India was due to depart the UK in just seven days' time and it was hoped that the assault force would, as Churchill put it, "mingle" with the other troops without drawing any unwanted attention.[21] As the 29th Brigade, along with No.5 (Army) Commando, was already assault-loaded on ships in Scotland in preparation for "Exercise 19", it was selected for the operation ahead of the Royal Marine Division. The 29th Brigade was, of course, well known to Sturges through the joint exercises with the Marines in Scotland.[22]

Another brigade would be required to support the 29th Brigade and, rather than tie up troops whose presence was urgently required in the Far East, Churchill had originally suggested that troops from the Belgian Congo could be utilized. This was considered impractical and instead the Chiefs of Staff decided that the reinforcements which were passing by Madagascar on their way to India could be used to support the 29th Brigade. Once the island had been seized, South African or East African soldiers could take over from the British troops, who could continue their passage to India.[23] The 29th Brigade would therefore be supported by the 17th Brigade Group (Brigadier G.W.B. Tarleton) of the 5th Division which was already under orders to sail for India in Convoy W.S. 17, due to leave the UK on 21 March. The stores and vehicles of the 17th Brigade had already sailed for Cape Town on 13 March in the transport ships *Empire Kingsley*, *Thalatta* and *Mahut* in Convoy O.S. 22, and in *City of Hong Kong* in Convoy O.S. 23, scheduled to sail on 23 March.

The 29th Brigade, commanded by Brigadier Francis Festing, consisted of the 1st Battalion Royal Scots Fusiliers,[24] the 2nd Battalion South Lancashire Regiment, the 2nd Battalion East Lancashire Regiment, and the 2nd Battalion Royal Welch Fusiliers. The number of transport vehicles allocated to this brigade was reduced to allow the inclusion of a mobile armoured force – 'B' Special Service Squadron of the Royal Armoured Corps. This was a composite unit formed from elements of the 9th Queen's Royal Lancers, the 10th Hussars and the Queen's Bays equipped with six Tetrarch light tanks, and the Royal Tank Regiment with six of the more heavily armoured Valentine tanks. The squadron was organized into two half-squadrons (one half-squadron of Valentines and the other of Tetrarchs) each of which were divided into one troop of three tanks, and one troop of two tanks with the unit commander in the remaining tank. For the voyage to Madagascar, two Tetrarchs and two Valentines were loaded into each of the assault ships *Keren*, *Karanja* and *Windsor Castle*.[25] The operation would include, for the first time, these tanks and other motor transport being waterproofed and driven ashore under their own power to land on beaches in a hostile country.[26]

Artillery support for the 29th Brigade was provided by two units – the 455th Independent Light Battery, Royal Artillery, armed with four 3.7-inch howitzers and two 25-pounders, and the 145th Light Anti-Aircraft Troop with 4 x 40mm Bofors.[27]

The 17th Brigade only learnt of its inclusion in *Ironclad* shortly before embarkation. This was "disconcerting news" for Brigadier Tartleton as his brigade was not tactically loaded nor had his troops received any training in amphibious operations.[28] The brigade consisted of the 2nd Battalion of the Royal Scots Fusiliers, the 2nd Battalion Northamptonshire Regiment and the 6th Battalion Seaforth Highlanders. The 17th Brigade's artillery support took the form of the 25-pounders of the 9th Field Regiment Royal Artillery. The whole force, which was designated Force 121, was under the command of Bob Sturges. Though his Royal Marine Division was no longer involved in the operation, Sturges was able to take many of the divisional staff with him to form the backbone of Force 121's headquarters.[29] Only four assault ships could be made available for the operation which severely limited the size of the assault force. In total *Keren, Karanja, Winchester Castle* and the Polish ship *Sobieski* could carry 323 officers, 4,753 other ranks and 115 vehicles. Of this number, 76 officers and 499 other ranks were allocated to Force Headquarters, including the Dock Operating Company, along with 38 officers and 328 men of the Royal Navy. This left just 209 officers and 3,926 other ranks for the fighting troops of the assault force.[30]

A strong Royal Navy squadron – Force H – stationed at Gibraltar, was ear-marked for *Ironclad*. The western Mediterranean could not be left unguarded, however, and before Force H could sail south other warships would have to take its place. As the Royal Navy's resources were severely stretched Churchill sought help from President Roosevelt. Churchill wanted US ships to be based at Gibraltar because he feared a reprisal from Vichy (as had happened after the attack on the French fleet) if Madagascar had to be taken by force. Churchill knew that the French would not jeopardize their relationship with the US by bombing Gibraltar whilst US ships were present.[31]

The President was prepared to assist with a naval contingent. Yet, rather than replace Force H at Gibraltar with an American squadron, Roosevelt preferred to take over all escort duties in the North Atlantic or send a number of warships to join the Royal Navy's Home Fleet. Ships from the Home Fleet would then be able to take over Force H's duties at Gibraltar. This last suggestion was the one eventually decided upon and Roosevelt agreed to provide a temporary reinforcement of two battleships, two cruisers, an aircraft carrier and a squadron of destroyers.[32]

Rear-Admiral Neville Syfret, Flag Officer Commanding Force H, was notified by the Admiralty on 13 March to prepare his ships for departure from Gibraltar at the end of the month. A week later, on the 20th, the Prime Minister, the First Sea Lord Sir Dudley Pound, and Sir Charles Portal, the Chief of the Air Staff, met at Chequers to discuss the six most urgent naval and air dispositions. Madagascar was second on the list.[33] That same day Syfret, who had been Churchill's Naval Secretary at the Admiralty,[34] was confirmed as Combined Commander-in-Chief of Operation *Ironclad*. The Admiral was told that "the operation must succeed whatever the cost" and that "no political or other considerations were to restrict his actions in achieving the object of the expedition".[35] *Ironclad* was, the Admiralty emphasized, "an operation of the first, *repeat first*, importance".[36]

Syfret was advised that the proposed forces would concentrate at Durban and that the naval contingent would consist of the battleship *Malaya*, the aircraft carrier *Eagle*, the cruiser *Hermione*, the destroyers *Laforey*, *Lightning*, *Lookout*, *Active* and *Anthony*, all from Force H, plus a second aircraft carrier, *Hermes*, another cruiser, *Devonshire*, and six other destroyers. In support of this powerful force were six corvettes, a flottilla of Bangor-class minesweepers as well as two Fleet Auxiliaries and the Hospital Ship *Atlantis*.

HMS *Devonshire* was escorting a convoy from the West Indies and would join Syfret at Freetown in West Africa. HMS *Hermes* was at Ceylon and was to meet the rest of the force at Durban, as were the minesweepers and the corvettes which were already in South African waters. However, *Hermes* was sunk by Japanese aircraft off Ceylon on 9 April and HMS *Indomitable*, with forty-five aircraft including nine Hurricane fighters, was added to Admiral Syfret's force. The other carrier, *Eagle*, required essential repairs and could not participate in any immediate action. She was replaced by HMS *Illustrious,* which was sailing directly from the US where she had been undergoing repairs. Amongst its forty-seven aircraft *Illustrious* carried twenty-five of the new US-made Grumman Martlet fighters. The entire naval contingent for *Ironclad* was designated "Force F".[37]

The planning for Operation *Ironclad* was conducted under conditions of the utmost secrecy for fear of inducing the Japanese to take the island for themselves before the British troops could complete their long journey round the Cape of Good Hope. There was also the possibility, as had been rumoured in the press and reported by the American embassy in London, of Vichy troops and "military supplies" being sent from Dakar to strengthen the garrison in Madagascar.[38]

Churchill, therefore, arranged for any ships passing round the Cape from Dakar to Madagascar to be intercepted by Royal Navy forces operating out of Cape Town. Such was the degree of secrecy surrounding Operation *Ironclad*, Field Marshal Smuts had not been told that the capture of Madagascar had at last been authorized and he questioned Churchill on the nature of the naval preparations being made in his country's principal port. Churchill did not explain these activities until 24 March, the day after the convoy had left Britain, and even then the South African Prime Minister was not given the code-name. The need for secrecy also meant that it would not be possible to warn or attempt to repatriate British nationals living in Madagascar.[39]

De Gaulle, for his part, was still pushing for Free French intervention in Madagascar. Following his letter to Churchill on 19 February 1942, he passed a "pressing note" to Anthony Eden in early April, reminding the Foreign Secretary of the "importance and urgency of the matter" and stressing that the participation of Free French forces in any operation against Madagascar was "essential".[40] Yet Churchill remained determined that de Gaulle should learn nothing about *Ironclad*. "The Free French are out of the business and should be kept out," the Prime Minister had told Eden. "But all the more is it necessary that we establish ourselves there."[41]

Churchill had received advice from Britain's Ambassador in Washington that the French Defence Minister, Admiral Darlan, might request assistance from the US if the Japanese were to reveal any intentions of occupying Madagascar but only providing that no Free French forces were used to defend the island.[42] It was also thought that there had been security leaks from the so-called French National Committee before the Dakar expedition, as it appeared that the colonists had been prepared for an attack.[43] The lesson learnt at Daker was that "no Frenchman can keep a secret",[44] and Churchill went to considerable lengths to prevent any word of the impending operation reaching the ears of the Free French. "It is of the greatest importance that de Gaulle's people should be misled about Ironclad", the Prime Minister told General Ismay. "Once they know, the secret will be out."[45] Churchill and the Chiefs of Staff agreed that the best policy was to say nothing rather than to try and deceive the French. But if de Gaulle should ask about Madagascar the official line was that "while, of course, we are watching the situation carefully, we are doing nothing for the present".[46]

This policy caused some embarrassment when General Catroux, one of de Gaulle's senior officers, proposed at the beginning of April to send Free French troops to Madagascar to start a Fifth Column. Such an action would be likely to put the authorities on the island in a state of high alert and possibly even induce them to extend mobilization. This was exactly what Churchill did not want but an outright refusal to assist Catroux might arouse the French general's suspicions. It was therefore decided to defer replying to Catroux for as long as was possible and then to create delays in shipping the troops to Madagascar.[47]

Frustrated with Britain's apparent disinterest in Madagascar, de Gaulle sought to achieve his objectives through another route. The country liable to be most directly affected by Axis occupation of Madagascar was South Africa. So a Free French representative, Colonel Pechkoff, was sent to Pretoria to urge de Gaulle's cause upon the South African Government. However, Premier Smuts had already been advised by the Foreign Office not to engage in any action that might alarm the Malagasy authorities. Churchill also agreed to keep Smuts fully informed of Britain's plans concerning Madagascar to allay the Field Marshal's fears and to counter Pechkoff's forceful arguments.[48]

Meanwhile de Gaulle continued with his own plans for an Anglo-French operation against the island, naming Admiral Muselier as the leader of the Free French forces that would "liberate" Madagascar.[49]

Because of the speed of the Japanese advance, Madagascar, which had been relatively unknown to the British public, suddenly became the subject of much media interest and the French Government felt compelled to state its position. On 10 March 1942, Charles Rochet of the French Foreign Office gave the American Ambassador a formal assurance that "neither the Japanese nor the Germans had made suggestions to the French Government with regard to the use of Madagascar as a base".[50] This message was repeated by the French Ambassador in Washington and was later confirmed by Pétain himself. It did not stop the press speculation. On 18 March there was a suggestion in the *Evening Standard* that troops were being sent from Dakar to Madagascar. Five days later the *Evening Standard* again reported on discussions being held in Washington between the US and Vichy concerning Japanese intentions towards Madagascar. The following day, the same newspaper printed a report from Pretoria which indicated that the Vichy regime had allowed the infiltration of a strong Japanese Fifth Column into Madagascar, which was actively at work.[51]

These reports triggered the inevitable retaliation by Paris Radio on the 24th: "The Anglo-Saxon press has opened a propaganda campaign against Madagascar. This press offensive corresponds in every detail to that launched against Syria before the invasion of that country by Anglo-Gaullist forces ... But will the United States officially attempt an open act of war against France, or will they once again delegate the job to de Gaulle?"[52]

This did not silence the "Anglo-Saxon" press, which was contemptuous of Vichy's active collaboration. A cartoon in the *Evening Standard* of 21 April, for example, shows the key to Fortress Madagascar being handed over to a party of Japanese visitors, and *The Economist* of 21 March observed that it was "an odd fact about minor Vichy officials that they are prepared to defend French territory to the last but only against the democracies". Twelve days later, *The War Illustrated* felt obliged to advise its readership to "WATCH MADAGASCAR!" It then went on to explain that "if the Japs could control Madagascar and its 135 airfields the Allies' lifeline with the Mediterranean and South Russia would be in the gravest peril ... If this island falls into Axis hands it will be one of the greatest strategic disasters of the war."[53]

All this press coverage caused Churchill much discomfort. As he later confessed, he felt a "shiver" every time that he saw the word "Madagascar" in the newspapers. "All those articles with diagrams and measured maps", he told the British nation in a radio broadcast after the capture of Diego Suarez, "showing how very important it was for us to take Madagascar and forestall the Japanese, and be there 'first for once', as they said, filled me with apprehension."[54] But the Government made no attempt to suppress the media. When it was suggested by the Joint Planners that the Government should "damp down" press interest in Madagascar, Churchill intervened. He saw such a move as "dangerous" and to discuss the subject with journalists as "more dangerous still"! It was far safer for the Government simply to appear disinterested in the matter.[55]

With so much attention being focused upon Madagascar, a cover story had to be devised for *Ironclad* but, as the 29th Brigade was to be assault-loaded and the troops issued with tropical kit, this would prove difficult. The problem was handed to a recently formed special section of the JPS – the Future Operational Planning Section – under the authority of Colonel Oliver Stanley. This was to be the first time that such strategic deception would be used to support an actual major offensive.

Stanley's assistant was the horror-fiction writer Dennis Wheatley. In his account of his war years, Wheatley explained that as the brigade was assault-loaded the given objective would have to be enemy-held territory. The eastern Mediterranean was out of the equation as there was no passage beyond Malta, which was under almost constant attack. The only possible alternative, as the planners saw it, was Burma, with the convoy going first to Trincomalee in Ceylon for re-grouping. To reinforce this story an officer flew out to Ceylon where he commandeered "scores" of buildings for use by the troops of the 29th Brigade during the two weeks that they were supposed to be re-forming before the assault on Burma. Equipment destined for Madagascar was packed into crates marked "Rangoon".[56] To prevent any possibility of a security leak, all the clerical work associated with the operation was dealt with by senior officers only.[57]

To help convince the French that the capture of Madagascar would not simply be another British colonial conquest, Churchill repeatedly urged Roosevelt to participate in the operation (even pleading with him to send just three or four "observers" with the expedition). But the President would not put his relationship with Vichy at risk by attacking French territory. When it became clear that the US was not going to be drawn into hostile action against Vichy, Churchill asked Roosevelt to at least demonstrate unambiguous support for the operation. He requested four things from the President:[58]

1. To allow the dropping of leaflets on the morning of the landing informing the French garrison that the operation had US support.
2. To send a token US detachment to join the occupying forces after the attack.
3. To inform the Vichy Government after the operation has taken place that it had US approval and support.
4. Make public that the above communication has been made to Vichy.

To such suggestions Roosevelt replied that "it would be unwise to identify the expedition in the manner indicated ... My reason for this is that we are the only nation that can intervene diplomatically with any hope of success with Vichy, and it seems to me extremely important that we are able to do this without the complications which might arise by the dropping of leaflets or other informal methods in connection with your operation."[59] Roosevelt had already sent Britain a considerable number of warships – there would be no further help from the United States.

In order to preserve the veil of secrecy surrounding the operation, another deception plan was formulated to cover the departure of the 29th Brigade from Scotland. The troops were told that they were to engage in *Exercise 19*, which was an amphibious exercise in Fife, and, to explain the movement of their heavy baggage, they were informed that the brigade was moving to new barracks. Only when the brigade was actually embarked were the men told that the exercise had been cancelled but their true destination was not revealed. The nature of the expedition, however, could not be concealed as landing craft remained suspended from the davits of the ships in place of the lifeboats.[60]

At 20.30 hours on 23 March, the expeditionary force embarked at Greenock for Britain's first offensive operation since Japan had entered the war. A vast convoy, its departure having been delayed by two days to allow the ships of the assault force to complete their preparations, sailed from both the Clyde and Liverpool and gathered in the Irish Sea. This was one of the "Winston Specials", Convoy W.S. 17, which was carrying 50,000 troops to the East. It was at that time the largest convoy ever to leave Britain.[61]

Despite the need for urgency, progress was slow as the convoy had to continually switch direction to confuse prowling enemy raiders. "All ships flew barrage balloons and manned anti–aircraft guns in defence against enemy aircraft," wrote the historian of the 5th Division. "The destroyer screen continually weaved in and out ever alert for submarine attack. The whole convoy turned this way to port and then that way to starboard at the command of the siren on the Commodore's ship."[62] Yet it would prove to be a comparatively uneventful voyage to Freetown with just one dangerous incident. Four days out from Britain the convoy was attacked by the German U-boat, *U-587*, but the close escort sunk the submarine before it could inflict any damage upon the troopships.[63]

On board one of the assault ships, the large passenger liner *Winchester Castle*, a combined operations room was set up for the two assault commanders, Captain Garnons-Williams of the Royal Navy and Brigadier Festing, along with their staffs. No.5 Commando (of 365 men) also sailed in *Winchester Castle*. The 1st Royal Scots Fusiliers sailed in *Keren;* the 2nd Battalion of the Scots Fusiliers was in *Oronsay* along with the Seaforth Highlanders. Such was the degree of secrecy surrounding the operation, the two Scots Fusilier battalions were unaware of the other's presence until after the transports had put to sea.[64]

As the convoy steamed towards the assembly port of Durban the commanders learnt that a second brigade of the 5th Division – the 13th Brigade under Brigadier V. C. Russell – would join the expedition as a floating reserve. This would give Sturges a total of around 13,000 men under his direct command.[65] It was felt that the forces deployed in the Syrian campaign had been inadequate and this had encouraged the French to resist with some prospect of success. This mistake would not be repeated at Diego Suarez – Sturges would have an overwhelming force at his disposal. But this additional brigade, Syfret was warned, could only be committed "in the event of unexpected opposition or for mopping up operations immediately after capture of objective". If there was no pressing need for the brigade to be used he was to arrange for its immediate dispatch to India.[66] The 13th Brigade was already sailing in W.S. 17, its men in *Franconia*, its motor transport in *Nainbank* and *Martand*.[67]

There was also an entirely new kind of vessel – a Tank Landing Ship. The increasing predominance of armoured fighting vehicles on the battlefield meant that if Britain was to attack enemy occupied territory her infantry would need the support of tanks. As early as 1940 Churchill had recognized this need and he called for the development of a ship which was capable of crossing oceans but which also had a draught shallow enough to allow tanks to be disembarked directly onto the shore.[68] Such a vessel was found in the tankers which were specifically built to cross the bar at the entrance to the Maracaibo channel in Venezuela. One of these type of ships, which became known as "Maracaibos", was to join the convoy at Durban. This was the SS *Bachaquero*. For the landing in Madagascar, however, *Bachaquero* carried a battery of 25–pounders and six trucks.[69]

The commissioning of *Bachaquero* was kept a closely guarded secret and until the day he actually saw the vessel its captain, Lieutenant-Commander A.W. McMullan, had never heard of a Tank Landing Ship. Trials were undertaken in Scotland and then followed, in October 1941, with *Bachaquero* sailing to Freetown. After a series of exercises in combined operations, *Bachaquero* was ordered to Durban for a re-fit. *Bachaquero* remained in South Africa and joined Syfret's force when it reached Durban.[70]

At 03.00 hours on the morning of 1 April, Syfret in *Malaya*, along with the destroyers *Laforey*, *Lightning*, *Active*, *Duncan* and *Anthony*, slipped out of Gibraltar under the cover of darkness, followed a few hours later by *Hermione*. Churchill, working late into the night as usual, cabled Roosevelt to say that the operation against Madagascar was going ahead as planned. "I hope," Churchill wrote, "that the Japanese will have missed their opportunity there".[71]

Whilst at sea the following evening Syfret received a signal from the Admiralty which warned him that the French battleship *Richelieu*, accompanied by three light cruisers, was likely to be leaving Dakar the next day, the 3rd. It was understood in London that the four French warships were returning to France, which would place them perilously close to the German occupying forces. Syfret was ordered to intercept, and he moved his squadron closer inshore. *Active*, *Anthony* and *Duncan* were topped up with fuel from *Malaya* ready for action whilst *Illustrious* and *Devonshire* rushed at top speed to re-fuel at Freetown. For the next three days the ships searched the ocean but nothing was seen of the *Richelieu* and, on the morning of 6 April, the Admiralty ordered Syfret to move on to Freetown as planned.[72]

As the convoy continued its journey south the weather became increasingly hot and, to the relief of all the troops, the tropical khaki uniform was issued to replace the heavy battle dress.[73] Keeping the troops occupied and fit was the greatest concern of the officers during the long voyage – in excess of 8,000 miles – in cramped conditions.[74] Sweepstakes were arranged, regular physical training exercises were carried out in the confined deck spaces, and obstacle races organized along the narrow gangways. The method adopted by the officers of the Royal Scots Fusiliers to keep the men in good physical condition was to march them round and round the open decks in full kit accompanied by the pipes of the regimental band. Lieutenant-Colonel Armstrong, who commanded the 1st Battalion, noted that this endless marching was just as boring to those who had to watch as it was to those that had to march! Despite such activities many, if not most, of the men were "hideously" sea-sick and the voyage was soon dubbed, by those below decks, as "vomit and vermin".[75]

After two weeks at sea the convoy reached the port of Freetown in Sierra Leone on Africa's west coast, but the troops were not allowed ashore. Whilst in port, planning conferences took place between the 29th Brigade and the 17th Brigade. This, naturally, led to increased speculation amongst the troops and it would appear that a number of the men correctly guessed the convoy's true destination, as the island of Madagascar on the map in the foyer of *Keren* bore an increasingly worn appearance. The presence of French-speaking Intelligence Officers as well as a "Political Branch" under Brigadier Lush in the expedition further confirmed the view amongst some that their objective was a Vichy-administered colony.[76]

Chapter 3

"Let's Risk Something"

L ord Mountbatten, Chief of Combined Operations, stood on the deck of the aircraft carrier *Indomitable* to salute the great convoy as it departed from Freetown on the second leg of its journey to Durban.[1] From this point on the exercises on board the ships became serious training sessions. A number of experienced officers from the 29th Brigade were exchanged for officers of the 17th Brigade and lectures were given on combined operations (which included advice on avoiding the local water and the local women!).[2] The troops also practised embarkation and disembarkation from landing craft on the upper decks. On those ships not carrying landing craft, mock-ups were built out of planks and benches.[3]

On at least four occasions the convoy's escorts went into action after reported submarine contacts. The destroyers, along with minesweepers and aircraft from *Indomitable*, would break away from the convoy, deploying depth charges and "hooting and shooting flares", much to the amusement of the bored soldiers on the troopships. A number of torpedoes were fired at the convoy but none found their targets.[4]

Axis forces were also on the move towards Madagascar. Continuing pressure from German leaders upon Japan to commit itself to some form of action in the western Indian Ocean obliged Nomura to meet Fricke again on 8 April 1942. The Japanese Admiral was at last able to announce the departure of a force of four or five long-range submarines and two auxiliary cruisers which would be employed from May to July off the African coast between the Arabian Sea and the Cape of Good Hope. The Japanese also moved against Ceylon. During the second week of April carrier-borne aircraft attacked Trincomalee, destroying its docks and harbour facilities. A large Japanese surface fleet was now also at large in the Bay of Bengal.[5]

This increased pressure from the Japanese caused the Chiefs of Staff to concede that "we are in real danger of losing our Indian Empire" and on 15 April Churchill expressed these fears to Roosevelt: "Until we are able to fight a fleet action there is no reason why the Japanese should not become the dominating factor in the western Indian Ocean. This would result in the collapse of our whole position in the Middle East, not only because of the interruption of our convoys to the Middle East and India, but also because of the interruption to the oil supplies from Abadan, without which we cannot maintain our position either at sea or on land in the Indian Ocean Area."[6]

This activity in the Indian Ocean prompted the German Ambassador in Tokyo to ask the Japanese Foreign Minister if these operations were part of a wider strategic plan or merely actions to harass the British. Foreign Minister Togo replied that they "had a general meaning and … in time they would also affect the western part of the Indian Ocean, so that Japanese conduct of the war would correspond with the German desire for a Japanese advance in the direction of the Near East."[7]

The destruction of the docks at Trincomalee and the presence of the Japanese fleet in the waters around Ceylon meant that the cover story for *Ironclad* had been rendered implausible and on 13 April Syfret was informed by naval cypher that the cover story had been changed. The new, false, destination was to be the Middle East and Sturges was authorized to permit "discreet leakage" of the change of plan to his troops when the convoy reached Durban. Meanwhile, arrangements were made at Alexandria for the reception of the expedition and an attack upon the Italian-occupied Dodecanese Islands in the eastern Mediterranean was openly discussed. As expected, the Italians soon learnt of the proposed operation and reinforced their garrisons on the islands. Though the Italians might have been deceived, the troops on board the convoy remained convinced that they were heading for the Far East.[8]

On 19 April, as the convoy approached the Cape of Good Hope, Syfret, in *Malaya*, accompanied by *Illustrious* and the destroyer force, put into Cape Town to meet General Smuts. The South African Prime Minister offered Syfret, himself a South African, the support of a squadron of the South African Air Force. The admiral was pleased to accept this addition to his strength, but the distance from South Africa to Madagascar prohibited these aircraft from taking an effective part in the attack upon Diego Suarez. It was therefore agreed that bombs and fuel for the SAAF would be shipped with the convoy to Madagascar and that the squadron would fly to Diego-Arrachart after the airfield had been secured and made serviceable. At the meeting Smuts seized the opportunity to express his long-held belief that the entire island should be subjugated and he told Syfret that he intended to cable this opinion to London the very next day.[9]

Churchill, of course, could not allow large numbers of troops to become embroiled in extended operations in the jungles of Madagascar whilst the situation in the Far East was so unstable. He explained this in a letter on 30 April: "We are not setting out to subjugate Madagascar, but rather to establish ourselves in key positions to deny it to a far-flung Japanese attack. A principal objective must be to get our best troops forward to India and Ceylon at the earliest moment, replacing them with garrison battalions from East or West Africa. Getting this place is meant to be a help and not a new burden."[10] However, Syfret was authorized to prepare for extending the objectives of the operation to include the capture of Tamatave and Majunga.[11]

Syfret spent just one night in Cape Town. Here he transferred his flag to *Illustrious*, as *Malaya* had been ordered back to Freetown. Its place in Force F was to be taken by the battleship HMS *Ramillies*, detached from the Eastern Fleet, which Syfret would join in Durban. The *Ramillies* was armed with eight 15-inch guns, one of which is still displayed outside the Imperial War Museum in London.

Syfret and his detachment left Cape Town at 07.00 hours on 20 April and met up with the rest of the convoy at Durban two days later. That same day South Africa broke off diplomatic relations with the Vichy Government. Because of this, and the close proximity of Madagascar, the South African authorities feared that they would have considerable difficulty in keeping the convoy's destination a secret. So before the convoy arrived in Durban a "false" rumour was spread around the port that the force was actually heading for Madagascar. At the same time, known enemy agents were fed the story that the rumour of an attack on Madagascar was really a cover to mask the true destination, which was Ceylon![12] Despite the fact that the destination of the convoy was now supposed to be the Dodecanese Islands, this rumour was reinforced by "hush-hush" briefings given to the naval officers in the convoy on an amphibious operation for the capture of Rangoon. Charts of Trincomalee and its approaches were also issued to senior personnel. Needless to say, stewards and orderlies on board the ships saw some of the charts and "got wise" to the operation. This news, Lieutenant-Commander Ballard recalled, reached the shore exactly "as it was intended to do".[13]

Regardless of where the troops were bound, they were given a tumultuous reception when they disembarked at Durban. Those ships and men destined for Madagascar remained in port for twelve days whilst the rest of the convoy steamed off to India. There was much to do in this time. The two brigades of the 5th Division were not prepared for amphibious operations and their vehicles had to be waterproofed and their guns and equipment re-stowed in preparation for the assault. Personnel and stores had to be re-allocated, maps and photographs distributed and, after the long sea voyage, wireless sets had to be tested and tuned, whilst all the armoured vehicles and motor transport of the assault force had to be checked, serviced and refuelled.[14] Altogether, 190 vehicles were unloaded, made ready for operations and reloaded onto the ships of the assault convoy within just sixty hours.[15]

The landing craft were also refuelled and then tested before being transferred to their respective assault ships, including the Motor Landing Craft, *Derwentdale*, which was made ready to take fourteen landing craft from various ships in the convoy.[16] An addition to the Field Security branch, the 151 Port Security Section, joined the assault force at Durban and a gang of Afrikaner dockers were employed to travel with the convoy to assist with the unloading of equipment at Diego Suarez. These men remained on the island, performing the same duties later in the year at Majunga.[17]

Little was known about Madagascar's defences and the Chiefs of Staff had requested that aerial reconnaissance of the Diego Suarez district should be undertaken, even at the risk of alerting the French. The SAAF had been detailed for this task.

Under the code-name Operation *Lunatic*, two long-range Maryland reconnaissance-bombers flew over Diego Suarez on 21 February. Heavy cloud obscured the target area, however, and the resultant photographs were unsatisfactory. The operation was repeated on 12 April, the aircraft flying from Lindi in Tanganyika.

The two planes separated as they approached Madagascar, with one Maryland photographing the area north of Courrier Bay and the other covering the road from the coast to Diego Suarez. Flying at between 12,000 and 6,000 feet, the Marylands were easily visible from the ground. Interestingly, the French immediately assumed that the planes were British and not Japanese, the colonials already perceiving their former allies as the greater threat.[18]

Again the Marylands encountered cloud over the approaches to Antsirane. But, together with some of the earlier photographs, a "mosaic" of the entire area was pieced together. The mosaic was then dispatched "by safe hand" to the Naval Commodore at Durban and presented to the Force Commanders upon their arrival in South Africa.

The first set of photographs had arrived just before the convoy left the UK, which enabled Sturges and his staff to select the landing beaches and plan their attack. A report from a British agent on the island, however, had noted the presence of barricades, artillery emplacements and machine-gun posts three kilometres outside Antsirane.[19] But the cloud to the south of Antsirane on the second reconnaissance hid these landward defences, which led Sturges and Syfret to believe that the only heavy armament in the area were the coastal batteries, particularly those on the Orangea Peninsula that guarded the entrance to Diego Suarez Bay.[20]

Whilst at Durban, Syfret and his staff finalized the details of the proposed operation against Majunga and Tamatave, which was given the code-name *Ad-Hoc*. Syfret also called a conference with all the commanding officers of the ships that would be involved in *Ironclad*, including the merchant ships. Even at this stage he was not prepared to divulge all the details of the operation, Malagasy place names being replaced by Scottish ones. After demanding "the utmost secrecy" from the merchant marine officers and warning them to be prepared to do "the most unorthodox things" in their ships, Syfret informed them that they "were proceeding on an expedition to make an assault landing somewhere"! [21]

Two hundred thousand leaflets had been printed which were to be dropped around Diego Suarez with an appeal to the French soldiers, sailors and airmen not to oppose the British landing. At the time that the leaflets were printed it was thought that the United States would be involved in the operation and half of them bore the Stars and Stripes alongside the Union Flag and the Tricolour. Reginald Colby, who was the Chief Information Officer (i.e. head of propaganda) for the operation, only learnt at Durban that the Americans would not join *Ironclad*. He was faced with disposing of 100,000 leaflets, any single one of which could reveal the destination of the convoy. As he could not dump them at sea, bury them or burn them on an open fire, he took them in a launch to the aircraft carrier *Illustrious* and fed the whole lot into the ship's boilers! [22]

Despite the advanced state of preparations for the attack upon Madagascar, a change in the French Government caused the War Cabinet to consider postponing the operation. Pierre Laval, a declared advocate of closer ties with Germany, had been installed as Minister of Foreign Affairs on 14 April. Two days later the Joint Intelligence Sub-Committee of the War Cabinet sat to consider the possible reactions to *Ironclad* by the Vichy Government now that Laval was back in power. Air attacks upon Bathurst (Gambia), Freetown and Gibraltar were considered to be likely and the possibility of France actually declaring war upon Britain was discussed.[23]

At another meeting ten days later, the Chiefs of Staff concluded that an attack on Madagascar would at least provide Laval with an excuse for granting further concessions to the Germans. The Chiefs of Staff recommended that the operation should be postponed until June, by which time the attitude of the French people towards Laval might have "crystallised".[24] This, the Foreign Office saw, was the Chiefs of Staff's "usual" malaise of cold feet when an operation was imminent and Eden's advice to the War Cabinet was that Laval would pursue his pro-German policy regardless of Britain and that the operation should proceed as arranged.[25] "It is silly planning things and then calling them off," complained Eden's Under-Secretary, Alexander Cadogan. "Lets risk *something*."[26] However, to explain the "necessary strategical background" of the operation to the French people, and hopefully minimize any public outcry which Laval could turn to his advantage, the Political Warfare Executive (PWE) arranged for the printing of 2.5 million leaflets which were to be dropped by the RAF on urban areas in unoccupied France. This would take place on the night of 5 May, following confirmation that the operation had begun.[27]

None of this satisfied General Brooke, who remained firmly opposed to the venture. As late as 1 May, just four days before the assault was to begin, he expressed his concerns to Churchill and Eden about the effect the operation would have upon relationships with Vichy. He feared that Laval would use the attack as justification for handing over Bizerta, Dakar and the remains of the French fleet to the Germans.[28] Brooke believed that such a response by the French would have a "serious, adverse effect on our power to prosecute the war".[29] Indeed, many people were becoming increasingly concerned about the nature and the degree of France's collaboration with the Axis Powers. France had recently transported food and vehicles to the Axis forces in Libya, and Italian aircraft had refuelled at the French airfield at Algiers.[30]

However, the prospect of a Japanese base in Madagascar had become Churchill's "haunting fear"[31] and he would not be dissuaded. "It was, of course, much easier to do nothing," Churchill argued at the Chiefs of Staff Committee meeting. "If the enterprise were abandoned, we should not have to take any risks [of retaliation by Vichy]. But having informed the President and General Smuts that we intended to carry out the operation at an early date, if we now reversed the decision and the Japanese walked into the Island, our inaction would take a deal of explaining away."[32] So the Chiefs of Staff were "kicked into"[33] sanctioning the operation and the PWE and the Joint Planners were authorized to prepare counter-measures against a possible Vichy backlash following the capture of Diego Suarez – including, if necessary, the bombing of Paris! "Nothing", Churchill told President Roosevelt, "must interfere with Operation Ironclad."[34]

Though the US President had not been prepared to endanger his relationship with France by actively supporting Britain's attack upon Madagascar he arranged for a message to be passed to the French Ambassador on the morning of "zero day" which was to state that "if for the defeat of the Axis powers it is desirable that American troops or ships use Madagascar in the common cause of the civilised peoples, we shall not hesitate to do so at any time".[35]

Roosevelt also prepared a broadcast for 29 April 1942 which, in very general terms, endorsed the action that Churchill was about to take. In one respect the timing of the broadcast was quite appropriate, in another it almost gave the whole game away! "The united nations will take measures if necessary to prevent the use of French territory in any part of the world for military purposes by the Axis Powers. The good people of France will readily understand that such action is essential for the united nations to prevent assistance to the armies and navies or air forces of Germany, Italy and Japan."[36] The press had been full of reports about Madagascar and this address all but confirmed the island could no longer remain untouched by the war. When Diego Suarez was attacked, less than a week after Roosevelt's broadcast, it might have come as a surprise to the French garrison, but it can hardly have been a shock.

Whilst the ships were being prepared for Operation *Ironclad* another, even more secret, enterprise was already in progress. As far back as November 1940, the representative of the Ford Motor Company in Madagascar, Percy Mayer, made contact with the UK High Commissioner in South Africa. Mayer, born a British Subject in Mauritius but since naturalized as a French citizen, offered to provide information on Madagascar and to help persuade the colonists to detach themselves from their allegiance to Vichy.

This message was passed onto London and, in January 1941, the Special Operations Executive (SOE) agreed to take control of Mayer's activities. Mayer's supervising officer was Lieutenant Wedlake, who set up a Madagascar "Mission" in Cape Town. The two men met on 13 March 1941 at Cape Town where Mayer was presented with a wireless set which he subsequently hid inside a false ceiling over his bathroom at his home in Tananarive.[37]

Mayer was to prove to be one of SOE's most successful agents of the war, later achieving the rank of Major. As the SOE Headquarters report on the operations in Madagascar explained, it was "typical of the man" that when the military and political situation prevented him from returning directly home from Durban, he found his own way back to Madagascar. He purchased a 27-foot yacht, dropped her overboard from a steamer in the Mozambique Channel and sailed the yacht single-handed 150 miles to land at Majunga![38]

Mayer was instructed to "influence Madagascar and Réunion in favour of the Free French, away from Vichy", either by "large scale" bribery of senior French personnel or by assassinating the Governor-General! The latter course of action was thought impracticable but Mayer was an acquaintance of the naval Commandant at Diego Suarez and commander of the French navy in Madagascar, Captain Maerten, whom Mayer considered a "foul player" and someone that could easily be bribed into changing his allegiance. "It might be possible to work on him by feminine intrigue", reported Mayer, "women being his weak point." The enthusiastic new agent received permission from London to approach Maerten, despite the fact that this would reveal his clandestine links with the UK. Yet Mayer had misjudged the French officer. Maerten, who had commanded a destroyer at Mers-el-Kébir when the Royal Navy bombarded the French fleet, firmly rejected Mayer's offer. Remarkably, Maerten did not expose his British friend.[39]

Mayer's first successful contribution to the Allied cause was in October 1941 when his French wife, Bertha, transmitted a wireless message informing Cape Town that a convoy of five ships had sailed from Madagascar. The convoy was intercepted by the Royal Navy and 40,000 tons of French shipping fell into British hands. As a result of this, the Germans prohibited Vichy from despatching reinforcements to any of their Indian Ocean colonies – even though the French were becoming increasingly anxious over the safety of Madagascar.[40]

Throughout the previous months, SOE's activities in the region had developed to the extent that an East African Mission had been formed under the general direction of Julius Hanau (code-name "Caesar"), who was based in London. The local head of the Mission, based at Durban from January 1942, was Lieutenant Colonel John Todd.

The Japanese entry into the war gave added impetus to the Todd Mission and Mayer was encouraged to expand his organization. No information exists to provide us with details of exactly how many people were recruited by Mayer, but there were possibly more than sixty individuals, both men and women. As these people lived on the island they, or their families, risked imprisonment or reprisal and their names were kept secret. They were identified simply by the letters DZ, followed by a number, i.e. DZ1, DZ2, DZ3, etc. Mayer himself was DZ6. This group of individuals included a mining prospector, a zoologist, the director of a meat canning factory – and possibly even the Anglican Bishop at Tananarive.[41]

The advent of *Ironclad* gave the organization in Madagascar the opportunity to prove its worth. Hanau flew down to Durban and met John Todd on 16 April. Six days later, Convoy W.S. 17 sailed into port and the two agents met Syfret and Festing to discuss the Mission's role in the coming operation.

Following the meeting at Durban, arms, ammunition, plus four wireless sets and code books were landed from the schooner *Lindi*, operating out of Dar-es-Salaam, on the beach at Majunga where they were concealed. Whilst Mayer was assisting with this operation, called *Frinton 2*, he received a signal from his wife to return immediately to the capital. At Tananarive Mayer was informed of the parts the local organization were to play in Ironclad.[42] These were:

1. To display a light on the island of Nosy Anamo to serve as landfall for the fleet on the night of the operation.
2. The provision of two pairs of guides to conduct the advance demolition parties to the two batteries defending the landing beaches.
3. Transmission by wireless during the period immediately preceding the operation of intelligence regarding enemy troop movements and the location of minefields, submarines and aircraft.

4. Provision of a special guide for attachment to the Force Commander to act as an advisor on local matters.
5. To cut the telephone land-lines connecting the coastal batteries with HQ Diego Suarez and with the aerodrome.
6. Immobilization of aircraft at the aerodrome.[43]

Mayer also suggested that a drinking party should be organized for the night of the assault landings. He planned to invite Maerten and the military commander, Colonel Claerebout, to the party and spike their drinks with "knock-out" drops!

Lindi also had a vital role to play in the operation. As the assault landings were to begin before dawn, the convoy would have to navigate the notoriously perilous waters of Madagascar's north-western coast in complete darkness. The only Admiralty charts of this area available to Syfret were dated 1892, so it was essential that the entrance to Courrier Bay was surveyed before the arrival of the task force.

Two members of the SOE had travelled to Dar-es-Salaam to buy a boat that would be suitable for the survey. They bought *Lindi*, an old sixty-foot-long former sailboat, now a diesel-powered, coastal schooner. With the vessel purchased, the rest of the team were flown in from Durban. These were Captain Van Veen, a reconnaissance specialist, Sergeant Tannahill, a weapons and explosives expert, and Legg, the wireless operator. After dropping off the wireless sets at Majunga and picking up two of Mayer's men, *Lindi* sailed up to Courrier Bay to undertake the survey and to meet up with Mayer.[44]

Despite the identity code of DZ, not one of Mayer's organization lived in Diego Suarez. As none of the men knew the area, they would have to be in position well in advance of the landings so that they could familiarize themselves with the ground. They would then have to lie low until the night of the attack. The party was to consist of Mayer's two men, plus Van Veen and Legg. The party landed at Ambararata Bay on the evening of 29 April.

It was essential that Mayer, who was to head the Mission's activities in Diego Suarez and who was to organize the drinking party, was able to move around overtly. He also needed his car. He therefore had to invent a good reason for driving all the way from the capital to the north. The plan he devised was quite brilliant.

Food was in short supply in the north due to the British blockade. Rice, the staple food, was grown in an area south of Diego Suarez but, because of poor road communications, it could only be transported to Diego Suarez by ship. The lack of shipping, because of the British blockade, had led to attempts at conveying the rice by dhow, but this had been largely unsuccessful due to adverse currents and strong winds. Mayer proposed to put forward a plan to the authorities in Diego Suarez to use lighters and tugs to move the rice to Courrier Bay and then across land to Antsirane, thus avoiding the long and dangerous sea route round the far north of the island. The brilliance of this plan was that the route suggested by Mayer was the exact one that the invasion forces were going to take and he would be able to travel repeatedly from Antsirane to Courrier Bay without arousing suspicion. It was also an entirely plausible scheme.

Almost immediately upon his arrival at Antsirane, Mayer made contact with all the senior civilian and military officials, including his friend Maerten. His arguments, and the desperate food situation, easily persuaded these people to consider his plan. The only objection came from Maerten, who pointed out that Courrier Bay was heavily mined. Mayer was so well received that he was able to wander freely round Diego Suraez and he even managed to visit one of the submarines – the *Bévéziers* – at anchor in the bay. To help him tour the area the French actually *gave* him petrol for his car, as fuel was strictly rationed!

On his third day at Antsirane, Mayer drove out to Courrier Bay, ostensibly to study the road conditions and the landing facilities for the rice operation. Here he met a French sergeant who commanded the defences of the bay and, after a drink or two, the sergeant took the British agent on a guided tour of the French positions. "We got very friendly", reported Mayer, "he showed me all over the defences, position of machine guns, signalling gear, gave me the number and composition of troops etc."[45]

In the days leading up to the start of operations Mayer drove around the entire area, meeting the local commanders and finding out exactly where all the French troops were located. No civilians were allowed onto the Arrachart aerodrome but this remarkable agent talked his way into the airbase (on the pretext of meeting a pilot friend who was landing there from Tananarive) where he was able to learn the exact strength and composition of the forces stationed there.

It was arranged that, whenever possible, Mayer would pass this information to the section hiding at Ambararata Bay who, in turn, were to transmit it to Durban, from where it was relayed to Syfret in *Ramillies*. Some of the information Syfret received during the passage from Durban was so significant that it prompted him and Sturges to re-write the orders for the assault, even though the original instructions for the operation had already been distributed. However, due to concerns that the entire expedition might be jeopardized if the section was discovered or if *Lindi* was seen cruising around the coast – and as much important information had already been obtained – it was decided to withdraw Van Veen and his men after just one day ashore. This message was signalled to Van Veen and, on the 30th, the section was re-embarked on *Lindi*. The boat then hid in the lee of a small island nearby until the night of the landings. Yet the return of Van Veen meant that Mayer could no longer contact Durban and he had to keep his final intelligence notes on his person. It nearly cost him his life.

Three days earlier the first ships had sailed from Durban. That evening the sealed orders were broken open and each captain finally learnt of his ship's role in Operation *Ironclad*. Even at this late stage, the operation could be cancelled and it was only on 1 May 1942, when final confirmation was received from London that *Ironclad* was to proceed as planned, that Force F's true destination was broadcast to each ship's company.[46]

The task force was divided into two convoys, both of which were to follow the usual shipping routes to the north of Madagascar to give the appearance of normal convoys heading to the East. The two convoys would not concentrate until the day before the start of the operation.[47] The first convoy, which consisted of six motor transport ships, two tankers and the Tank Landing Ship (LST), set off from Durban on 25 April. The convoy was escorted by *Devonshire*, with two destroyers and the 3rd Escort Group. Three days later a "fast" convoy left Durban which included the troop transports, the assault ships, *Ramillies*, *Illustrious*, *Hermione*, and a further six destroyers. *Indomitable*, which formed part of the Eastern Fleet, was not scheduled to join the assault force until the morning of 3 May.[48]

Earlier in the day, back in London, Churchill had invited the Chiefs of Staff to lunch at 10 Downing Street. The Prime Minister, and indeed the whole country, needed a victory after the succession of disasters in the Far East, and General Brooke noted in his diary that Churchill was elated and excited at the prospect of the attack upon Madagascar.[49] Later a message of encouragement, which reflected Churchill's mood, was sent to the force commanders: "Ironclad may be the first star in what we all feel is assured to be a glittering firmament." Diego Suarez would be taken, Churchill then told General Wavell, "by the use of strong forces and severe, violent action".[50]

Chapter 4

"Ironclad Begun"

Madagascar, known to the French as "la Grande Ile", is the fourth–largest island in the world. It is over 900 miles long and 350 miles across at its widest point and, along with its dependencies, Mayotte and the Comoros Islands, it comprises an area of around 240,000 square miles, which is greater than France itself and four times the size of England and Wales. The island is largely composed of malarial swamps, dense jungle, high mountains, deep ravines and dry plains, whilst its forbidding coast is fringed with reefs and sandbanks. Movement across the island is generally only possible along the roads, which are poor, and on the railways, which are few. Madagascar has a tropical climate with summer monsoons and average day-time temperatures of around 30°C. The region around Diego Suarez (named after a Portuguese adventurer who landed and terrorized the area in the mid-sixteenth century) is dry and hot for most of the year, with ninety per cent of its annual 900mm of rain falling between December and April. In 1941 Madagascar had a population of 3,500,000, including 25,000 French and assimilated French.[1]

At the extreme northern tip of Madagascar is the Andrakaka Peninsula. The narrow isthmus by which it is joined to the mainland is formed by two deep cuts, on the east side Diego Suarez Bay and to the west Courrier Bay. The anchorage in Diego Suarez Bay is enclosed by two, almost encircling arms of land, leaving a narrow, easily defended channel as the bay's only entrance. On a spur of land, known as the Diego Suarez Peninsula, which projects into this magnificent bay, is the town and naval base of Antsirane which, in 1942, had a population of 30,000. Diego Suarez had been a military camp since 1885 and an independent French colony for ten years before being incorporated into the rest of Madagascar. Its defences were originally constructed in 1904 but during the First World War many of the guns were removed and sent to France. In the 1920s, Diego Suarez was partially re-armed, though some old guns remained in use.[2]

After the Allied attack upon Dakar the fortifications at Diego Suarez were strengthened and, following the reconnaissance flights over the area by the SAAF, all the defences had been fully manned.[3] At Antsirane were the barracks of the *2me Régiment Mixte de Madagascar* (*RMM*), consisting of three battalions of French, Senegalese (recently arrived by ship from Jibuti) and Malagasy soldiers. Their numbers had been increased during the preceding weeks and now totalled 3,000 men of whom 800 were Europeans. There were also around 4,000 French naval personnel in and around Antsirane.[4]

In March 1941, a survey of Madagascar's defences was undertaken by the Vichy War Ministry. In its conclusions the survey's report recommended an

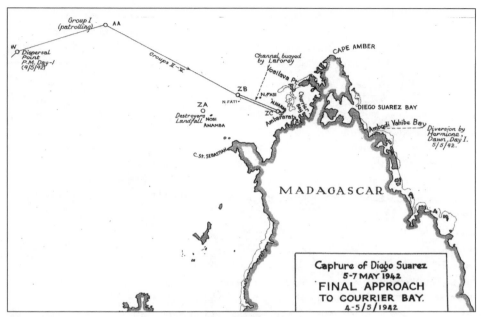

MAP 2: The approach route taken by the invasion fleet from the dispersal point towards Courrier Bay on the 4 and 5 May 1942. The route was marked by SOE at a point just north of Nosey Anamo (marked on this map as Nosi Anamba), in the form of a flaming torch displayed by the crew of *Lindi*.

"augmentation" to the island's air forces, an improvement in the mobility of the general reserve by equipping it with motorized transport (coupled with the development of the island's road network) and the modernization of the artillery, including an increase in the number of anti-tank and anti-aircraft weapons, particularly at Diego Suarez, Majunga and Tamatave.[5]

Only one of these recommendations had been implemented, this being the increase in the island's air defences. All that had existed before Annet's arrival were a few old Potez 29 and Potez 25 biplanes which were used in reconnaissance and communications duties. On 1 July 1941, a squadron of modern Morane-Saulnier MS 406 fighters, *Escadrille* 565, was established at Arrachart airfield near Diego Suarez. This was followed on 23 July by the formation of another squadron, *Escadrille* 555, of Potez 63–11 twin-engine bombers, at the capital Tananarive. *Escadrille* 565 had between eighteen and twenty aircraft, whereas 555 had just seven Potez bombers. In February 1942, there was a change in these dispositions. The two fighter and bomber squadrons were merged to form the *Groupe Aérien Mixte*. The air group's main base was Invato-Tananarive, with a detachment at Diego-Arrachart which was kept in a state of constant readiness.[6] Though Darlan informed Annet on 24 March that he would receive a reinforcement of a further 30 aircraft and 400 men, it was too late – Convoy W.S. 17 was already at sea.[7]

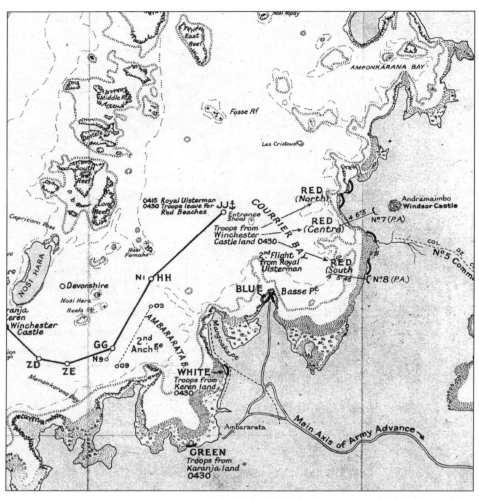

MAP 3: The approach route and location of the landing beaches at Ambararata and Courrier Bays on 5–8 May 1942.

Altogether there were some 8,000 troops on the island with the *1er Régiment Mixte de Madagascar*, artillery sections, a company of engineers and a motorized reconnaissance detachment at the capital Tananarive, in the centre of the country. The remainder of the troops, consisting mainly of artillery sections and reservists, were distributed around the island. If the Vichy authorities were to call for full mobilization their force could be increased to 30,000 men, though it was unlikely that the additional troops would be fully armed or equipped.[8]

To the south of Antsirane was Arrachart airfield where the detachment of the *Groupe Aérien Mixte* was permanently stationed. The aircraft at Arrachart consisted of both Potez 63–11 bombers and MS 406 fighters. The Potez 63–11 was officially classified as an army co-operation and reconnaissance aircraft but it seems to have been widely utilized as a light-bomber and could carry up to eight 50kg bombs. The MS 406 was the principal fighter aircraft of the French *Armée de l'Air*. It had a top speed of over 300 miles per hour and was armed with a 20mm cannon and two machine guns. It had performed creditably against the *Luftwaffe* in the battle for France. Over 1,000 of these planes were produced but by 1942 they were considered to be obsolescent. The main base of the *Groupe Aérien Mixte* was at Tananarive where, in addition to a squadron of MS 406s, there was a flight of Potez 63–11s, a number of old Potez 25 reconnaissance and ground attack biplanes with a 500lb bomb load, and general purpose Potez 29s which were used mainly for casualty evacuations.[9]

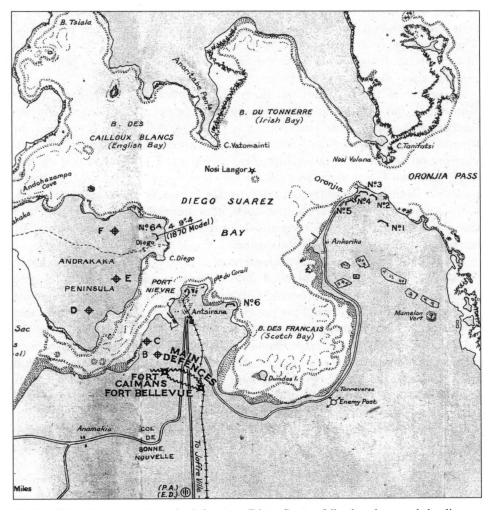

MAP 4: The advance on the main defences at Diego Suarez following the assault landings at Ambararata and Courrier Bays

The entrance to Diego Suarez Bay was defended by heavy batteries, with searchlights on both arms. At the harbour mouth was one battery of four 320mm guns on fixed mountings and three other batteries equipped with smaller ordnance.[10] A mining barge containing twenty-five mines was moored close to the shore at this point, which, in the event of an attack, could lay a line of mines across the harbour entrance. Further south on the Orangea Peninsula there was a battery of two 80mm field guns in a small, Foreign Legion-style fort known as Mamelon Vert, which projected into the sea to guard the eastern approaches. Altogether, there were seven coastal batteries in and around Diego Suarez, mounting a total of twenty large calibre guns. Mines had also been used to seal the comparatively open beaches of Courrier Bay. Laid in two lines in July 1941 by the vessel *L'Ocean*, these 111 mines stretched from the islet of Nosi Famaho to the shore.[11]

Little was known of any landward defences other than the presence of a range of field works with gun emplacements, but it was thought that these were not armed. There were, however, two mobile batteries of 75mm and 65mm field guns and an anti-aircraft battery at Arrachart airfield. In addition there was a heavy anti-aircraft battery at Lazaret Point.[12]

At anchor in the bay were the sloop *D'Entrecasteaux*, the auxiliary cruiser *Bougainville* (an armed merchant ship mounting three 135mm guns) and the submarine *Beveziers*, which had fought at Dakar in 1940 where it crippled the British battleship *Resolution*. Three other submarines and the sloop *D'Iberville* were out on patrol.[13] The cargo ships, *Ile-Bourbon* and *Foch*, were also in the bay, along with two Greek ships and two Italian ships – one a freighter, the other a passenger liner. A German freighter, *Wartenfels*, was under repair in the dry dock. It was known that there were ample stocks of ammunition at Diego Suarez and the cases marked "medicines" recently delivered by the auxiliary cruiser actually contained bombs, mines, shells and explosives.[14]

Though the attitude of the French garrison could not be predicted, maximum resistance was expected and planned for, especially as Laval had recently been demanding a Japanese occupation of Madagascar to pre-empt a British or Gaullist attack.[15] Annet had also stated his position in March by declaring publicly that "Madagascar has but one will, to remain French. For this she does not need the aid even temporarily of any other nation ... she will be able to face ... any menace of aggression from whatever source it may come."[16] Despite all of this, Churchill still hoped that the French would not fight back and he suggested to the Chiefs of Staff that during the middle of the attack a launch flying the white flag should steam into Diego Suarez and offer "the most tempting terms for capitulation"![17] The suggestion was rejected but the rules of engagement under which the British troops were to operate stipulated that they should not be the first to open fire, except against aircraft and submarines.[18]

As a direct assault upon Diego Suarez had been discounted by the Joint Planning Staff, the plan of attack was to land the troops in Courrier Bay and the adjacent, but smaller, Ambararata Bay. According to 121 Force's operational instructions, "an early and rapid advance towards the objective accompanied by tanks, carriers and artillery would impress the badly equipped enemy ... who will be more likely to give up the struggle if they can be convinced that our attack is in great strength and that their defence is inadequate to meet it."[19] The infantry would therefore march across twenty miles of rough terrain to approach Antsirane from the south-west without waiting for the motor transport to be unloaded.

A diversionary attack was also arranged. At Zero Hour the cruiser *Hermione* would undertake a fake bombardment of Ambode Vahibe Bay to the south-east of Antsirane. As a further distraction, dummy paratroopers would also be dropped in the inaccessible country around Mahagaga on the direct route from Ambode Vahibe to Antsirane.[20]

Complete sets of orders were produced and distributed to each ship. These included instructions for the consolidation of Diego Suarez immediately after its capture and for the possible secondary assaults upon Majunga and Tamatave.[21]

It was understood that the approaches to Courrier Bay and Ambararata Bay were mined and that the beaches were defended by two coastal artillery batteries, No.7 of four 164mm guns and No.8 of four 138mm guns. There was also an armed observation post on a rocky promontory at the northern edge of Courrier Bay referred to, and still known today, as 'Windsor Castle'.[22]

The attack was to be made on a broad front across six beaches, and was modelled on recent, successful Japanese operations. Though command and control would be more difficult, if the landing was opposed the attackers would be likely to breakthrough somewhere, whereas if the assault was concentrated on a narrow front the attack might never succeed if that point was heavily defended.[23] For the assault landings, three beaches along the northern half of Courrier Bay were nominated as North, Central and South 'Red Beach'. A single beach at the south-western tip of Courrier Bay was 'Blue Beach', with 'White' and 'Green' beaches further south in Ambararata Bay. No.5 Commando, with one company of the East Lancashire Regiment under its command, was to land at Red Beach and capture the two batteries and the observation post. They were instructed to put the French guns out of action, but not to destroy them. The Commandos and the East Lancs would then march across the Andrakaka Peninsula to the north-west of Diego Suarez Bay – a distance of just ten or eleven miles. The Andrakaka Peninsula, however, is separated from the naval base at Antsirane by more than a mile of water, but it was hoped that the Commandos would find some means of crossing the water to attack Antsirane from that side.[24]

The main attack upon Antsirane would be made by the bulk of the 29th Brigade. The first wave of the brigade, consisting of the Welch Fusiliers and the 1st Royal Scots Fusiliers, was to land at White Beach and Green Beach. Mayer had warned Syfret that Blue Beach was defended by six light and six heavy machine guns, concealed in nests, manned by a company of Senegalese troops. It would be the job of the Welch Fusiliers, immediately after landing, to move a detachment north to take the Senegalese from the rear and occupy Blue Beach.[25]

Once the beaches had been secured, the Welch and the Scots were to advance eastwards across the Ambararata Plain to attack Antsirane from the landward side.

This was a march of some 18–20 miles. The second wave of landing craft would deliver the remainder of the East Lancs to Blue Beach, and the South Lancs to White and Blue beaches. These two battalions would follow the advance of the two Fusilier battalions upon Antsirane.

The next to land would be Tarleton's 17th Brigade. Elements of this brigade would take over control of the beach area and the coastal defence batteries. The remainder of the 17th Brigade would follow the main body of the 29th Brigade to support the attack upon Antsirane on day two or three of the operation. Once Antsirane had been taken the 17th Brigade would move through the town and capture the French positions that guarded the harbour entrance to allow Syfret's ships to enter Diego Suarez Bay. Tarleton was also ordered to send a battalion to assist the Commandos if they encountered stiff opposition on the Andrakaka Peninsula. The 13th Brigade would remain on the troopships in the bay as the force reserve.[26]

With confirmation that the operation was to proceed not being received until 1 May, there were only three days to sort the various platoons into landing craft loads, to study the landing tables, to issue ammunition and to test the weapons by firing them into the sea.[27] The photographs taken by the SAAF were shown to the troops, and cloth models that had been made of the landing beaches were used to demonstrate exactly what was expected of each platoon and section.[28]

When Antsirane had been secured, the third phase of the operation would then begin – an attack by the land forces, supported by naval bombardment, against the coastal batteries on the Orangea Peninsula which defended the entrance to Diego Suarez Bay. The earlier decision to extend operations to include the capture of Tamatave and Majunga was countermanded by the Chiefs of Staff on 3 May because of the pressing need to rush the 13th and 17th brigades on to India, where the military situation had deteriorated further.[29]

The landings were to feature an entirely new body of troops. This was a specialized unit whose function was to land with, or ahead of, the first wave of troops to take control of the landing beaches. Formed from Navy personnel, the duties of this unit included marking out and consolidating the beachhead, keeping personnel and equipment moving through the beachhead as quickly as possible, helping to moor the landing craft, supervising ammunition and supply dumps on the beach, marking safe passages for the wounded returning to the ships, supporting the attacking troops if they met stubborn resistance, and acting as a rearguard in the event of an evacuation. This unit was so successful that the Royal Naval Commandos (also known as the 'Beach-head Commandos') were formed later in 1942.

Another embryonic military unit included with the *Ironclad* forces was a branch of Army Intelligence called 'Field Security'. At this time its functions were rather ill-defined but they included making contact with British agents and the capture of enemy spies. Surprisingly, Field Security appears to have been well-informed (no doubt by Mayer) and had been provided with lists of both Allied sympathizers and German spies in northern Madagascar.[30] A small number of Field Security personnel were attached to each battalion of the 29th Brigade. They were to enter Antsirane with the leading formations of their respective battalions to seize the town's key civilian installations. These were listed as the Defence HQ, the Government Residency, both police stations, the post and telegraph office, the power station, the reservoir, the prison and the bank.[31] The Expeditionary Force also included a Political Warfare officer who would land armed with soap, scent and toothpaste to distribute amongst the locals. Quite how it was thought the French would respond to this gesture, after being bombed and shelled into submission, was not explained![32]

The aerial support for the landings was to involve all nine squadrons from *Indomitable* and *Illustrious* and included a variety of aircraft types – Albacores, Sea Hurricanes, Fulmars, Swordfish and Martlets. The Fairey Swordfish was a torpedo, spotter and reconnaissance aircraft which was armed with two machine guns and one 18-inch torpedo. The Albacore, designed by Fairey to supersede the Swordfish as a torpedo–bomber, could carry one 1,610lb torpedo, six 250lb or five 500lb bombs. The Sea Hurricane, Fairey Fulmar and the Grumman Martlet were specialist carrier-borne fighters. Of these, the Fulmar was also used as a reconnaissance plane and a light bomber with two 113kg bombs. The Fulmar's crew included a navigator to ensure that the pilot found his way back to the carrier!

Eight Albacores of 827 Naval Air Squadron (NAS), along with a number of Sea Hurricane 1Bs from 880 NAS and three Fulmar IIs all from *Indomitable*, were given the tasks of attacking the airfields and dropping leaflets upon Antsirane and Arrachart. On their first run the Albacores were to scatter the leaflets. Five minutes later they were to repeat the run, this time bombing the airfield. If there was any movement by the French aircraft before the expiry of the five minutes, the Albacores were to attack immediately. The Hurricanes would follow a few minutes later to complete the work of the Albacores. The three Fulmars were to attack Vohemar aerodrome, which was situated seventy-two miles to the south of Arrachart. This would prevent Vohemar being used as an advanced operational base for the French aircraft at Tananarive.[33]

Of the remaining aircraft from *Indomitable*, three Albacores were to undertake air support for the transport ships at anchor in Courrier Bay and patrol over Diego Suarez Bay. Two Fulmars or Sea Hurricanes were to provide continuous fighter cover over Antsirane town and harbour whilst another two fighters were to provide the aircraft carriers with defensive cover. The rest of *Indomitable*'s Albacores were to undertake seaward reconnaissance and act as a reserve strike force.

Eighteen Swordfish of 810 and 829 squadrons from *Illustrious*, escorted by eight Martlets, were to "sink at sight" any submarines in the harbour and any surface ships seen under way or attempting to get under way. One Fulmar and one Swordfish were to provide the ground forces with tactical reconnaissance whilst six other Swordfish and six Martlets were to give the military whatever direct air support was necessary. Three Swordfish with two Martlets as escort were to drop the eighteen dummy parachutists and one Swordfish was kept on standby to provide aerial observation for the warships bombarding the defences on the

Orangea Peninsula. Rear-Admiral Boyd (*Indomitable*), Senior Officer, Aircraft Carriers, was told that after the immobilization of the French air forces and submarines his first priority was the protection of the convoy and the military landing. Therefore, the rest of *Illustrious*'s aircraft were to assist *Indomitable*'s fighters in protecting the transports and the beaches.[34]

At noon on 4 May 1942, the two convoys from Durban, plus the *Indomitable* with two destroyers from the Eastern Fleet, converged upon the pre-arranged concentration point about ninety-five miles to the west of Cape Amber at the northernmost tip of Madagascar. This was a dangerous time for the British force as there were now nearly fifty ships assembled off the Malagasy coast. All radio transmissions were prohibited until Zero Hour and communication was limited to visual signalling during daylight hours only. If Syfret had to postpone the operation at the last minute, due to adverse weather or some other unforeseen occurrence, radio silence would be maintained – for days if necessary. Only when the attack had begun would contact be made with London. The possibility of an intervention by Japanese forces was so keenly felt that all the available ships of the Eastern Fleet, including two battleships, one aircraft carrier, five cruisers and seven destroyers, patrolled the seas between 130 and 220 miles to the east of Diego Suarez throughout the operation. Long-range Catalina flying-boats had also begun to fly reconnaissance patrols deep into the Indian Ocean and these continued until after the capture of Diego Suarez.[35]

All the ships involved in *Ironclad* were instructed to "give first priority" to engaging any Japanese naval units they encountered. If a Japanese force approached the western Indian Ocean which was inferior to the combined strength of Force F and the Eastern Fleet, Somerville was ordered to concentrate all these forces to achieve the destruction of the enemy. If, on the other hand, the Japanese arrived with a superior force Somerville had been given the authority to cancel the entire operation and withdraw all the ships.[36] It was therefore "with some relief", as Bob Sturges later wrote, that darkness fell with this vast armada undetected by enemy aircraft or surface vessels.[37]

For the assault, the ships were divided into five groups. Group I was the covering force of *Ramillies*, *Illustrious*, *Indomitable*, *Hermione* and seven destroyers. This group left the main body at 14.30 hours to take up its positions to the north-west of Cape Amber. The remaining four groups, with a combined total of thirty-four ships, were under the command of Captain Oliver of the *Devonshire*. He had to take this convoy eighty-eight miles to the main anchorage off Courrier Bay through narrow and hazardous waters, with the last half of the journey in darkness.[38] The French considered the approach to Courrier Bay to be impossible at night and Syfret fully expected to lose some of his ships on the broad reefs that surround the bay.[39]

At 18.00 hours the destroyers *Laforey*, *Lightening* and *Anthony* were sent ahead of the convoy to make landfall and establish an accurate position. For this they would have to locate the light on Nosi Anambo which it was hoped that *Lindi* had

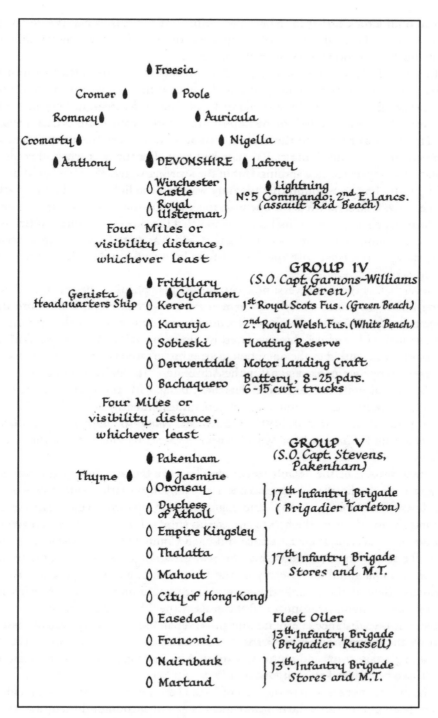

PLAN 1: The cruising order of the invasion fleet on the final approach to Madagascar and the landing beaches.

placed on the rock earlier in the evening. After a minor scare when the destroyers almost attacked a small island with torpedoes, thinking it was an enemy ship, the white light was spotted glowing in the darkness.

In actual fact, the crew of *Lindi* had found that it was impracticable to place a light on Nosi Anambo. They had also discovered that the island's position had been charted incorrectly (it was found to be one and three-quarters of a mile further to the west) and before the imposition of radio silence this crucial piece of information was relayed to the convoy.[40] To accurately mark the point where the deep channel led into Courrier Bay they had to anchor the boat where it could be seen by the approaching warships. But in the swirling waters the boat could not be held steady. The crew found that the only way that the light could be kept facing in the correct direction was for one man to sit astride the mast and turn round as the boat swung about on its anchor. So it was that the success or failure of Britain's largest amphibious assault since the First World War rested upon a single person clinging to a frail mast with one hand whilst he waved a home-made torch with the other![41]

Nevertheless the destroyers, now certain of their position, began to lay buoys along a narrow, fifteen-mile-long channel as far as Nosi Hara, little more than three miles from Ambararata Bay. The destroyers then waited at the entrance of the channel with signal lights displayed until the arrival of the convoy. With his forces now committed to the operation, Syfret broke radio silence and transmitted the pre-arranged, ciphered signal to the Admiralty: "IRONCLAD begun."[42]

The two aircraft carriers were detached along with the destroyers *Paladin*, *Panther*, *Javelin* and *Inconstant* to operate independently under Rear-Admiral Boyd, some thirty-five miles off Cape Amber. *Ramillies*, with *Lookout*, *Active*, *Pakenham* and *Duncan*, kept within visual supporting distance of the assault convoy.

The approach of the assault convoy to Courrier Bay was led by the corvette *Freesia* with the flotilla of minesweepers in echelon on either side, followed by the destroyers *Anthony*, *Laforey* and *Lightning*, and then the cruiser *Devonshire*. Behind *Devonshire* were the first of the assault ships – *Winchester Castle* and *Royal Ulsterman* – carrying the East Lancs and No.5 Commando. At a distance of four miles, or at maximum visibility, was the next group of ships. Three corvettes led *Keren*, *Karanja* and *Sobieski* carrying the South Lancs and the Scots and Welch Fusiliers. Behind the assault ships were *Derwentdale* and *Bachaquero* with the 29th Brigade's motor transport and the guns of the 9th Field Regiment.

Once again a distance of around four miles separated the third group of vessels. Led by the destroyer *Pakenham* and the corvettes *Thyme* and *Jasmine* were the remaining troop ships and motor transport ships carrying the men and materiel of the two brigades of the 5th Division.[43]

The first anchorage, just to the west of Nosi Hara, was reached without incident. From this point onwards the minesweepers began to encounter difficulties. At one stage all four vessels lost their sweeps after sailing too close to one of the smaller islands and then, as they neared the second anchorage, they entered the minefield.

The mines, which were moored to the sea bed, floated six to eight feet below the low-water mark and were spaced about 150 feet apart.[44] Altogether seventeen of the mines were cut.

The assault ships and transports reached the deep waters of the bay at around 02.00 hours. It was as near to the shore as the ships dare approach until every mine had been swept. "For an hour or so the normal illumination within the ship had been replaced by red lights to provide some measure of adaptation to the darkness on deck," recounted an officer on board *Karanja* with the Welch Fusiliers. "We began to assemble in silence broken only by the slapping of water against the side of the ship, now at anchor, and the occasional chink of metal on metal which provoked a prompt and hoarsely whispered 'Quiet there.'"[45] The troops had spent the previous day resting and sleeping, now they were wide awake and about to embark upon the first large-scale combined operation Britain had ever attempted.

Earlier in the night Mayer had cut the telephone line connecting the Courrier Bay batteries with Defence Headquarters at Antsirane. He then waited for the start of the landings to help guide the British troops and pass on the information he had gathered since the 28th, when the last transmission had been made to Durban. The withdrawal of the other agents at Ambararata meant that Mayer could not attend the drinking party in the town but he had already learnt that the knock-out drops he had been given were only effective for two and a half minutes!

Not having been told the exact time of the landings, Mayer waited until 02.40 hours and then, thinking that the attack had been postponed, he returned to Antsirane. There he was arrested following a report that he had been trying to obtain military information from a French soldier. The notes intended for Sturges were still in his pocket!

He was taken to the Naval Headquarters where he was imprisoned, and his room at the hotel was searched. Though Mayer managed to tear up his notes the French police were able to piece them together. It was all the evidence the police needed. Mayer was charged with espionage and was told that he would be shot.[46] But, by then, the attack upon Diego Suarez had started.

The first wave of landing craft carrying the Commandos, and the attached company of the East Lancs, set off from the dispersal area at 02.18 hours. Two of the landing craft collided with each other and the troops had to be trans-shipped in mid channel, and all the Landing Craft Assault (LCA) heading for Red Beach South mis-read a pre-arranged signal and ran aground before reaching the beach.[47]

As the landing craft sped towards the shore one of the mines detonated in the minesweeper *Romney*'s sweep. Everyone braced themselves for the expected barrage from the French coastal batteries. But all remained silent ashore. Fifteen minutes later, at 03.15 hours, a second mine exploded. It seemed inconceivable that the French could sleep through both explosions but, to everyone's amazement, the peace of the warm spring night returned and remained undisturbed.[48]

The Commandos landed in Courrier Bay shortly after 04.30 hours, one hour before dawn. As the French did not believe that ships could enter the bay at night no guards were posted and the Commandos silently crept ashore unobserved. A correspondent for the *Daily Telegraph* recorded the rest of the story: "Wearing special rubber-soled boots, each one knowing his life depended on silence, our men stole in noiselessly … We split into four pre-arranged parties and finding no opposition spread out fanwise to comb the hillside where the battery was located.

"In the first cast we missed the guns – they were so beautifully concealed. Then in the first glimmer of daylight we made out some huts below us so some of us went down there. We crept in and found they were barracks with the crews from the battery fast asleep … They came tumbling out, holding their hands up in surrender. They were all coloured troops and the whole thing was over just like that!" [49] After securing all the prisoners, the Commandos rendered the guns temporarily unserviceable by removing the breech blocks, and then fired three green Verey flares into the sky to signal their success to the waiting assault ships.[50]

Leaving one section with the guns, the rest of the Commandos moved inland. One troop of Commandos encountered two French officers who had been hiding in the grass. Despite facing overwhelming odds the French officers fired at the Commandos and one of them, showing considerable bravery, leapt up and stabbed one of the Commandos in the arm. Both were killed. The Commandos next reached a small barracks complex which they found in the dark by following the telegraph wire which ran between the battery and the barracks.[51] At the barracks six Europeans and ninety Malagasy were taken prisoner. The two troops which landed at Red Beach South found that their first objective, No.8 Coastal Battery, did not exist.[52]

All did not go entirely satisfactorily for No.5 Commando, however, because the pinnacle of the promontory of Windsor Castle had been turned into an infantry post occupied by a combat group. This was found to be an extremely strong position, more than 1,200 feet high, the upper slopes of which were sheer rock, the only access being up a single stairway cut out of the rock. The French held this post all day and the following night, stopping every attempt to scale the precipitous face of the rocks with small-arms fire, grenades and bombs from a 60mm mortar.[53]

Though the observation post in their rear remained in enemy hands, the main body of the Commandos, with two Bren gun carriers, assembled at the pre-arranged rendezvous point two miles inland and at 09.00 hours began the march upon Diego Suarez village. One troop was left behind to guard the prisoners and to continue the attack upon Windsor Castle.

The advance across the Andrakaka Peninsula was led by the Bren gun carriers, each packed with men armed with automatic weapons. A small body of French troops was waiting in prepared defensive positions across the peninsula's isthmus, supported by two 65mm field guns. But at the sight of the Bren gun carriers the French abandoned their defences and retreated eastwards to their main base of the *Camp des Tirailleurs* near the village of Diego Suarez. Here, after just a few minutes of "half-hearted" gun-fire, the defenders surrendered and the village was taken. A further 17 Europeans, 100 native troops and 2 coast defence batteries were captured.[54]

The Commandos "diplomatically" hoisted both the Union Flag and the Tricolour on the flag-staff at the summit of the 300-foot high crag of Cap Diego.[55]

With all the French artillery commanding Courrier Bay in British hands, the landing craft of the main assault force, loaded with soldiers and weapons, made their way to the beaches escorted by corvettes. The time was 04.32 hours.

At this moment the heavy guns of *Hermione* opened fire with star shells on the eastern side of the island in the feint bombardment upon Ambodi Vahibe Bay, the most likely alternative landing place. At the same time the cruiser began making smoke and dropping burning tar barrels to simulate the approach of a convoy.[56]

As soon as *Hermione* opened fire, Captain Laporte, commanding the Orangea batteries, telephoned Defence Headquarters at Antsirane. Within ten minutes, Colonel Claerebout had called together his senior officers and the warning signals and sirens sounded around the town.[57]

Thirty minutes earlier, just before 04.00 hours, the first aircraft had left the decks of *Illustrious* and *Indomitable* stationed to the west of Cape Amber. The aircraft were ordered to keep more than seven miles from the shore until fifteen minutes after zero hour and then to attack from the east coast, i.e. the opposite direction from the assault landings.[58] From Admiralty charts, maps and the photographs provided by the SAAF, relief models of the Diego Suarez area had been made for each aircraft carrier. These enabled the flight crews to become familiar with the terrain in the different light conditions that they would experience.[59]

The Swordfish of 810 and 829 squadrons flew from *Illustrious* in three waves of six aircraft each. The first wave, armed with torpedoes, arrived over the bay at 05.00 hours. Spotting *D'Entrecasteaux*, the six Swordfish released their torpedoes in the direction of the French sloop. All the missiles missed their target. But one of the torpedoes, which had passed under the *D'Entrecasteaux*, struck the *Bougainville*. A medical officer on the *D'Entrecasteaux* recorded the action in his diary: "Rushed to the deck just in time to see the stern of the Bougainville lifted in an enormous column of water. She breaks in two aft and begins to sink slowly." The guns of the auxiliary cruiser, which had just got under way, continued to fire on the British aircraft even as the ship was sinking. But at 05.05 hours *Bougainville* was hit again. "This time", wrote Jean Hanlon, "a fresh triangular fragment slides slowly beneath the water in the midst of an impressive cloud of smoke."[60]

The second wave, carrying depth charges, spotted the submarine *Bévéziers* trying to move away from the jetty into deeper water. Three aircraft, diving in line astern, depth-charged the submarine, which soon began to list to starboard. *Bévéziers* caught fire just before she sank.

All this had been achieved within minutes of the opening of the attack, though it cost the squadron five aircraft. This included one of the Swordfish which failed to reach *Illustrious* when its engine stalled just 100 yards from the carrier. Its crew was rescued by the destroyer *Javelin*.[61]

The surviving crewmen from *Bougainville* and *Bévéziers* later joined the French infantry defending Antsirane. Amongst these was the unfortunate captain of *Bourgainville* who, having survived the burning and sinking of his ship, was killed in the trenches outside Antsirane with a rifle in his hands.[62]

By the time that the third wave from *Illustrious* arrived over the bay just a few moments later, the French gunners were at their posts and the Swordfish met severe anti-aircraft fire from the shore batteries and the ships. The commander of the Cap Diego battery even rowed out into the bay in a small boat to gauge the effectiveness of his guns, exposed continuously to the attacks of the Fleet Arm. He was later recommended for the *Médaille Militaire*.[63]

In their first pass the planes dropped the leaflets and bombed the battery at Lazaret Point, before making another attack upon *D'Entrecasteaux*. This time the sloop was set on fire and it ran aground in Andohazampo Cove.[64] During this a shell from the battery hit the engine of the flight leader, Lieutenant Everett, who was forced to make an emergency landing. The Swordfish came to a halt upside-down on the beach inside the eastern arm of the bay. Everett and Pilot Officer Graves were captured and taken prisoner. The following day Everett and Graves had the unfortunate experience of being in prison in Antsirane whilst the town was bombed by their own squadron.[65]

Predictably, the leaflets made no impression upon the French. Annet later claimed that the British message would have received "touching attention" had it not been preceded by the bombing of the French ships and the killing of French sailors. Instead, as Syfret revealed in his operational report, "what the inhabitants did with the leaflets would surprise their originators"![66]

The airfield was targeted by the first wave from 831 Squadron, using bombs and incendiaries. At 05.00 hours, eight Sea Hurricanes from 880 Squadron set off from *Indomitable* to complete the work of 831 Squadron by destroying "anything and everything of military importance left on the aerodrome".[67]

The Hurricanes arrived over the target area just as dawn was breaking and attacked in two sections of four aircraft. Though they encountered flak, by the time the Hurricanes broke off and returned to *Indomitable* two Potez 63 bombers and two elderly Potez 25 biplanes were on fire as well as five Morane fighters and, unfortunately, a civilian aircraft. Some of the hangars were also hit and a stray bullet killed the detachment commander Lieutenant Rossigneux.[68]

At this stage of the battle the French still believed that the British attack was coming from the south-east. Because Mayer had cut the telephone line from Windsor Castle, Claerebout was completely unaware of the landings in Courrier Bay and he sent his only mechanized unit, the *Détachment de reconnaissance motorisé*, southwards to counter the dummy parachutists.[69] These had been dropped by three Swordfish, each carrying six dummies in their bomb racks, near a police post (so they would not drop unseen) in a valley north of Col de la Herte.[70] To reinforce the impression that the British attack was from the east, the *Hermione* moved north towards the Orangea Pass to engage the batteries at Cap Miné. However, the

164mm guns of Le Point de Vue battery out-ranged *Hermione's* main armament and the cruiser was forced to withdraw.[71]

These diversions had worked well, but by now the entire garrison was awake and under arms, including those officers who had just gone to bed after what had been, despite Mayer's absence, a late and "rather boozy" night at the house of a woman called Natalie.[72]

At Green Beach the 1st Royal Scots Fusiliers waded ashore through the knee-deep water with the Welch Fusiliers reaching White Beach at approximately the same time. A journalist with *The Daily Telegraph* described the scene: "Through a powerful broadcasting amplifier a bronzed 22-year-old beachmaster was shouting orders to a dozen landing craft, a hundred yards out, telling them at which point to beach. They came in one after another like trains arriving at a terminus." [73]

'C' Company was the first to land at Green Beach, quickly organizing one platoon to form a perimeter guard around the beach. All equipment had to be man-handled and the laborious task of unloading machine guns, mortars, food and ammunition began. However, after detaching the necessary landing craft for the Commandos at Red Beach, there were only sufficient craft remaining to land on the first trip 580 men of the Royal Scots, 512 of the Royal Welch and 14 Bren gun carriers, as well as the beach parties, signals, engineers and medical detachments.[74]

The second run by the landing craft used for the Commandos on Red Beach took the remainder of the East Lancs to Blue Beach at Basse Point. "The sea was very choppy, and waves were breaking over the landing craft," wrote one member of the East Lancs. "Before very long we were all wet through, and we couldn't see exactly where we were going."[75] As the landing craft neared the shore they were met by small-arms and machine gun fire from around fifty Senegalese infantry. "Machine-gun bullets lashed the sea into feathers of foam", wrote the naval officer directing the operation, "and several penetrated the hull of the landing craft."[76] Some of the lifeboats of *Royal Ulsterman*, with Bren guns mounted in the bows, were also used in the run to Blue Beach and the Lancashires were able to return fire.[77] As planned, one company of the Welch Fusiliers was sent northwards to Basse Point. Faced with overwhelming numbers from the front and the rear, the Senegalese fled in disorder. Their huts were then burned to flush out those who had attempted to hide. With this the last of the beaches had been secured.[78]

It had taken the landing craft two hours to deposit fewer than 2,400 men on the shore and the main anchorage had still not been swept of all its mines. It took another hour to clear the mines, by which time the tide had fallen and the wind had strengthened to Force 8.[79] Blue Beach was now the only beach that could still safely be used and *Bachaquero*, carrying the 29th Brigade's transport and attached artillery, had been ordered to move through the swept channel to Blue Beach at approximately 06.00 hours. But more mines were found in the anchorage and *Bachaquero* had to wait until midday before she was able to reach a mooring position off the beach. However, it was discovered that the rocks and the gradient of the beach made a landing impossible, and *Bachaquero* was faced with the prospect of having to unload its cargo by derrick onto small landing craft. It would take approximately two days to unload all the guns and vehicles in this fashion. After all the trials and exercises, the crew of the *Bachaquero* were hugely disappointed.[80]

There were also continuing problems on Red Beach. Machine-gun fire from the French post on Windsor Castle continued to hamper movement across the beach and, at 11.26 hours, *Devonshire* was asked to bombard Windsor Castle. Instead of trying to shell such an elevated position Captain Oliver launched his on-board Walrus sea-plane. The aircraft flew ten bombing runs and, later, Albacores and Hurricanes joined in the attack, but the defenders defiantly clung to their eyrie.

As the aircraft attacked Windsor Castle, *Devonshire* received a signal from the Senior Officer Minesweepers that *Auricula* had struck a mine. Boats were sent to take off the crew. Though she did not actually sink, *Auricula* was too badly damaged to tow to harbour and the minesweeper was abandoned and left floating at anchor.

Another attempt was made to evict the French from Windsor Castle when the destroyer *Laforey* was ordered to bombard the position with its 4.7-inch guns. Captain Hutton opened fire at 15.26 hours. After twenty-nine rounds a white flag appeared on the summit of the position. Hutton flashed a signal to the French post "come down or we continue". The Beach Station reported to *Laforey* that the French were leaving their posts and the Commandos went up the rock to take the surrender. Either this was a bluff or the French changed their minds, but they returned to their posts and drove the Commandos back with grenades, wounding the troop commander, Captain Heron. *Laforey* was asked to re-engage the French position and, at 16.58 hours, Hutton fired a further thirty-six rounds. This time the destroyer scored a direct hit on the living quarters just below the summit, but the French continued to hold their ground. *Lightening* and *Cromarty* joined *Laforey* and more than 100 shells were fired at the French post, but to no avail.[81]

Further attempts were also made by the Fleet Air Arm to sink *D'Entrecasteaux*. A little after 12.30 hours, two aircraft from 810 Squadron dived from 4,000 feet and straddled the sloop's bows with bombs. One of the bombs hit the French ship, penetrating the platform deck and exploding. *D'Entrecasteaux* then turned and made its way across the bay to the shallow water of the Cul de Sac Gallois. At 14.45 hours, six more aircraft took off from *Illustrious* and located the sloop beached in a sandy cove. The Swordfish attacked, their bombs exploding on and around the stricken vessel. The sloop was then raked by the aircraft's guns: "15.00. Ten very heavy machine gun attacks – the moral effect is terrific," wrote Jean Hanlon. "It is a veritable hail ... Shots penetrate to the very centre of the ship. On the spar-deck, chunks of wood jump in the air. Our funnels are on fire. A dense cloud of smoke envelops us. Everything is torn up, twisted, bent and broken." Though seriously damaged, *D'Entrecasteaux* fought back and three of *Indomitable*'s planes were hit in the attacks on the sloop, two of which were put out of action for several days.[82]

Back in Courrier Bay, as *Bachaquero* was weighing anchor opposite Blue Beach a fast motorboat rushed alongside carrying the news that a suitable landing spot had been found in Red Beach.[83] Following in the wake of the minesweeper *Cromarty*, which had to cut adrift two mines as the ships approached the beach, *Bachaquero* at last came to a halt on firm ground. But the LST had run onto a bank, or false beach, and there was still a great depth of water beyond the bow. All was not lost, however, as a form of portable wooden jetty was lashed onto the ship and three Bren gun carriers were able to drive off *Bachaquero*, through much shallower water at the end of the jetty, and onto the beach. Unfortunately the next three vehicles became waterlogged and had to be pulled ashore by ropes by fifty or sixty soldiers, working at times up to their necks in water.[84]

It was now 17.15 hours, and the tide had risen making it impossible to land any more vehicles unless *Bachaquero* could be moved higher up the beach. So Lieutenant-Commander McMullan withdrew *Bachaquero* about a mile offshore, stopped and pointed the ship's bows at the beach. He ordered "full speed ahead" and charged towards the shore.

Two hundred yards from the beach McMullan cut the engines as the ship rushed towards the land. The soldiers on the beach cheered the ship as it crashed through the bank until they realized just how fast *Bachaquero* was travelling towards them and then they turned and fled! For the first time in warfare a Tank Landing Ship had landed on a hostile beach. The rest of *Bachaquero's* cargo was rapidly discharged and at 19.00 hours McMullan wriggled his now much lighter ship off the bank and into deeper water.[85]

Chapter 5

"The Crack of the Shells"

Whilst the munitions were being hauled ashore in Ambararata Bay, 'C' and 'D' Companies of the Royal Scots Fusiliers along with the battalion reconnaissance group, led by Lieutenant-Colonel Armstrong, sought out a path through the mangrove swamps which encompassed the beach. Speed was essential if the desired element of surprise was to be achieved. But the effort of shifting, quite literally, tons of equipment by hand had exhausted the Fusiliers and Armstrong ordered a ten-minute rest before pushing on towards Antsirane. Stopping, even for this brief period of time, was considered dangerous. For Armstrong it was a "hard" decision to make.[1]

The dusty track, which ran from the coast to a poorly maintained road, was soon located. This road linked the villages of Ambararata and Mangoky and led to the main Antsirane—Arrachart road. The Welch Fusiliers reached the junction of the track just ahead of the Scots. By winning the race to the road the Welch earned the privilege of marching directly upon Antsirane whilst the Scots, who were still feeling "wet and miserable", were given Arrachart airfield as their objective.[2]

The lead was taken by a few cyclists and motorcyclists until the Bren gun carriers overtook the column at Mangorky, some five miles east of Courrier Bay. Fortunately, the appearance of the column seemed to leave the villagers "unmoved" and one even managed to greet the invaders with a "good morning" in passable English.[3]

Though still early morning, the hot, tropical sun bore down upon the invaders who, with their motor transport still at sea, had to drag their weapons, ammunition and sufficient stores to sustain the brigade in the field for the next forty-eight hours, in hand-carts.[4] Beyond the mangroves was the wide, open Anamakia Plain, which was a wilderness of undulating grassland. The tall, brown grass was interspersed with roads and sandy mounds from which cacti sprung. There was also the occasional area of cultivated arable land forming green in a sea of brown. The rough and uneven road to Antsirane crossed this dry plain which, because of the uneven ground and irregular vegetation, was ideal for sniping or ambush. Yet, as Sergeant Croft-Cooke observed, "there was no sound of firing, no glimpse of the enemy, nothing to break the warm peace of the day except the occasional rattle of a Bren carrier."[5] As the morning wore on a strong wind developed which whipped up the dirt from the road and the men were soon covered in a fine, red dust.

The Welch Fusiliers' march along this road was without incident until they approached Anamakia village. Here a French naval officer, *Capitaine* Yvernat, and three ratings who, they claimed, were returning from an aborted fishing trip, were captured by one of the leading Bren gun carriers. It was now 08.15 hours.[6] As had been planned, the leading battalion was carrying a letter from Admiral Syfret to the French Governor-General. This was handed over to Yvernat, who was allowed to return to Antsirane in his own vehicle. In the letter Syfret assured the French Fortress Commander that Britain had no interest in a permanent occupation of Madagascar. The island was French, Syfret wrote, and would remain French. Those members of the garrison who were prepared to co-operate with the British would be permitted to remain in office with their salaries paid for by HM Government. Those who were determined to oppose the British forces would be repatriated to France if they held French passports. The French Commander was asked to reply, either by radio or through an officer bearing a flag of truce.[7] Having already broadcast a response to the leaflets dropped by the Fleet Air Arm that "Diego Suarez will be defended until the end in accordance with the traditions of the army, the navy and French aviation",[8] there was little prospect of Colonel Claerebout now surrendering. But the letter gave the garrison a final warning. If the French chose to resist, the island would be taken by force.

The return of the naval officer to Antsirane (at approximately 09.00 hours) with Syfret's letter only served to inform the French commander of the direction of the main British attack, and was later considered to have been a serious mistake.[9] In fact the French had not been as easily deceived as the British imagined. Concerned with the "worrying and abnormal" silence from No.7 Battery, *Capitaine* Yvernat had been sent from Antsirane to investigate the situation and to check the telephone line, before he was surprised and captured at Anamakia. The commander of the Windsor Castle detachment had also taken action and had sent a runner to Diego Suarez at 06.30 hours and another at 06.45 hours with details of the British attack. By 10.00 hours the French at Antsirane had a good indication of the size and composition of the force that would soon descend upon them.[10]

The French commander immediately despatched a company of Senegalese light infantry to delay the advance of the 29th Brigade. As a ground attack was now imminent he also moved three companies of his troops into position along the extensive line of defences on the landward side of the Antsirane peninsula.[11]

The Senegalese delaying force hurriedly occupied a prepared position on the Anamakia road which included dugouts and well-camouflaged, concrete machine-gun emplacements. The position was situated on the forward slope of a ridge which commanded the Col de Bonne Nouvelle at the point where the road turns northwards towards Antsirane, some fifteen miles from Courrier Bay.[12] The Col de Bonne Nouvelle was the last of a series of strong defensive positions which faced to the west. None of these positions had been manned and it was only when the French learnt of Festing's advance that the Senegalese *tirailleurs* were rushed forward in lorries to occupy the Col de Bon Nouvelle defences.[13]

Meanwhile, the 29th Brigade pushed rapidly eastwards into the Anamakia Plain, reaching the Col de Bonne Nouvelle at around 11.15 hours. Festing's Bren gun carrier was now leading the advance and when the Senegalese opened fire his driver became the first casualty of the engagement, shot in the hand.[14] It was immediately apparent that a frontal assault upon such a position would be costly and so two companies were sent round the flanks of the hill whilst Festing called for armoured support from the tank squadron.

Though the last of the twelve tanks was not landed until 10.00 hours, as soon as the first four were ashore Major Simon had led two Valentines and one Tetrarch forward to assist the infantry. Captain Palmer remained on the beach in his Valentine to assemble the rest of the squadron. Simon's three tanks now rumbled up to Anamakia village and were called into immediate action. It was the first time in its history that Britain had used tanks to support an amphibious operation.[15]

Followed by the rest of the Welch Fusiliers and supported by two 3.7-inch howitzers of 455th Light Battery RA which had also just arrived,[16] the tanks drove towards the French position. The tanks, however, could not scale the heights nor could they bring their guns to bear directly upon the defenders. Once it was evident that the tanks could make little impression upon the Col de Bonne Nouvelle the defenders reopened their fire upon the advancing Fusiliers. Festing and his Brigade Major, who had joined the attack in their Bren gun carrier, were caught in this fire and forced to abandon their vehicle at the foot of the ridge and take cover behind a bank.

The Welch Fusiliers were halted by the French machine guns until late in the afternoon when four more tanks and the South Lancashire Regiment reached the front. The South Lancs had remained as a floating reserve on board *Sobieski* during the initial assault. As the landing had been completely successful, the South Lancs were ordered to land at 07.00 hours and follow the other battalions of the 29th Brigade in two parties at one hour's interval. By the time that the landing craft had disgorged their cargoes and returned to the transport vessels in the main anchorage, a strong wind had developed. The ships were dropping second anchors with the wind increasing to Gale Force 8, creating hazardous conditions for the soldiers and sailors alike.[17] Nevertheless, the landing craft were loaded for another trip and the first party of the South Lancs, which included the battalion HQ, was ashore by 08.30 hours. At approximately 14.00 hours this leading party caught up with the rest of the brigade at the Col de Bonne Nouvelle.[18]

Continued shelling by 455th Light Battery drove the French out of their forward positions into a trench in the rear of the position. This gave the attackers their chance. Under the cover of the howitzers and tanks the Welch Fusiliers, supported by the South Lancs, stormed up the hill and finally took the ridge at bayonet point, though some of the defenders escaped and made their way back to Antsirane.[19] The position on the Col de Bonne Nouvelle was taken at the cost of two officers killed and a number of Fusiliers wounded, and it had held up the entire brigade for five hours. Thirty men of Lieutenant Philippe's *1er Compagnie de 1/2 Régiment Mixte de Madagascar* were killed; almost all those taken prisoner were wounded.[20] It gave Festing a clear warning of the stubborn resistance that was to come.

At 15.15 hours the advance upon Antsirane re-commenced with the Bren gun carriers of the two Fusilier battalions taking the lead, behind which were the companies of the Scots Fusiliers marching on either side of the road. The Welch Fusiliers, exhausted by their assault upon the French positions, were allowed to recuperate before following the rest of the column towards Antsirane.[21]

Whilst the main body was held up at the Col de Bon Nouvelle the two leading Valentines had continued along the road towards Antsirane. They encountered and destroyed two trucks of French reinforcements heading towards Bon Nouvelle (one of which was transporting a machine-gun) shortly after midday to the north of Con Barriquand.[22]

Joined by the two Tetrarchs of Lieutenant Carlisle's troop, the tanks moved on along a good, fast road until they entered a flat plain. The Valentine troop was about 400 yards ahead of the Tetrarchs when a heavy-calibre gun opened fire on their left. The tanks continued to advance confidently, believing that the French had no weapons capable of stopping a heavily armoured Valentine. Though they were unaware of it at the time, the tanks had driven to within range of the French 75mm guns on the main Antsirane defences.

The Vickers-Armstrong Valentine had a crew of three with a driver, gunner, and the commander who also acted as radio operator and secondary gunner. The tank was armed with a 2-pounder main gun and a 7.92 Besa co-axial machine-gun. The Tetrarch Light Tank MK VII also had a three-man crew and carried exactly the same weapons as the Valentine but it lacked the heavy armour of the Valentine, which at 16.26 tons was twice the weight of the Tetrarch.[23] Neither was a match for the French 75mm guns.

More heavy French guns joined in the action as the Valentines traversed their 2-pounders and returned fire. The leading Valentine was hit almost immediately and the driver killed. The second heavy tank, carrying Major Simon, was also hit by the 75s using solid shot. The driver, Trooper Bond, managed to pull himself through the driver's hatch but, as he climbed out, he fell forward underneath the rolling tank. He died with the tank on top of him as he begged Simon to shoot him.[24] The tank rolled forwards 150 yards down the road before being destroyed by volleys from French guns on both sides of the road.

Instead of deploying away from the road, the Tetrarchs followed their troop commander down the road in single file. The first Tetrarch was struck and its officer killed. The vehicle then caught fire and the driver was so severely burnt that he later died of his injuries. A second Tetrarch was also hit and began to burn. Its commander pulled the machine-gun from its mounting on the turret and leapt from the burning tank. Gathering together all the unwounded men from the tank crews he led them against the French artillery on foot. It was a brave but futile gesture. Rifle and machine gun fire from the Antsirane defences soon had the tank crews pinned down, though one man, Sergeant Grimes, ran the gauntlet of the enemy fire several times to recover more ammunition from the stranded tanks. The officer of the sole surviving Tetrarch halted his tank in dead ground further back and then crawled forward on his hands and knees to see what assistance he could provide. Simon ordered him to return and inform Brigade HQ of the situation. On the way back the tank encountered and destroyed another lorry-load of French reinforcements which was trying to infiltrate by a different road.

Meanwhile, French infantry from the Antsirane defences tried to encircle Simon's tiny force. Three times the French tried to surround the tank crews but were held at bay until 15.45 hours. With one of their officers fatally wounded and most of their ammunition gone, the crews were captured.[25]

The reckless and unsupported attack by the British tank squadron had cost the expeditionary force eight of its twelve principal armoured vehicles. Only one Valentine and three Tetrarchs were left fit for service.

Behind the tanks the infantry trudged towards the French positions, led on by the Scots Fusiliers. All along the route French snipers harassed the British column but their marksmanship was poor and they inflicted few casualties. A few French aircraft had also attacked the invaders. When news of the British landing reached Tananarive, the rest of the *Groupe Aérien Mixte* were flown up to the airfield at Anivorano, some fifty miles from Diego Suarez. From there three Potez 63s had attempted to bomb the vehicles of the column at 13.00 hours and two Morane fighters had machine-gunned Blue Beach at 17.07 hours. Greatly outnumbered, the French lost a further two aircraft in these sorties.[26]

As the 29th Brigade approached the Antsirane perimeter defences, Festing, Stockwell and Armstrong met to consider their options. The loss of the tanks had been a severe blow and none of the heavy artillery had yet been landed. The nature and extent of the French defences was unknown to the attackers and Festing had not been provided with a sufficiently detailed map of the area (though he was later to complain that "excellent" French maps could have been purchased locally for just five Francs each!)[27]. What was clear to the British commanders, however, was that the French were well prepared and a direct assault without artillery support would be hazardous in the extreme. Yet night was fast approaching and Festing wanted to seize Antsirane before the French troops at Tananarive could be mobilized.

At 17.30 hours, with only thirty minutes of daylight left, the attack upon Antsirane began. The only available mortar detachment laid down a smokescreen ahead of the surviving tanks. The capture of Major Simon left the remaining tanks under the command of Captain Palmer. He decided to attack with a cavalry-style charge into the guns in the hope of taking the gunners by surprise. It was, as one man would later write, like the charge of the Light Brigade all over again. With Palmer's Valentine in front and the Tetrarchs behind in an arrow formation, the remnants of the squadron charged through the smoke at full speed. Sergeant Clegg of the Hussars recalled the attack vividly: "As soon as we were clear of the pampas grass all hell descended on us. How the few of us survived I shall never know. The crack of the shells as they flew over the turret and around us sounded as if the artillery was on our hull." [28]

The tanks tried to make for the cover of a wood but two of the tanks were hit, one of which was Palmer's Valentine. He and his crew bailed out and made a run for cover. One of Palmer's men fell and the Captain turned and ran back to help him. Sergeant Clegg saw what happened next: "As he caught hold of the fallen trooper, a high-explosive shell fell on them. One moment they were there, as if held motionless, and in that terrible flash they were gone." Captain Llewellyn Palmer was recommended for the Victoria Cross.[29]

Meanwhile, 'C' Company, 1st Royal Scots Fusiliers, led the infantry attack, with one platoon on the left of the Antsirane road and two on the right. 'D' Company was in close support. The ground, which was partly grassland and partly cultivation, sloped gently down towards the French defences with a single, small ridge forming the only undulation in otherwise flat terrain. "As we neared the town it was still broad daylight," recalled Corporal Butterfield of the Signals Platoon. "There was a big open field in front of us. We went across that field in open formation as if we were going on a Sunday school picnic. They were waiting for us to get in range of their machine-guns and then they opened fire on us."

This heavy fire from machine-guns and snipers brought Lieutenant Thompson's platoon on the left of the road to a halt after just 100 yards. A number of men were hit with Thompson himself being wounded twice. "The guy in front of me went down, shot through the neck. I knew I had also been hit but felt no pain", Butterfield later wrote. "It was utter chaos. Moaning and groaning all over the place."[30] Thompson was treated at the regimental aid post but insisted on returning to his platoon which was still stationary and under fire.

The two platoons on the right of the road actually reached the first line of the Antsirane defences, which consisted of an anti-tank ditch. This obstacle was around seven feet wide with sheer walls seven feet six inches high. It was as far as the Scots were to go.[31]

With no immediate prospect of success from the main assault, 'D' Company tried to turn the right flank of the position. By this time night had fallen and the Fusiliers could make little headway in the dark against concentrated enemy fire. The South Lancs coming up alongside the Scots experienced the same difficulties. "Any movement forward over the open ground", recalled Major Manners, "was immediately met by a hail of machine-gun fire."[32]

It was apparent that the French were well organized and determined to resist. Armstrong called off the attack and reported in person to Brigade HQ (which had been set up in a corrugated-iron building bearing the unlikely name of 'Robinson's Hotel') to explain the situation to Festing. The Brigadier agreed to postpone the attack until the following morning. The South Lancs took up perimeter positions whilst the Scots Fusiliers were ordered to remain where they were for the night with fighting patrols to be sent out at intervals throughout the night to maintain contact with the enemy.[33]

When he returned to the front Armstrong was told that that some of 'D' Company's platoons were missing. Armstrong went forward to the anti-tank ditch were he found just two wounded Fusiliers. Armstrong helped the men back to the battalion where he found the "missing" platoons.

Amongst these was a section of 17 Platoon which had been pinned down in the anti-tank ditch. The French had placed a machine-gun to fire along the ditch but concrete sectioning in the ditch limited the line of fire and gave the Fusiliers some degree of protection. The platoon was ordered to withdraw but the men could not risk moving from behind the sectioning. Fusilier Bernard Grehan explained how the deadlock was broken: "Someone shouted 'Bloody hell, they're coming!' Some Senegalese were walking along the top of the ditch and shooting down at our blokes. I could see we weren't going to get out of this, so I stood up and fired a couple of shots at the Senegalese. I don't think I hit anyone but it made the Senegalese jump down. This was our chance to run for it because the machine–gunner could not fire in case he hit his own men." The section escaped and Fusilier Grehan, promoted to NCO, received a Mention in Despatches.[34]

Festing had hoped to catch the French off guard by mounting an immediate attack upon Antsirane. He had certainly succeeded in surprising the defenders, as the positions at the Col de Bonne Nouvelle had only been partially manned and bridges on the main approach prepared for demolition had been taken intact before the French could respond. But the consequent lack of reconnaissance and the speed of the attack had led to much confusion.[35] The attack also lacked sufficient force to penetrate the Antsirane defences, both in infantry and artillery. Though the first of the guns of the 455th Light Battery had now joined the infantry, the flat ground and mixed vegetation in front of the anti-tank ditch meant that the gunners were unable to find a suitable point to set up an observation post.[36] The 25–pounders of the 9th Field Regiment RA had experienced great difficulty moving through the dense bush around Red Beach and they had yet to reach the front.[37]

These defences, though formidable, were far from new, having been designed by General Joffre in 1909 when he was fortress commander at Diego Suarez.[38] It is usually stated that the British had no knowledge of these defences even though Mayer had transmitted details of the fortifications to Durban whilst the assault convoy was at sea. This information was relayed to East Africa Command HQ in Nairobi but there the message was lost or ignored and was not passed on to the Force commanders.[39] Furthermore, if Festing would have looked more carefully at the map he so severely criticized, he would have seen the word "Ouvrage" marked where the French defences were located. This is the French word for "work", i.e. defensive work. The British officers, it later transpired, misinterpreted this as meaning factory or "works" and had disregarded it.[40]

There was also an Intelligence Note submitted to the War Office less than three months earlier, which listed six named fieldworks linked by a line of entrenchments. This line (referred to in French documents as the G-H Line) ran from shore to shore across the neck of the Antsirane Peninsula along a low ridge, about two miles south of the port itself. The fortifications were almost three-and-a-half miles long and consisted of a continuous trench system, protected by a hedge of barbed wire,[41] supported by a substantial fort on either end of the line – Fort Caimans to the west and Fort Bellevue to the east. Both forts overlooked the open shore line at their respective ends where steep slopes covered with scrub ran down to join the mangrove swamps bordering the sea.[42]

Along the length of the trench system were emplacements for 75mm guns, well-sited observation posts, and pillboxes armed with mortars and machine-guns. Parts of these defences were set in concrete like a Maginot Line in miniature. There were also a number of mobile (bullock-drawn) 75mm guns hidden in the "swathes" of sugar cane. The French positions were cleverly camouflaged and well-concealed amongst the tall crops, making the pin-pointing of targets from the air extremely difficult and completely impossible from the ground.[43]

Approximately 1,400 yards ahead of this line was the anti-tank ditch which extended for a short distance on either side of the three roads that ran south from Antsirane through or round the French defences. Without ladders or without digging a ramp neither infantry nor tanks could surmount this obstacle. Once inside the ditch the attackers were robbed of forward vision and were under intense and accurate fire from the main defensive armament. Of the three roads, the road to the west, along which the advance had been made from Courrier Bay, and the central road to Arrachart airfield and beyond to Joffreville, passed directly through the French defences. The 75mm guns situated in the pillboxes above the trench network could fire down these roads for a distance of approximately 1,000 yards. The third road travelled to the east of the defences along the coastline but it was defended by a number of detached strongpoints and also came under the fire of the 75mm gun mounted on the top of Fort Bellevue.[44]

Sturges and Festing now had to consider their options. Only a full-scale attack, using every available man and gun could, succeed against such defences, but the men of the 29th Brigade had marched eighteen miles in tropical heat and in wet clothes along a very bad and dusty road. They had carried all their own weapons and dragged their ammunition and stores behind them on hand-carts. The brigade had been fighting and marching since before dawn and some of its units were still on the road. "By now", wrote an officer with the Welch Fusiliers, "all were hot, tired and edgy."[45] To balance this, the brigade's transport, including the rest of the guns of 455th Light Battery, was now on its way to the front and the leading units of the 17th Brigade had also landed.[46]

Oransay and *Duchess of Atholl* with the troops of the 17th Brigade had reached the anchorage at 11.00 hours. Disembarkation began fifteen minutes later. "As we entered our landing craft, we watched in astonishment at the furious gunfire rocking the island as the task force ships and aircraft let rip," one of Tarleton's brigade later recalled. "Those massive guns thundered for a good eighty to ninety minutes and we were treated to the magnificent spectacle of our air forces battering distant positions and swooping low to strafe the intended beach-heads."[47]

The first battalion to land was the 2nd Battalion, Royal Scots Fusiliers, which took over the beach areas, releasing the last elements of the 29th Brigade and 5 Commando. However, the landings were still not complete when darkness fell at 18.00 hours and they did not re-commence until the moon was up at 22.30 hours. Disembarkation continued throughout the night, with each company moving off along the road to Antsirane as soon as it had formed up.[48]

The hospital ship *Atlantis* had anchored in Courrier bay and as the men of the 17th Brigade marched towards the front to join Festing's exhausted force, the wounded from the fighting passed the other way: "We saw infantrymen themselves being brought back on stretchers or limping, the blood flowing freely," remembered a sergeant of the Seaforth Highlanders. "It was a nightmare to behold at night. 'Christ, it's hell up there!' some of them warned us ... In all, the prospects seemed horrific."[49]

Day one of the Battle of Diego Suarez was over and the great naval base was still French territory. The attempt at surprise had failed; indeed it was the attackers who had been surprised by both the formidable French defences and the organized efficiency of the defenders. Festing was far from happy with the situation he found himself in, as he was subsequently to report: "There appears to be a tendency when collecting information about possible theatres of operation to concentrate on the study of such things as personalities of army commanders, political undercurrents and such information as is available from the Encyclopaedia Britannica and Baedeker. The information most valuable to an assault commander is the information about *military installations and defences and numbers and calibre of troops.*"[50]

Festing now had to concentrate all his resources for a conventional direct assault against a prepared enemy position. The lack of information about the French fortifications meant that all he could do was plan for full-scale frontal assault to bludgeon his way through the defences. For this he needed the whole of the 29th Brigade, all the available artillery, the few remaining tanks, the aircraft of the Fleet Air Arm and the guns of the Royal Navy.

Chapter 6

"Savage Hearts"

The British troops settled down as comfortably as was possible in such an alien environment. French tracer rounds had caused a heath fire which raged around the perimeter of the 29th Brigade's positions.[1] But, apart from the occasional crack of a sniper's rifle, the French guns were quiet.

There was little rest, however, for any of the men. Breakfast was called for 02.00 hours and shortly afterwards the 1st Scots Fusiliers mounted the first of the fighting patrols – led by Armstrong in person. The patrols were designed to harass and confuse the enemy whilst the attacking troops moved into position, and to maintain the pressure upon the French.

Sturges planned a frontal assault upon the French line with the Scots Fusiliers and the East Lancs, whilst the South Lancs attempted to turn the French flank. The Welch Fusiliers, who had taken up a position around La Scama astride the Ambararata road, were to form the reserve.

So, as the Scots and the East Lancs hurried through breakfast, the South Lancs moved to the west of the Antsirane defences. In three columns, fifty yards apart, the South Lancs marched up to the coast road in the darkness. Their objective was to turn the right flank of the French position along the open beach. Once past Fort Caimans, the South Lancs were to take the Antsirane defences in the rear at daybreak from the direction of the cemetery. To help the South Lancs, the Scots Fusiliers and the East Lancs were to distract the French by sending out "noisy" patrols between 04.00 to 05.00 hours. Dawn was expected at 05.30 hours – Zero Hour for the attack upon Antsirane.

At this time the Fleet Air Arm was to bomb Antsirane. This would be followed by a simultaneous assault on the front and rear of the French positions. If the main assault succeeded in breaking through the French line, the Welch Fusiliers, spearheaded by the remaining tanks and the battalion's Bren carriers, were to take up the advance and push on to capture Antsirane. General Sturges, no doubt expecting heavy casualties and hoping that his men would restrain themselves once they had captured the enemy positions, sent the troops this message: "Speed and savage hearts in the attack. Tolerance in victory."[2]

The howitzers of the 455th Light Battery had moved up during the night to take up a position on the left of the main Antsirane–Ambararata road to support the dawn attack. The four guns formed a line to the north of the meat canning factory with a platoon of the Welch Fusiliers deployed as local defence for the artillery. The 9th Field Regiment had also managed to land all its guns and one of its two batteries, 28/76 Battery, was travelling slowly towards Antsirane. It would not be in position and ready to lend its weight to the attack of the 29th Brigade until much later in the day.[3] The second battery, 19 Battery, had been unable to land at Blue Beach because of the discovery of a number of unswept mines in the channel. The battery landed further north in Courrier Bay but the artillery vehicles could not break through the thick jungle to reach the Ambararata road. Instead, 19 Battery moved across country to Diego Suarez North from where, it was hoped, it could shell the French positions from the rear.[4] During its march the artillery had been fired at by the French sloop *D'Entrecasteaux* and the Sea Hurricanes from *Indomitable* were summoned to deal with the valiant French sloop.

"We flew in low all the way to the sea, over the low bare hills of the northern part of the island," Hugh Popham of 880 Squadron recalled, "until the great harbour opened up in front of us, with the sloop in the shallows to the north of the town. She had steam up and as we raced across the water, she let loose volumes of oily smoke that blew in a dense cloud towards us. One after another we tore into her, guns blazing. The tracer showed up briefly as it went sparkling into the smoke; our tracers going in and theirs coming out. I held it, thumb hard down and that intoxicating drumming of eight machine-guns shaking the whole aircraft into the smoke until, a yard or two in front of me, the mast and aerials suddenly loomed up. I hauled back on the stick, and we went wheeling round for another run."[5]

D'Entrecasteaux was then bombed by *Indomitable*'s Swordfish. One of the bombs penetrated the deck and exploded, setting the vessel on fire. Despite her condition, *D'Entrecasteaux* continued to use her guns until she was finally silenced by the destroyer *Laforey*, which fired eighty-six shells at the sloop. *D'Entrecasteaux* was beached and survived the war despite having been hit sixteen times by bombs and shells.[6]

Some forty Marines from the sloop, including a gunnery observer, had also landed on the Andrakaka Peninsula the previous evening, recapturing some ground from No.5 Commando. The French Marines, armed with light machine guns, established themselves in the thickly wooded hills overlooking the road between Courrier Bay and Cap Diego. Until radio contact was lost when *D'Entrecasteaux* was abandoned by her crew, this force directed the guns of the sloop on to British vehicles passing along the road. The Marines held out for another day before being captured by the Commandos. The French claimed to have inflicted forty-seven casualties upon the British, losing only two of their own men.[7]

In readiness for the main attack, the 1st Scots Fusiliers moved up to the anti-tank ditch at about 03.00 hours in two columns to the right of the central road. Because of their recently acquired knowledge of the area, 'B' Company and 'D' Company led the way followed by 'C' and 'A' Companies on the left and right respectively. The 3-inch mortars travelled with 'C' Company and Battalion Headquarters was with 'A' Company. The East Lancs lined up on the left side of the road.[8]

Meanwhile, the South Lancs had reached the western shore of the isthmus. They had moved off at midnight on a compass bearing in what was described as a "square formation". The pace set was 100 yards in five minutes with a stop every fifteen minutes to maintain contact and to check on the formation. It was a very dark night and despite these precautions the battalion became widely spread and all contact was lost with one platoon of 'A' Company.[9]

Having reached the shore, at around 04.30 hours, the battalion re-deployed into two columns. The right-hand column – 'B' Company, 'A' Company (less the missing platoon) and Battalion HQ – moved across open ground along the beach and passed the line of the Antsirane defences quickly and unchallenged. However, one platoon of 'B' Company, which had become detached from the rest of the column, stumbled across an enemy picket and suffered five casualties including the platoon commander, who was killed.

The column on the left of the road had to pick its way through rocks and mangroves in single file. As 'C' Company approached the flank of the French defences it was stopped by heavy fire from Fort Caimans. 'D' Company was ordered to move round the left of 'C' Company but this was also pinned down by fire from the fort. To add to the column's problems, snipers were firing from a nearby house and causing casualties in both companies. It was at this moment that Private Craddock of 'D' Company jumped up and charged across twenty yards of open ground towards the house. The French opened up on Craddock with rifles and light machine-guns but he ran round the back of the house and rushed the defenders, shooting three and bayoneting the remaining four. This was too much for the enemy troops near the house and they surrendered. For this remarkable act of bravery Craddock was awarded the Distinguished Conduct Medal.[10]

As dawn broke, the right-hand column, led by Lieutenant-Colonel West, moved behind the enemy lines and reached the Ana Bozaka Barracks. The barracks were found to be unoccupied but as the column moved off it came under fire from a wood on the left. The commander of 'B' Company, Major Northcote, ordered one of his platoons to lay down suppressing fire whilst he took another platoon round the enemy flank. As he led his men into the attack Northcote was hit in the chest, and the platoon, having suffered further casualties, fell back. Northcote, who was severely wounded, was taken prisoner along with the other casualties. Northcote was later awarded the Military Cross.[11]

The battalion was now in some difficulty. Both columns were under fire and were completely separated from each other, and both had taken casualties. Two platoons were missing and, due to a problem with the radios, neither column was able to make contact with Brigade HQ. Festing had no idea what had happened to the South Lancs and he feared the worst, but he was still determined to continue with the main attack.[12]

By Zero Hour all units were in position, and precisely on time the aircraft of the Fleet Air Arm dived from the sky. Levelling out almost at ground level, the attack was carried out with great determination and much noise, but little effect. "Heavy explosions shook the earth as bomb after bomb screamed to its billet," reported one eye-witness. "One Swordfish came diving down, unloading its bombs. Anti-aircraft fire came up again but the plane, still diving, opened up with its machine-guns spitting a trail of tracer bullets towards the ground."[13]

Flares were dropped to help the aircraft locate the French gun positions but the emplacements were so cleverly concealled that no positive sightings could be made. The only way that the pilots could pinpoint the exact positions was by circling the area just 200 feet from the ground hoping that the French would reveal themselves by trying to shoot them down. Some of the naval pilots simply dropped their bombs as close as possible to where it was thought the batteries were located.[14] The bombs from one of 810 Squadron's Swordfish hit an arms dump behind the French line which caused a "spectacular" explosion, but another Swordfish was shot down by anti–aircraft fire and crashed in flames.[15]

The renewal of the British attack triggered a programme of planned sabotage by the French. This included the destruction of two large oil tanks and the burning of fuel and materials dumps to prevent them falling into British hands.[16]

For an hour the guns of the Royal Artillery shelled the French positions.[17] The end of the bombardment signalled the beginning of the infantry assault and the Scots Fusiliers led the charge from the anti–tank ditch. Immediately they encountered very heavy and accurate fire. Casualties mounted rapidly as the battalion approached to within a few hundred yards of the enemy. To the right of the road 'B' Company encountered a concentration of fire from a group of huts which the leading section dealt with using hand–grenades. The company pushed on towards the main French line until stopped by shelling from mortars and by well–sited machine–gun cross–fires.

"The determination of all ranks to get through", wrote one Scot, "was magnificent." But the French defences were well hidden and the lie of the land made it difficult for the attackers to see where the enemy fire was being delivered from. Some men got beyond the ditch but, exposed in open ground, they were compelled to seek cover and the attack began to falter.[18] "If only more French and their colonials had fought [against the Germans] like that in France in 1940!" one wounded Scot complained bitterly.[19]

'D' Company also found itself under intense fire on an open ridge and the men went to ground. The Company Commander ordered his men to pull back from the ridge to the shallow valley behind and then work their way round to the right flank. But the runner sent to the forward units with this message was wounded and the order was not delivered.

With the Scots Fusiliers pinned down, when the East Lancs moved towards the French line its right wing was exposed to flanking fire. The East Lancs could not advance past such intense fire and so the Bren gun carrier platoon was sent on a wide detour to the right to locate the French guns. Unfortunately, Lieutenant Arnold turned inwards too early and the carriers passed in front of the French artillery. Five carriers were hit before Arnold was able to extricate the remnant of his platoon. Though only three carriers returned, some of the crews crawled back to the battalion over the course of the following few hours.

After the failure of the Bren gun carriers both the Scots and the East Lancs were ordered back to their start lines, but many men were left stranded, either unaware that the order had been given or unable to move.[20] Amongst the latter were two crew members from one of the disabled carriers of the East Lancs; Private Robert Ward dragged his wounded colleague, Private Cross, out of the damaged vehicle and remained with him under fire for fifteen hours before medics were able to reach the two men.[21]

The two battalions went into a defensive perimeter, covering the ridge above the anti-tank ditch. At first only 120 of the Scots Fusiliers managed to make their way back to the start line. The rest were scattered across the ground in front of the defences, unable to withdraw. A number of men, including Captain Coulter and Captain Evetts, crept towards the French line to try and rescue the stranded Fusiliers.

After repeated forays, during one of which Coulter was knocked unconscious by a French shell, most of the Scots were brought back to safety. Some, however, could not be reached and they had to remain under cover or trapped in shell holes until night fell. One man, Sergeant Knox, had penetrated so deeply into the defensive system that he was only able to return to Battalion HQ at the end of the battle. Another man, Lieutenant Reynier, found himself alone in the heart of the French positions armed with nothing but a hand-grenade. Instead of taking cover, he moved forward to attack a machine-gun section protecting one of the 75mm gun emplacements. Though he was spotted by the defenders and hit by a bullet in the mouth, Reynier managed to pitch his grenade into the slit of the emplacement. But the opening was protected against just such an eventuality by wire netting and the grenade bounced back, wounding Reynier a second time. "That action is one of a brave man," a French officer wrote later. "I believe I can tell you that, for you can be certain the French can pick one out." Reynier received the Military Cross.[22]

At 05.53 hours Syfret ordered *Devonshire* to make its way towards the Orangea Peninsula and to be in position to bombard the batteries at the entrance to Diego Suarez Bay at noon. The cruiser reached a point ten miles to the east of Orangea at 10.00 hours to find *Hermione* already in action with the coastal batteries. *Hermione* signalled that she was running low on ammunition suitable for such an engagement, having already fired more than 100 rounds. But as *Devonshire* herself had no ammunition to waste, and as the guns on the Orangea Peninsula could not be used against the land forces attacking Antisrane, Captain Oliver ordered a cease-fire.

When Diego Suarez was in British hands the guns would be needed to help defend the harbour and it made no sense to destroy the batteries. The two cruisers remained on station, taking it in turns to stay in range of the shore whilst the other stood out to sea. Two such large ships in comparatively stationary positions would be ideal targets for submarines and so four minesweepers were put on anti-submarine duties in the area around the Orangea passage.

Though the frontal attack was faltering, behind the enemy lines the South Lancs were creating havoc. Lieutenant-Colonel West had ordered the remnants of his command to split up and cause as much disorder as possible and 'B' Company – now led by Major Osborne – had managed to sever the French line of communications with Antsirane. Osborne had captured a wireless station on the road to Antsirane in the hope of making contact with the rest of the battalion. Though he failed to call up either Battalion or Brigade HQ, Osborne took up a defensive position astride the road. Despite a number of attempts to dislodge Osborne and his men, 'B' Company, alone and unsupported, successfully blocked the road all day, preventing petrol, water and munitions from reaching the French forward line. 'B' Company did not re-join the battalion until daybreak the following morning.[23]

The missing platoon of 'A' Company had even more success. It came across two strong enemy posts, overran both of them, and killed or captured their entire garrisons. The platoon, commanded by Lieutenant Hall, also broke up or captured a number of other bodies of French troops which it encountered. The platoon itself had taken casualties and when Hall finally disengaged and returned to Brigade HQ with more than 250 prisoners he had just seven men left under arms!

The actions of Osborne, Hall and West (who alone claimed to have shot over thirty-five of the enemy) behind the French lines caused a great deal of disruption in the rear of the defenders and seriously undermined their confidence. Some of the South Lancs got within 200 yards of the rear of the French line and fired at the backs of the defenders, whilst others captured a body of around 100 pack horses and mules of the Vichy artillery and caused them to stampede, creating even more confusion. Little wonder that in the afternoon some of the Malagasy troops were spotted retreating back to Antsirane.[24]

If Sturges had been aware of the chaos being caused by the South Lancs he could have thrown his reserve brigade at the French line to exploit this success and Antsirane might have been captured that morning.[25] Yet none of this was known, or indeed apparent, to the British commander. In fact heavy fire from the French guns compelled the howitzers of the Light Battery to withdraw from La Scama. All four howitzers had been put out of action by the French artillery and an ammunition limber had been set on fire. The command post had also been destroyed by a direct hit and the battery could no longer communicate with its forward observation post. An officer and two signallers had crept into the anti-tank ditch ahead of the Scots Fusiliers during the night to establish an observation post. From before dawn Lieutenant Brandon directed the fire of the battery with his head above the parapet of the ditch to observe the fall of every round fired, until the command post was hit and his position overrun by the enemy.[26]

The howitzer section pulled back from La Scama to the Col de Bonne Nouvelle, where the battery's two 25-pounders, along with the guns of the 9th Field Regiment, were shelling the French positions.[27] This concentration of fire against La Scama seemed to indicate that the French were preparing a counter-attack and Stockwell organized the Welch to receive the enemy. He placed the battalion Bren carriers on rising ground near the hotel and stationed three companies in defensive positions on either side of the road. Though the counter-attack did not materialize, the French continued their aggressive defence, bringing up a mortar on the right flank which inflicted casualties amongst Stockwell's 'B' Company.[28]

At 09.30 hours Sturges called together his two brigadiers, Festing and Tarleton, to discuss the deteriorating situation. According to Admiral Boyd of the *Indomitable*, "nearly everyone was under the impression that the battle was a ninety per cent failure. We had suffered heavy casualties in the 29th Independent Brigade. The 17th Brigade was inadequate, untrained and badly run ... The enemy were determined and their defences were well laid out."[29] With the South Lancs missing, it appeared that casualties were already considerable and that the operation might cost Britain more than 1,000 men. This figure was relayed to London and announced by Churchill in his address to the House of Commons on 7 May 1942.[30] To add to Syfret's problems, his ships were running alarmingly low on fuel and water. It was, as Sturges later recalled, "an unhappy moment".[31]

The government in France had also been made aware of the British landing and, in what Pétain described as Madagascar's "tragic hour", Annet had been cabled with the instruction that "resistance must continue by every means and to the last cartridge".[32]

This was followed by a message from Admiral Darlan: "Once again the British, instead of fighting their enemies, seek the easiest path of attacking a French colony far from the metropolis. Marshal Pétain has asked you to defend Madagascar, and I know that you have responded patriotically to his appeal. Firmly defend the honour of our flag. Fight to the limit of your possibilities and make the British pay dearly for their act of highway robbery.

"The whole of France and its Empire are with you at heart. Do not forget that the British betrayed us in Flanders [the evacuation from Dunkirk], they treacherously attacked us at Mers-el-Kébir, at Dakar, at Syria, that they are murdering civilians in the metropolitan territories ... Defend yourselves. You are defending the honour of France. The day will come when England will pay."[33]

Though the attack had clearly failed, any form of disengagement or delay, however temporary, was out of the question. The local administrator had called up all the reservists in Antsirane and a wireless message sent by Mayer's wife from Tananarive indicated that the French forces in the capital were being assembled for a move north to assist the garrison at Diego Suarez.[34] The authorities in Vichy had even made an appeal for assistance from the Japanese![35] But what Sturges described as his "main worry" was the large French detachment at Camp d'Ambre near Joffreville. This detachment might at any moment descend upon the rear of the 29th Brigade and sever its communications with the rest of the Expeditionary Force.[36] If Sturges could not achieve a quick breakthrough he might find himself fighting on two fronts against an ever-increasing enemy force. Consequently, the generals decided that the 29th Brigade should continue to harass the enemy positions throughout the remainder of the day. Then, as soon as it was dark, the whole of the comparatively fresh 17th Brigade, supported by the 29th, would make a grand attack directly against the French line. In preparation for the attack the French defences would be subjected to an intensive bombardment until fifteen minutes before the start of the attack. Consequently, from noon onwards the Fleet Air Arm bombed Antsirane and the 25-pounders stepped up their efforts from the Col de Bonne Nouvelle whilst the warships shelled the French batteries and pounded the Orangea Peninsula.[37]

The Fleet Air Arm had been active all day with a number of Martlets patrolling the skies over the beaches and the anchorage, with others providing aerial reconnaissance for the ground forces. At 06.00 hours, four Potez 63 bombers were spotted flying up from the south. A journalist with Festing's headquarters watched as the Fleet Air Arm closed in upon the intruders: "Suddenly two of our fighters came swinging up beneath them. One shot high above his quarry, and with a half roll, came down like a kestrel on a pigeon." The bombers broke formation but one failed to escape. "Burning like a magnesium starshell in that bright morning sky he held his course a little longer before plummeting down from the blue zenith, leaving his tragic plume of smoke behind."[38] One of the French planes attempted to bomb vehicles on the road from Courrier Bay, the other two flew on towards the anchorage. All three were shot down by the Martlets.[39]

It was another long day for the men of the 29th Brigade. Constant sniping, accurate shelling from the French 75s and the occasional well-directed mortar round kept the men pinned down in and around the anti-tank ditch. "The cry of 'Stretcher Bearer' here and 'Stretcher Bearer' there began with monotonous regularity," recalled an officer of the East Lancs. "One wondered whether one would be next on the list."[40]

In one incident, Fusilier Bunyan of 'C' Company, Scots Fusiliers, was sitting in the ditch with his section commander, Corporal Bell, when a grenade landed between them. Bunyan grabbed the grenade and shouted to his comrades who were able to dive for cover. Bunyan saved the section but he was, quite literally, blown in two. He was recommended, posthumously, for a Victoria Cross.[41]

Before the bombardment re-commenced at noon there was a lull in the fighting, the silence broken only by the occasional crack of a sniper's rifle. During this quiet period more men were able to return to their units, the snipers being driven off by the East Lancs setting fire to the bush.[42]

At around 15.30 hours Festing made a personal reconnaissance of the French positions to gauge the effect the bombardment was having upon the defenders. He concluded that the garrison was at last showing signs of weakening and he ordered the forward companies to send out fighting patrols to test the French resolve. Patrols by the Bren gun carriers attracted less fire than previously and another patrol by the remaining tanks penetrated closer to the defences than had been possible before. The patrols of the Scots Fusiliers had even more success, taking fifty prisoners.[43]

Earlier the threat upon Festing's rear, from the detachment at Camp d'Ambre, was eliminated when 288 men of the *3/2me RMM* were surprised and captured on the Joffreville road as they were being moved from their camp down to Antsirane.[44]

Sturges, meanwhile, had returned to *Ramillies* to request further assistance from the Navy to coincide with the frontal attack by the 17th Brigade. He arrived on the flagship "hot, begrimmed and unhappy," Syfret recalled, "things were not going well." Sturges was "emphatic" that the attack must be carried out before the moon rose at 23.00 hours, as the French positions were too strong to be captured in moonlight or daylight in the absence of strong artillery support. Any further delay to give the troops time to rest, Sturges told the Admiral, "would be playing into the enemy's hands."[45]

Sturges asked Syfret for a party of Royal Marines to distract the enemy by landing in the rear of the Antsirane positions "to take the Frenchmen's eye off the ball." As a result, at about 14.30 hours, Captain Martin Price, commanding the Royal Marine detachment on board the flagship, was instructed by the Admiral to prepare a force of fifty Marines for immediate deployment. "We want you to cause a diversion by attacking the town in reverse," Price was told. "You will go ashore from *Anthony*. Your objective is the Artillery Commandant's house, which dominates the southern end of the town. We want you to turn to the north as many rifles as possible that are now pointing south at the Army and prevent enemy reinforcements being available for a counter-attack."

It was intended that the Marines would link up with No.5 Commando, which was expected to have crossed the bay and penetrated as far as Antsirane docks. Sturges made no secret of the fact that he thought the mission was highly dangerous and he rated the Marines' chances of success as "four to one against". Syfret was equally pessimistic: "*Anthony*'s chances of success I assessed as about 50%, my advisors thought 15%, and of the Royal Marines I did not expect a score to survive the night."

It was extremely unlikely that, if the attack failed, the *Anthony* would be able to return. If she did manage to surprise the coastal batteries on the way in, the French gunners would be watching and waiting for her on the way out. But the situation had become so desperate that Sturges believed it was worth the risk, "even", the General conceded, "if the destroyer is lost".[46]

Syfret, who believed that the intended quick capture of Antsirane had failed, was becoming increasingly concerned with the turn of events: "The night attack, planned in a hurry, to be carried out by tired troops against very strong positions, had only a 10% chance of success. Prolonged operations, which we so much wished to avoid, was the unpleasant alternative … The next few hours were not happy ones."[47]

Price assembled the selected men and divided them into six sections and a Headquarters Section. As well as personal weapons, each man was issued with three grenades and the HQ Section included six Lewis machine guns and a 2-inch mortar.

The Marines were embarked in *Anthony* which, shortly after leaving Ambararata Bay, ran into a heavy sea and most of Price's men, accustomed to the steadier movement of the big battleship, were soon sea-sick! Nevertheless, the *Anthony* steamed the 100 miles or so round Cape Amber to the Orangea coast and at 19.45, two hours after nightfall, the destroyer began its approach to the entrance of Diego Suarez Bay. Lieutenant-Commander Hodges had never seen this coast before and the Orangea Pass is nothing more than a narrow break in the cliffs with dangerous reefs skirting the northern approaches. Though the high ground behind prevented the entrance from being silhouetted against the night sky, Hodges charged for the gap at twenty-two knots. It was, according to *The Times*, "the most astonishing incident of the whole undertaking".[48]

A searchlight on the Orangea Peninsula was switched on, its beam picking up *Anthony* as it crossed the harbour entrance. The shore batteries immediately opened fire upon the destroyer, but *Devonshire* was circling some six and a half miles to sea and the cruiser responded with its 8-inch guns. With *Devonshire's* second salvo the searchlight went out. *Anthony* also replied with her two rear 4.7-inch guns and the French batteries fell silent. One of the pilots from 881 Squadron had provided Hodges with a rough sketch of the positions of the wrecked French vessels in the harbour and *Anthony* crossed the bay unscathed. However, the defenders were now fully alerted and as the ship approached the main jetty it was met with machine-gun fire from the jetty itself and from the hill above.[49]

No.5 Commando was supposed to be waiting at the jetty to help with mooring the destroyer but this unit had failed to carry out its instructions. Every published account states that the Commandos did not cross the harbour because they were unable to locate any suitable boats. In fact two boats were found, both in good working order, but the Commandos' commanding officer lost his nerve, according to his medical officer, "from being without alcohol for twelve hours"! Despite repeated appeals by his junior officers the commanding officer remained "too dithery" and the crossing was not even attempted.[50]

In the darkness and without the assistance of the Commandos, the *Anthony* over-shot the jetty. Due to strong winds Lieutenant-Commander Hodges could not risk turning the destroyer in such close proximity to the shore and he reversed engines and backed up to the jetty. The Marines had to disembark from the stern by clambering over the destroyer's depth charges![51]

A tall warehouse at the end of the jetty protected the Marines from much of the enemy fire as they assembled into their sections and moved off through the dockyard which was still burning after the raids by the Fleet Air Arm. Price led his party towards the town. With a map taken from a book on coastal pilotage as his only guide, Price soon became lost. But, after stumbling through a cattle pen full of water-buffalo, Price found his way to the Artillery Commandant's house, which was occupied without opposition.[52] Price then sent Lieutenant Powell with three sections further down the road. Powell got as far as the naval barracks where he came under fire from guards at the gate-house. Powell's men replied with grenades and, moments later, the Commandant and his men marched out waving a white flag.

As Powell was accepting the surrender, a French drummer began to make a signal. Believing that they had been lured into a trap the Marines leapt at the bewildered drummer. When the Commandant explained that the man was about to sound the "cease-fire", the Marines humbly apologized!

In the barracks, Powell found three British Army officers, fifty other ranks and three Fleet Air Arm personnel who had been captured earlier in the fighting. Amongst the captives was Percy Mayer who told Powell that he had been sentenced to death and was due to be shot as a spy the very next morning.[53] Price then gave two of the released British officers and Mayer the task of examining papers found in the Artillery Depot for information. Powell searched the barracks and found it well stocked with weapons, including 2,000 to 3,000 rifles and a number of heavy machine-guns. Just one Marine was wounded, being accidentally shot in the leg by a comrade.[54]

Price had achieved his objective and had prevented any reinforcement of the main French defences by troops from the naval barracks. He had also prevented heavy street-fighting, which would have caused many casualties and much damage to the town itself. *Anthony* relayed the news of the success of the mission back to *Ramillies*: "Operation completed successfully – coast defence gunners require further practice."[55]

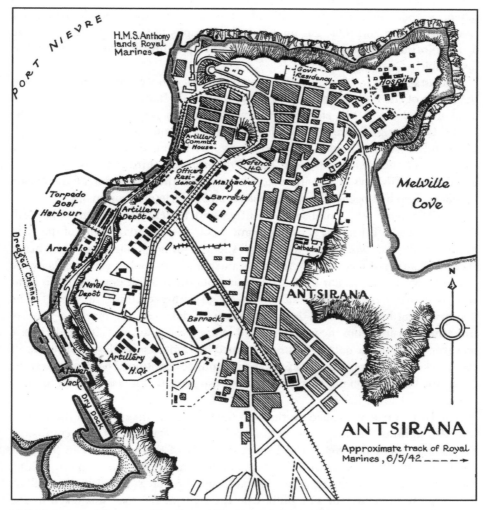

MAP 5: A map of the town of Antsirana (Antsirane), in Diego Suarez, showing the approximate route taken by the Royal Marines having been landed from HMS *Anthony*, 6 May 1942.

The attack of the 17th Brigade was scheduled to take place as soon as night had fallen but Sturges delayed the assault by two hours to coincide with the landing of the Marines. As it transpired, the last units of Tarleton's brigade reached the battlefield in poor condition with only an hour to go before the start of the attack, the men having disembarked throughout the previous night and marched all day. "Through that scorching day we plodded on," recalled an officer of the Seaforth Highlanders. "Before long, man after man began to drop at the side of the road, completely exhausted, and by the evening we were barely conscious of our actions."[56]

An attempt had been made by the 2nd Batttalion, the Northamptonhire Regiment to reconnoitre the ground over which they were to attack. However, the terrain proved too restrictive and in the daylight they were unable to even approach the start line. Tarleton's weary troops therefore had no knowledge of the French defences, their objectives were difficult to pick out on the ground, their maps were inadequate and they had no aerial photographs to study.[57] As the historian of the Northamptons made clear, it was "difficult to imagine circumstances less favourable to success".[58]

The attack was to be delivered on both sides of the western road, which was the sector of the line closest to the guns at the Col de Bonne Nouvelle, on a front of about 600 yards. The start line was a track which ran at right-angles to the road.[59] On the right were the 2nd Northamptons and on the left the 6th Seaforth Highlanders. As the Highlanders were only 180 strong they were joined by 'A' Company of the Welch Fusiliers. The 17th Brigade's third battalion – the 2nd Royal Scots Fusiliers – was in reserve along with the remainder of the Welch Fusiliers, who had been temporarily placed under Tarleton's command.[60]

At 20.15 hours the bombardment lifted and fifteen minutes later the 17th Brigade moved off from the start line, some 1,200–1,400 yards in front of the main French positions. "We moved forward in silence and not a sound could be heard except the swish of feet through the grass and a few soft-spoken commands by the officers," wrote Lieutenant Ronald Morton. "Suddenly a rifle cracked out in front and, as if that was the signal, the enemy let go with everything they had." The bombardment had done little damage to the fixed defences, and machine-gun fire from the forts and from the trench poured in upon the attackers.[61] In the darkness, however, much of the defensive fire was aimed high and it passed over the heads of the attackers. "A wave of fire swept over the ground," continued Morton, "and the din of the bullets cracking over our heads was so great that it was difficult to make oneself heard above it."[62]

The British troops pushed on through the fire and as they reached the French line the fighting became very confused. Taking advantage of the confusion, Sergeant Jones of the Welch Fusiliers rushed one of the machine-gun pillboxes on the left of the road which he seized, single-handed, at bayonet point, killing the three men working the gun. Twelve other French soldiers in the pillbox immediately surrendered. The pillbox on the right of the road was taken by the Northamptons, though its capture resulted in two of the battalion's senior officers being wounded.[63]

Likewise, the Seaforth Highlanders were ordered by Tarleton to charge the French lines with fixed bayonets. "Gentlemen", the Brigadier called to the men through a hand-held megaphone. "Things are pretty desperate and we have to get this thing settled as quickly as possible."[64] The Highlanders stripped off their packs and to the sound of the regimental war cry they went into "furious" action. It was to result in some of the most savage hand-to-hand fighting the 17th Brigade would ever experience.

"French Senegalese troops were still firing mortars horizontally at us and drilling machine-gun fire into our ranks," recalled Sergeant Stockman. "Somehow we just kept moving, driven by some inexplicable group momentum ... And this with men dropping left, right and centre, some looking literally torn to shreds." Stockman ran into a Senegalese soldier and, after a moment's hesitation, thrust the bayonet so fiercely into his opponent that it emerged on the other side of the African's body. "At first, I did not realise the ferocity with which I had stuck him and then found to my horror that I could not pull it out again. I had to fire a round, twist savagely and then pull, in order to disengage it from his body.

"The sight of what happened then made me quite sick. A burst of blood lashed over me and down the barrel of my rifle. I recall vomiting, then pulling myself together and continuing with the forward advance deep into the Vichy positions."[65]

One sobbing Highlander was left with just a ragged, bleeding stump after cornering a Senegalese trooper who fought free by biting through the Scot's arm. Another of Tarleton's men, having used all his ammunition, was left facing three Africans with just his bayonet: "I pulled off the bayonet as they jumped me and I managed to prick them back," the Scot later explained to his comrades. "I couldn't have got the third one hard enough and he came at me again. I had to take off his head with a slash of the bayonet."[66] But, finally, after two days of fierce fighting, the British broke through the French defences.

Tarleton's first objective was to reach a line north of the village of Antanambad, two miles beyond the trench network. This was accomplished at 23.00 hours. The success signal was given which was the cue for the reserve battalions, the 2nd Scots and the Welch, to advance. The two Fusilier battalions moved through the French defences and reached the outskirts of the town. There was still sporadic sniping and the tanks and Bren gun carriers which accompanied the advance reduced speed so that the infantry were protected by their armour.

When they reached the town there was considerable confusion and in the native quarter some of the houses were on fire. At about 01.00 hours, a Bren gun carrier crew of the 2nd Scots Fusiliers entered the Defence Headquarters and captured Claerebout and Maerten. These two officers formally surrendered to Festing at 01.45 hours.[67]

Though the Joffre Line had been breached the two forts were still intact and 'C' Company of the South Lancs remained engaged with the defenders in Fort Bellevue throughout the night of the 6th. 'D' Company, having suffered a number of casualties, was withdrawn. The fort was far too strong for just one company to take by storm so Lieutenant M.R. Emsley, the senior platoon commander, attempted to bluff the French into surrendering. On the morning of the 7th, Emsley, along with his Company Sergeant Major, crept across the open ground and until he reached the wall of the fort. The two men then stood up and demanded the surrender of the fort. The French commander was not fooled and he told Emsley that he was now a prisoner. Remarkably, Emsley persuaded the French officer to agree upon a ten-minute truce and the Lieutenant and his CSM escaped back to 'C' Company's lines. M.R. Emsley's "initiative and fearless conduct" earned him the Military Cross.[68]

Just before daylight Sturges arrived in Antsirane and took over from Festing. Though all fighting had ceased in the town, the defenders in the two forts were still offering resistance and firing upon the vehicles on the road, and a platoon of the Scots Fusiliers was still pinned down in the anti-tank ditch where, through a breakdown in communications, they remained until after midday.[69]

Sturges' main concern now was not the forts, which were surrounded and could not hold out for much longer, but the batteries on the Orangea Peninsula which were preventing the Royal Navy from entering Diego Suarez Bay. Detailed French maps of the area had fallen into Syfret's hands, which showed the strength of the Orangea positions, including the extensive Ankorike Barracks. The French had built a defensive line facing southwards, protecting the batteries from land attack. To reach these positions the 17th Brigade would have to capture Fort Bellevue, then march for approximately twelve miles along a difficult road and negotiate a narrow defile at Anbotolamba that was overlooked by Fort d'Ankorike. The fort was on top of a very steep hill which dominated the approaches in all directions and was armed with two 80mm guns.

Sturges estimated that the operation would take several days and result in at least 300 casualties. He therefore wanted to give the defenders on the Orangea Peninsula the chance to lay down their arms peacefully, in the hope of avoiding such a prolonged and costly operation.

In order to allow a negotiated settlement, and not wishing to precipitate further fighting, Sturges ordered the 17th Brigade – supported by the 25-pounders of 28/76 Battery – to advance only as far as Fort Bellevue, whilst the 13th Brigade (which had landed in Courrier Bay at daybreak on the 6th) was moved up from Blue Beach to occupy the airport. Unfortunately, Sturges had earlier called for a naval and aerial bombardment of the Orangea batteries. The attack was timed to begin at 09.00 hours and *Ramillies*, *Devonshire* and *Hermione* had already formed line of battle off the Orangea coast.[70] Sturges was now worried that once the fighting started it would be very difficult to approach the French positions with cease-fire proposals and he asked Syfret to delay the bombardment. But the Admiral could wait no longer: "I was tired of this shilly-shallying and parleying for which I had given no authorisation, and which was keeping the Fleet steaming up and down in dangerous waters, consequently I informed the General that I intended to commence a 15 minute bombardment to encourage the enemy to surrender."[71]

Urgent messages were sent back to the fleet but a few rounds were fired before the signal reached *Ramillies*. "It was a tense moment," remembered Sturges. "The Royal Navy and the Fleet Air Arm were straining at the leash to give all they had got to the Orangea peninsula, and with the opening of the bombardment by the Ramillies, I fully expected everybody on both sides to join in."[72]

Fortunately for all concerned, when the bombardment stopped the cease-fire held and negotiations were able to begin. Lieutenant-Colonel Stockwell drove up to the French positions with a white flag, a bugler and two bottles of gin! These wise tactics were soon rewarded with the surrender of all the forts and batteries held by the French, though one of the Orangea batteries was not actually evacuated until the following morning.[73]

Syfret's minesweepers swept the narrow channel of the Orangea Pass and by 16.20 hours the channel and the harbour were declared clear. Forty minutes later *Ramillies*, followed by *Hermione* and two destroyers, entered Diego Suarez Bay. Though the rest of Madagascar remained firmly in Vichy hands, the vital supply route to the East had finally been secured.

The three days of fighting resulted in more than 1,000 casualties. The British suffered the loss of 109 men killed or missing and 283 wounded. Throughout the course of the operation the Fleet Air Arm flew 361 sorties (152 *Indomitable*, 209 *Illustrious*). Seven aircraft were lost in action and two during landing on the carriers. Another five aircraft were damaged but repairable. A total of 236 bombs were dropped of which 76 were incendiaries and 160 were conventional 250lb bombs. Against the French submarines, twenty-four depth charges and five torpedoes were dropped. The Royal Navy fired 669 rounds, almost a third of which were in the failed attempts at destroying Windsor Castle. HMS *Auricula* was the only vessel lost by the Royal Navy.[74]

Syfret made an immediate award of twenty-one medals with a recommendation by the admiral for more than 230 further decorations, including 3 Victoria Crosses. Syfret himself was elevated to a KCB. and Sturges was created a CB[75]

French casualties numbered almost 700 men. Of the seventeen French aircraft that were destroyed, seven were shot down in aerial combat by the Grumman Martlets of 881 and 882 squadrons, the rest were hit on the ground. All the French naval vessels engaged in and around Diego Suarez were either sunk or crippled. The native French Air Force and Naval combatants were awarded a medal for their actions in the battle, many of whom were cited for the *Médaille Militaire* and the *Legion d'Honneur*. More than 150 French Army personnel were also recommended for awards, 43 of which were posthumous. Colonel Claerebout, though interned in the UK, was promoted by Vichy to *Général de Brigade*.[76]

The rest of Force 'F' steamed into the anchorage the following day and, at 17.30 hours on 8 May 1942, Admiral Syfret formally accepted the surrender of Diego Suarez on board his flagship.

The next day Churchill sent the following message: [77]

Prime Minister to Admiral Syfret and General Sturges

I congratulate you cordially upon the swift and resolute way
in which your difficult and hazardous operation was carried
through. Pray give all ranks my best wishes and tell them
that their exploit has been of real assistance to Britain
and the United Nations.

Add for 29th Brigade only:
I was sure when I saw you at Inveraray nine months ago
that the 29th Brigade Group would make its mark!

Chapter 7

"End of an Era"

Sturges' first task at Antsirane was to round up and disarm all the French combatants. This took most of the remainder of the day, and it was not until 17.00 hours that more than 6,000 French prisoners were assembled in the Avenue de France and marched away to their barracks where they were temporarily jailed.[1] Jim Stockman was shocked to see just how large the French garrison had been: "We lined up on either side of the road with fixed bayonets and stood to attention. The first senior French officer came marching along the road with a white flag. I shall never forget the sight. He had a sword drawn, bearing the flag, and his troops were marching on behind.

"The sight that passed us gave me a jolt in the stomach. There were literally thousands of highly professional French, Foreign Legion [*sic*] and Senegalese troops, and with them, an impressive array of cannon, heavy mortars, machine-guns and boxes of ammunition."[2]

The last French troops to be captured were those stationed at Joffreville, the only other sizeable town in the Diego Suarez area. This place was held by a party of French naval ratings commanded by a Petty Officer. They had been ordered to resist any small bodies of troops that might attempt to take the town and it was not until 11.00 hours on 8 May1942 that they were told of the cessation of hostilities. A Bren gun carrier patrol then entered Joffreville later in the day.[3]

The long-term imprisonment of such a large body of troops at Antsirane was completely impractical and Syfret decided to ship them to South Africa, where the British and French casualties had already been sent.[4] A limited number of French nationals, who were prepared to sign an agreement not to take up arms against Britain, and who wanted to remain on the island, were permitted to stay in Madagascar.[5] The rest sailed for Durban on 20 May in *Oransay*, which carried 111 French officers, 836 French other ranks and ratings, 402 Senegalese, 55 Germans, 70 Italians, 5 civilian officials, 26 wives and 44 children.[6]

When the prisoners reached South Africa and learnt that they could escape internment by joining the Fighting French, all of the Senegalese volunteered to enlist with the Gaullists. The French soldiers, on the other hand, remained staunchly loyal to Pétain and when one of de Gaulle's personal representatives tried to persuade them to re-enlist with the Fighting French he was pelted with pennies. Back in Antsirane, the Malagasy troops were disarmed and confined to barracks and a curfew was imposed upon them which lasted several weeks.[7]

The crew of *Wartenfels* was also taken prisoner. These men had volunteered to help defend Antsirane during the battle but their offer was scornfully rejected by the French. The crew had scuttled *Wartenfels* and sabotaged the pumping apparatus of the dry docks. Both were later repaired successfully. Amongst the German crew were six men who appeared on Field Security's "Black List" as "Agents of Propaganda and Information". When, on the day following the capture of Diego Suarez, it was discovered that two of these six "spies" had escaped and were believed to be making for Tananarive, Sergeant Croft-Cooke of Field Security took it upon himself to pursue the missing Germans.

Croft-Cooke, in his book *The Blood-Red Island*, tells of this thrilling adventure which took him through the jungles and rivers and dusty red roads of northern Madagascar on his motorcycle. "There were fallen trees, cracks, rocks, loose fine sand which sent me skidding askew across the road, rotten wooden bridges and stony fords, sudden stampedes of cattle in front of us, sharp climbs up craggy hillsides ... all the time the parching dust from the dry red earth, the crimson dust which clung to eyelids, stuck to wet lips, choked throat and nose, coloured our khaki shirts, our knees, our arms." Crofte-Cooke eventually caught up with, and arrested, the two German agents at Maromandia near the eastern coast more than 300 miles from Diego Suarez.[8]

Another task for Field Security was to deal with the Gaullist sympathizers who had been interned by the Vichy officials. In the Prison Civile, Croft-Cooke found just six Gaullists – four seamen and two soldiers. Though these individuals expected to be released as soon as the British took over Antsirane the delicate political situation made that impossible. They had to remain in prison under the protection of the Scots Fusiliers for nearly two weeks before tempers had cooled sufficiently for these men to be allowed back into the community.[9]

After securing the prisoners Sturges, who was to remain Fortress Commander until the end of all hostilities in Madagascar, ordered his troops to prepare Antsirane and Diego Suarez for defence against counter-attack. In the planning of Operation *Ironclad*, it had been considered that a large force might be sent from French West Africa to join Annet's remaining troops in mounting a counter-offensive. It was estimated that a full brigade group, supported by battleships, cruisers, destroyers and submarines, could be dispatched from Dakar, though such a force would not be able to reach Madagascar in less than three weeks.[10]

The French Navy had already attempted to attack the ships in Courrier Bay and off the Orangea Peninsula. A little after 05.00 hours on the 7th, an aircraft from *Illustrious* had depth-charged the submarine *Le Héros* outside the reefs to the north-west of the bay. *Le Héros* had been some 500 miles north of Madagascar escorting a cargo ship from Diego Suarez to Djbouti when the British landings began. Commander Lemair had turned back to fight after receiving a message from Maertens ordering the patrolling submarines to close in on Diego Suarez and sink any British ships they saw.[11]

Le Héros had been spotted by Sub-Lieutenant Alexander, who was part of a flight of six British aircraft engaged in anti-submarine patrols around Courrier Bay and Diego Suarez. Flying at 1,000 feet Alexander saw the submarine on the

Churchill (left) watching a landing craft and Valentine tank being released into Loch Fyne during his visit in the summer of 1941. (Imperial War Museum; H11177)

HMS *Ramillies*, flag-ship of Force F, off Madagascar. (Imperial War Museum; A8858)

The Special Operations Executive vessel M/V *Lindi*. (Imperial War Museum Department of Documents, the Papers of H. Legg)

The crew of the *Lindi* constructing the torch which would guide the assault convoy into Courrier Bay. (Imperial War Museum Department of Documents, the Papers of H. Legg)

Courrier Bay as seen from Windsor Castle, looking towards Basse Point. No.7 Battery is located on the high ground on the right of the photograph. (Author)

The great natural rock monolith of Windsor Castle as viewed in 1942. (Courtesy of A. Lowe)

The infantry post on the summit of Windsor Castle. (Author)

One of the 138mm gun emplacements of No.7 Battery at Courrier Bay. (Author)

Part of the barracks complex at the rear of No.7 Battery at Courrier Bay. (Author)

One of the machine-gun posts above Red Beach that was overrun by No.5 Commando. (Author)

The remains of a Potez 63-11 bomber being inspected by British Officers in the hanger at Arrachart airfield. (Imperial War Museum; A8997)

The French Air Force hanger now sits abandoned at the end of the modern runway at Arrachart airport. (Author)

A view of Antsirane, taken in 1942, looking towards Port Nièvre. (Courtesy of A. Lowe)

A British despatch rider in Antsirane opposite the Malagasy infantry barracks. The motor-bicycle is a Harley Davidson. (Courtesy of A. Lowe)

A damaged gun emplacement of No.6 Coastal Defence Battery. (Author)

The entrance to the dry dock at Port Nièvre. (Author)

The pillboxes, adjacent to the main Antsirane road, which formed the centre of the French defences. (Imperial War Museum; A8888)

The same pillboxes today. (Author)

The central gun emplacement of Fort Caimans as seen today. (Author)

Looking southwards from Fort Caimans, in the direction from which the British attacks were delivered on 5 and 6 May. (Author)

The crumbling remains of the Scots Fusiliers Memorial which today stands beside the Antsirane road. (Author)line of the dawn attack on 6 May. (Courtesy of A. Lowe)line of the dawn attack on 6 May. (Courtesy of A. Lowe)

The crumbling remains of the Scots Fusiliers Memorial which today stands beside the Antsirane road. (Author)

Dismounted cannon of the 320mm coastal battery at Cape Miné. (Author)

One of the 100mm guns of the Poste Opitque battery overlooking the narrow entrance of the Orangea Pass. (Author)

The entrance to Arrachart airport. Note the French Air Force insignia above the portal. (Author)

The vast panorama of Diego Suarez Bay as viewed from Fort d'Ankorike. Antsirane is in the middle distance, and in the far distance the range of heights, which includes Windsor Castle, can just be distinguished. (Author)

The Naval depot in Antsirane, attacked by the Royal Marines during the night of 6 May. (Author)

The memorial in Antsirane to the Japanese submarine that attacked HMS *Ramillies* in Diego Suarez Bay. (Author)

Some of the Royal Marines, from HMS *Ramillies*, after their daring night attack of 6 May. (Imperial War Museum; A8865)

Men of the 2me Regiment Mixte de Madagascar after the surrender of Antsirane. (Imperial War Museum; FLM1072)

Corporal Bernard Grehan (seated) pictured with a fellow NCO of the 1st Battalion Royal Scots Fusiliers. (Author)

The pipes of the Royal Scots Fusiliers lead the victory parade through Antsirane after the French surrender. (Courtesy of A. Lowe)

The wreck of the French sloop *D'Entrecasteaux* in Diego Suarez Bay. (Imperial War Museum; A9405)

A conference after the surrender of Antsirane between (from left to right) Festing, Syfret, Sturges and Captain Howson R.N., who was Syfret's Chief of Staff. (Imperial War Museum; A8995)

British troops landing at Tamatave. (Imperial War Museum; K3483)

British Bren gun carriers in the streets of Majunga. (Imperial War Museum; FLM1217)

British troops looking down at the Betisboka bridge which had settled in just a few feet of water and was still passable after French attempts at its demolition. (Courtesy of A. Lowe)

Huts forming a typical Malagasy village in 1942. (Courtesy of A. Lowe)

Men of No.5 Commando interrogating French prisoners. (Courtesy of J. Jepson, Combined Operations Association)

The Lysanders of No. 1433 Flight over Madagascar. (Imperial War Museum; MAD294)

Another Vichy road block! Men of the South African 1st Armoured Car Commando prepare to haul away a felled tree with their Marmon–Herrington Armoured Car. (Imperial War Museum; MAD 173)

The 25–pounders of the 56th East African Artillery firing at the French positions on the Andriamanalina Ridge. (Imperial War Museum; MAD 122)

A Ford 1-ton truck on the road heading southwards towards Antananarivo. (Courtesy of A. Lowe)

The statue of Marshal Joffre in Antsirane. (Author)

Sovereignty restored. General Legentilhomme arrives at Tamatave to assume the post of High Commissioner, as the representative of the Free French National Committee. (Courtesy of A. Lowe)

surface making directly for the anchorage in Courrier Bay. Alexander dropped down to 100 feet to confirm his sighting, passing over the submarine. Now certain of his target, Alexander turned to make a second run as the submarine began to dive. As he closed upon the French boat Alexander released his depth charges, which fell on both sides of the submarine. The boat was blown back to the surface and then, slowly, the submarine began to sink. Survivors from *Le Héros* were picked up and interrogated on the assault ship *Keren*.[12]

A second submarine, *Le Monge,* which had been escorting a convoy to the Vichy island of Réunion, had also returned and had placed itself off the entrance to Diego Suarez Bay in an attempt to attack *Indomitable*. At 07.56 hours on the morning of 8 May, *Le Monge* sighted the approaching aircraft carrier and launched her torpedoes. *Indomitable* took evasive action, with one of the French torpedoes passing just forty-five yards ahead of her bows. *Indomitable*'s escorting destroyers, *Active* and *Panther*, raced forward and depth-charged the submarine. *Le Monge* sank with the loss of all sixty-nine hands.[13]

Another of the three submarines which had been on patrol on 5 May, *Glorieux*, had been at Majunga from where she was ordered north to attack the ships in Courrier Bay. By 10.05 hours on the morning of 6 May, *Glorieux* was twenty miles to the west of Diego Suarez. The submarine submerged and tried to move within striking distance of the British fleet. However, its periscope was seen by an Albacore operating from *Indomitable*, and *Capitaine* Bazoche had to turn and run to the north. Later in the afternoon, having evaded its pursuers, *Glorieux* again attempted to approach the ships in Courrier Bay. At 14.35 hours, Bazoche had *Indomitable* within his sights at just 12,000 yards. As it closed upon the aircraft carrier the submarine was detected by *Indomitable*'s escorting destroyers. Bazoche dived down to thirty metres and once more escaped to the area around Cap Ambre. When night fell, the submarine was able to surface and re-charge its batteries. For the next two days *Glorieux* cruised the area around Courrier Bay at periscope depth seeking to engage the British ships, but the defensive patrols of the destroyers kept the submarine out of range. On the night of 8–9 May, *Glorieux* received a signal from Vichy informing her that Antsirane had been taken. The submarine was ordered back to Majunga, and later she sailed to Dakar after joining the sloop *D'Iberville* off the coast of Angola.[14]

The French had also made another attack from the air. Early on the morning of the 7th three Morane fighters had approached Courrier Bay from the south-west. As on the 6th, the Martlets from 881 Squadron were on patrol over the beaches and the section leader immediately attacked the first of the French fighters head-on. The Morane was hit in the wings and the engine, and it was forced into the sea. The other Martlets followed their section leader into the attack and both remaining Moranes were shot out of the sky.[15]

Apart from a single reconnaissance patrol over the Indian Ocean carried out by a Kawanishi H6K flying boat from its base in the Andaman Islands, the Japanese had not intervened during Operation *Ironclad* and on the 8th the Eastern Fleet stood down from its covering role.[16]

Yet Churchill still feared a major Japanese offensive against Diego Suarez and plans to dissuade the Japanese from mounting an assault were put before the Chiefs of Staff. The Prime Minister suggested that announcements should be made that Diego Suarez was to be turned into a second Singapore. But this was rejected by the Chiefs of Staff as they felt it might provoke the Japanese into attacking before the British had become too well entrenched. Instead it was decided to "decry in public" the importance of Diego Suarez whilst secretly improving its defences.[17] Admiral Fricke and Admiral Normura did indeed meet just five days after the surrender of Antsirane to discuss the situation in the Indian Ocean. The German Chief of Staff "urged" the Japanese Attaché to recommend action against Diego Suarez as "the enemy position in Madagascar was still precarious and that an immediate Japanese counter-attack had every prospect of success".[18]

Meanwhile, the 17th Brigade took possession of the positions on the Orangea Peninsula with one company of the 2nd Scots Fusiliers taking over the fort at Mamelon Vert. The 29th Brigade occupied the defences in and around Antsirane and began constructing an elaborate trench system covering the airfield and the road from the south.[19] The 13th Brigade formed an outpost line on high ground some three miles south of the airfield. The army also took over the coastal artillery batteries but, in what Syfret described as a "grave oversight", no trained Coast Defence personnel had been included in the expeditionary force. As the batteries were an essential part of the defences of Fortress Diego Suarez, Syfret had to delegate technical officers from the warships to train the infantry in rudimentary artillery techniques.[20] The tanks damaged in the attack upon Antsirane were recovered and taken to the naval arsenal where Royal Electrical and Mechanical Engineers had set up their workshop. The engineers found that the French shot had bent, but not penetrated, the tanks' armour and they were able to straighten the plates and put the vehicles back into service. The engineers were also able to repair the guns of the coastal batteries which had been hit in the battle, and working parties from *Ramillies* stripped *D'Entrecastreaux* and *Bouganville* of all their "useful" guns and equipment.[21]

The Admiralty now wanted Diego Suarez to become the principal operational base of the Eastern Fleet. Somerville disagreed. Until the entire island had been subjugated, Diego Suarez would never be entirely secure and, the Admiral argued, improvements made at Antsirane would eventually benefit France and not Britain. Instead Somerville chose Kilindini in Kenya as his main fleet base and Antsirane was destined to be used as a repair base for cruisers and destroyers, and as an assembly port for convoys.[22] But the docks had been severely damaged during the battle (including some cases of sabotage) and until they could be repaired most cargoes had to be landed on the Courrier Bay beaches or in Diego Suarez Bay and transported overland. There was a huge amount of material to be landed to support the British forces and moving it across country was difficult, time-consuming and a drain on fuel reserves. As *Glorieux* was still at sea, Syfret needed the ships to be unloaded as quickly as possible. A civilian labour office was therefore set up by Lieutenant-Colonel Dean of the Pioneer Corps which took over the Malagasy prisoners. Along with 100 Arab dock labourers, up to 2,000 Malagasy prisoners were put to work each day re-building the docks, clearing the beaches and repairing the roads. Later, when these men were released from the French Army and allowed to leave the barracks, they continued to be employed as civilians.[23]

On 11 May, Syfret advised the Admiralty on the size of the garrison that he considered would be required to hold Diego Suarez against attack: 1 infantry brigade group, 2 garrison brigades with eight Bren gun carriers per battalion, 1 independent machine-gun company, 1 regiment of field artillery, 1 heavy and 1 light anti-aircraft regiment, 1 squadron of Valentine tanks and 1 squadron of armoured cars, plus all the associated support units including signals and a dock operating company. Syfret also recommended that another fighter squadron should be sent to support the contingent of the South African Air Force reconnaissance/bombers which would be based at Arrachart.[24]

Syfret also had to deal promptly with the civilian population of Antsirane. He had promised the French civil servants that they could retain their positions and salaries if they co-operated with the Allied forces. This was re-stated at a meeting in the Town Hall where a ten-foot-high poster portrait of Marshal Pétain had been so recently displayed.[25] Here the police, schoolmasters, clerks, and the municipal and customs officials were asked if they wished to continue in their existing posts. But the French officials were concerned that if they volunteered to serve under the British they might lose their pensions. As an American observer explained, "Their personnel folders, and the money they had paid into the retirement fund, were not with General de Gaulle in London. They were in Paris, in Occupied France, and Vichy had access to the documents."[26] What they wanted was to be ordered to continue with their jobs. Reluctantly, the Chief Political Officer, Brigadier Lush, had to order them to carry on as normal, which the French administrators, happy that their pensions were no longer in jeopardy, did quite willingly. The senior government officials, however, refused to collaborate with the British and all of them chose instead to be repatriated to France.[27]

Brigadier Lush, whose responsibility it was to organize the civilian authorities in maintaining the normal functions of the provincial government, soon found that the local officials were happy to work with the British but they were not prepared to countenance any interference from de Gaulle. On 10 May 1942 Lush wrote to London to explain the "universal hatred against the Fighting French [which] was expressed by all sections of the community." If the Gaullists were to be allowed into Madagascar, Lush told the British Government, "law and order in the Occupied Territories ... could not be guaranteed". Of even greater concern was that the introduction of the Free French would, according to Lush's telegram, antagonize British sympathizers in the rest of Madagascar and jeopardize any future operations.[28]

The capture of Diego Suarez was greeted with much acclaim in the Allied press. "There will be a feeling of immense relief in every one of the United Nations over the fact that at last we have beaten the Axis to an important move," *The New*

York Times commented on 5 May. "The British occupation of Madagascar takes the initiative away from Japan in the great battle which will soon begin for the command of the Indian Ocean ... Madagascar in Allied hands is as much a defeat for Germany as Japan."

A statement from Washington on the same day made it clear that if France was not able or willing to defend its territories from the Axis then the Allied Powers would be compelled to seize the French colonies on behalf of the United Nations. The occupation of Diego Suarez was, according to a Reuters report, "the end of an era in relations between the Allied nations and Vichy" and a break with the French Government was accepted as now being inevitable.[29] Indeed, the operation was immediately denounced in Vichy as an act of unnecessary aggression and by Berlin, which described the attack as "a breach of international law".[30]

The Nazi-controlled Paris press went even further by threatening retaliatory action: "The French Colonial Army is intact, and thousands of young Frenchmen are waiting for the opportunity to avenge the murder of their brothers ... There are British colonies in Africa ... they are within our reach."[31] Such vitriolic language was stifled after Roosevelt made it clear that "any warlike act permitted by the French Government against the Government of Great Britain ... would of necessity have to be regarded by the Government of the United States as an attack upon the United Nations as a whole". The US also declared that "if essential to the common cause" it would not hesitate to send troops and ships to support the British in Madagascar.[32]

In the UK also, the capture of Diego Suarez had stirred up a major political storm. Not only had de Gaulle been kept completely in the dark about the operation but he first learnt of the British action when he was woken at 03.00 hours in the morning with a telephone call from the Reuters press agency to be told that the British were landing at Diego Suarez!

Free French headquarters, not wishing to expose its impotence, was quick to release its own statement to the press in which it declared its satisfaction with the British move. It claimed that most of the 25,000 French in Madagascar were "for" de Gaulle, thereby implying that the attack was being undertaken on behalf of the Free French against Vichy.[33]

More privately, however, de Gaulle was "staggered"[34] by the blow dealt to him by his allies and a long, angry, and in parts threatening, letter was sent by the French National Committee to the British Foreign Office on 6 May. "The action now going on", wrote M. Dejean, the French National Commissioner for Foreign Affairs, "may have direct and imminent repercussions on the Fighting French forces and territories ... the British action against Madagascar may well shock many French people even amongst those most faithful to the Allied cause."

Dejean warned the Allies that the Free French could not accept their exclusion from the operation and that the future of France and its relations with the Allies would depend upon the extent of the French National Committee's "active share" in the war.[35] De Gaulle was so incensed that for six days he refused Anthony Eden's request to discuss the matter.

In his first public address after the attack, a speech to the House of Commons on 7 May, Churchill did little to dilute de Gaulle's anger. After praising the conduct of the British troops, he said, almost as an afterthought, that "the French also fought with much gallantry and discipline. We grieve that bloodshed has occurred between the troops of our two countries, whose people at heart are united against the common foe. We trust that the French nation in time will come to regard this episode as a recognisable step in the liberation of their country, including Alsace-Lorraine, from the German yoke."[36]

The next day the Foreign Office went one step further when it issued a public statement which reiterated the terms offered to Claerebout in an effort to show that the authorities in Madagascar had been given every opportunity to join the Allied cause before the first shot had been fired: "Simultaneously with the first landing of British troops at Courrier Bay," ran the statement, "and long before any active resistance was encountered, the British force commanders, on the instructions of H.M. Government ... informed the authorities that Madagascar would remain French and, after the war, would be restored to French sovereignty ... The force commanders also announced the intention of the United Nations not only to restore their trade with the island, but to extend to Madagascar every economic benefit accorded to French territories which had already opted for the Allies."[37]

Churchill also referred to Madagascar in his next speech, two days later, but he still failed to offer the French any clear guarantees about the island's future. Discounting Vichy's "bluster and protest", he claimed that Britain held Madagascar "in trust for that gallant France which we have known and marched with, and whose restoration to her place among the great Powers of the world is indispensable to the future of Europe. Madagascar rests under the safeguard of the United Nations."[38]

When de Gaulle and Eden did finally meet, the Foreign Secretary's assurances that Britain would restore Madagascar to France after the war or at any time that the occupation of Madagascar was no longer essential to the Allied cause, did nothing to alter de Gaulle's belief that Britain was trying to steal France's empire. As for the reasons given by Eden for excluding Fighting France from the operation – principally that Britain did not want to take responsibility for sending Frenchmen to fight Frenchmen – de Gaulle took them "for what they were worth". Eden could not understand the General's attitude. Surely, he said, "General de Gaulle would rather have the British than the Japanese in Diego Suarez?"[39]

Eden told de Gaulle that Britain had no designs upon Madagascar and that he wanted the French administration to continue to function in the colony. This was even worse news for de Gaulle as it meant that the Vichy organization on the island would be left in place. De Gaulle was utterly opposed to such a measure. "Either it will come off, and the result will be the neutralisation of a French territory under allied guarantee – which we will never accept," de Gaulle insisted. "Or it will not come off, and in few weeks' time you will have to undertake alone, in the interior of the island, an expedition which will begin to look like a conquest."[40]

De Gaulle was entirely correct (as events would prove) and Eden agreed to publish the following communiqué which was broadcast on 13 May 1942: "It is the intention of His Majesty's Government that the Free French National Committee should play its due part in the administration of the liberated French territory." [41]

Taking Eden's words at face value, de Gaulle began to arrange for Free French forces in East Africa to be transported to Diego Suarez.[42] The announcement, however, caused enormous embarrassment in Diego Suarez for Brigadier Lush, who had been trying to gain the co-operation of the local officials with assurances that the Free French would not be invited into Madagascar. "No-one can understand why we had to utter a word about the Free French in Madagascar," Admiral Somerville complained to his wife. "All it did was to make the whole population hostile and what the next move is I'm dammed if I know."[43]

Alan Brooke was also alarmed with what he saw as Eden's "mad desire" to appease de Gaulle, which would only provoke further resistance from the colonials if Britain attempted to extend its occupation across the rest of the island. "Eden's support of de Gaulle", Brooke wrote in his diary of 2 June, "will go near losing the war for us if we do not watch it." [44]

Yet the British Government's declaration did not say when the Free French would be allowed into Madagascar. Though this provided some comfort for the colonists, it did not satisfy de Gaulle, who, seeing no immediate prospect of being allowed into Madagascar, threatened to leave Britain and take the Fighting French to the Soviet Union. The General even went as far as writing to the Free French colonies telling them to prepare to "renounce" their association with the Allies and asking the Soviet Ambassador Bogmolov if his government would agree to receive the French National Committee.[45]

Churchill had anticipated a strong reaction from de Gaulle and he had imposed a travel ban on the General which prevented him leaving the country. "I think it would be most dangerous to let this man begin again his campaign of Anglophobia," Churchill told Eden, "which he is now more than ever attracted to." Six weeks later Churchill repeated his concerns. "There is nothing hostile to England this man may not do once he gets off the chain."[46]

Yet the British occupation of Diego Suarez did provide de Gaulle with an opportunity to rally another Vichy colony to the Cross of Lorraine. Just eleven days after the landings at Courrier Bay de Gaulle began to make arrangements for Free French forces to invade Réunion which, no longer able to call upon military support from Madagascar, was accomplished later in the year with no assistance from Britain.[47]

If Britain, an island, was to carry the war to her enemies she could only do so by amphibious operations. Indeed, from North Africa, to Italy, the Pacific and eventually Normandy, combined land, sea and air operations led the great assaults upon the Axis Powers that brought about their destruction. As the first such Allied expedition of its kind Operation *Ironclad* was studied in detail by Britain's military planners.

After the operation the Assault Force Naval Intelligence Officer (Commander Wedlake) and the Force Naval Signal Officer (Lieutenant-Commander Butler) were flown back to the UK to report. They were asked by Mountbatten to prepare a lecture (*Operation Ironclad: The Madagascar Expedition*) which was given to the Staff of Combined Operations Headquarters and the Staff of the Combined Training Centre at Inveraray. The operation was seen to be of such importance that the lecture was given to General Eisenhower and General Clark on their *first* night in the UK after their arrival from the USA. Butler was then sent to the United States where he gave the lecture to all the key military and naval personnel.[48]

Many other reports on Operation *Ironclad* were written and submitted to the War Office and the Admiralty. The first of these reports, and arguably the most relevant, was that of Admiral Syfret. He produced a forty-three page summary of the operation which included four pages of "Observations" and ten of "Detailed Lessons". The first comment in his report was on the importance of naval and military staffs, shipping, landing craft and troops being specifically trained together in combined operations. As he pointed out, the assault landing by the 29th Brigade followed by a twenty-mile march and a prolonged battle was "without precedent". Such an achievement was only possible because of the extensive training which the 29th Brigade had undertaken throughout the previous twelve months. Without such specialized skills, Syfret wrote, "the operations could not have been mounted under the conditions they were."[49]

Syfret's other recommendations included the separation of the Force HQ from the assaulting troops, increased use of armoured vehicles and the construction of larger and faster landing craft and more tank landing ships. The Admiral also considered that beach-head personnel, such as the Royal Naval Commandos employed so successfully at Courrier Bay, should be permanently established.[50] All of these recommendations were implemented before the end of 1942. To avoid confusion with the Army Commandos, the Royal Naval Commandos were identified by letters rather than numbers. Eventually there were twenty-two Royal Naval Commandos, the ones deployed at Diego Suarez, being the first, were A and B Commandos. The Royal Naval Commandos were to become vital components of every subsequent combined operation.[51]

The difficulties experienced by *Bachaquero*, the Tank Landing Ship, provided another valuable lesson. The landing in Courrier Bay had shown that where the coastline prevented the ship from reaching the beach, some method of bridging the distance between ship and shore had to be found. The result was that *Bachaquero*, and her sister ships, were each adapted to carry six sixty-foot-long sections of causeway. The causeways were constructed and the ships re-fitted in time for Operation *Torch*, the Anglo–US invasion of French North Africa in November 1942.[52]

Another important innovation in combined operations was conceived from a suggestion by Admiral Boyd. He noted that the Fleet Air Arm could have saved a great deal of flying time between their parent ships and the battle area if Arrachart airfield had been captured and turned into an air base rather than simply neutralized by air attack. From Boyd's observation the self-contained mobile airfield was developed. Known as the Mobile Operational Naval Air Base (MONAB) Organization, it was used very successfully in the Pacific theatre later in the war.

Ironclad had been the scene of the first extensive use of waterproofing of tanks and motor transport. Of the 200 waterproofed vehicles which landed on the beaches, approximately 10 per cent suffered mechanical failure. Most of the failures were from the transport of the 17th Brigade, which landed during the night and sank in deep water, but a few of the 29th Brigade's Bren gun carriers also failed – due to insufficient waterproofing of the engine compartment – when they were swamped on board the landing craft. Another lesson learnt.[53]

One of the great successes of the operation was found in the dummy parachutists. The French unit sent to stop the supposed parachutists was Claerebout's best-equipped company composed of his finest men.[54] Though this unit was ordered back to Antsirane as soon as Syfret's letter reached the town, it was robbed of its primary function – that of a mobile fighting force. Dummy parachutists were used again by Britain as decoys, perhaps most notably in Operation *Overlord*.

Finally, as the first major British offensive in the era of radio broadcasts and instant wireless communications, Syfret found himself faced with a new problem – one which has become familiar to all military commanders – that of dealing with the media. To handle the correspondents that travelled with the expeditionary force and those that arrived subsequently, Syfret advocated the appointment of a "Press Liaison Officer" to the staff of future operations.

Britain's next large-scale combined operation, the raid against the French port of Dieppe, took place just three months after *Ironclad*. The raid – code-named Operation *Jubilee* – was planned as a "reconnaissance in force" to test Hitler's Channel defences and as a rehearsal for the eventual re-invasion of Europe. In fact the raid was a political gesture, to appease the Russians who were demanding a second front in Europe, and not a military necessity. Though Commander Wedlake was appointed to the Planning Staff, Admiral Syfret's main recommendation – that the military and naval units involved should train together for at least six months – was disregarded due to political pressure for immediate action. As a consequence the raid was a complete disaster with the assaulting troops being repulsed after suffering 68 per cent casualties.

Chapter 8

"Shabby Deal-Making"

With Diego Suarez secure in British hands, the question of extending Allied control to include Madagascar's other major ports was once again raised. "Tamatave and Majunga, as well as other ports, have been regularly used by French submarines, and can be so used by Japanese," Jan Smuts reminded Churchill. "Madagascar authorities are violently hostile. After capture of Diego no material resistance is likely at present, but if time is given to organize resistance we may have a stiff job. Control of Madagascar is all-important for our lines of communication in the Indian Ocean and no risk can be run." Churchill wrote to Syfret on 15 May and told him that if he could seize the two ports in the next few days he could use both the 13th and 17th Brigades in the operation. If the Admiral thought this impractical then the two brigades of the 5th Division must be shipped on to India without further delay. Madagascar, Churchill explained, "must be a security and not a burden. We cannot lock up active field army troops there for any length of time."[1]

After the savage resistance already displayed by the French, Syfret replied that he considered it unlikely that Majunga and Tamatave could be taken as quickly as Churchill required. So the Admiral was instructed by the Prime Minister to make Diego Suarez secure with "minimum forces" whilst working towards achieving full collaboration with the French throughout Madagascar by peaceful means. Churchill wanted "matters to simmer down" in the hope that at least some form of temporary arrangement, or *modus vivendi*, could be reached with the Governor-General. This was to be engineered with the promise of financial assistance and trade deals as well as the threat of further military action if no satisfactory compromise could be found.[2]

The manner in which the occupying forces conducted themselves was therefore of great importance. This message was relayed to the troops in the first edition of a British forces newspaper published in Antsirane, in which the men were told that "on the behaviour of each of us towards the French population of Diego Suarez will depend much of the future of Anglo–French relations".[3]

Consequently, and despite Smuts' repeated appeals for the whole of Madagascar to be subjugated, confirmation that no further operations were to be undertaken, at least for the foreseeable future, was received from London on 17 May.[4] As a result of this instruction, Force F was broken up. Throughout the course of the 19th and 20th of the month the ships dispersed. *Indomitable*, *Illustrious* and *Devonshire* joined the Eastern Fleet and other ships, including *Hermione*, returned to Gibraltar. On the 23rd the assault ships departed for Kilindini and the remaining destroyers steamed to join Admiral Somerville. This left *Ramillies* with just two corvettes to protect it from enemy submarines.

Syfret was unhappy with this arrangement. He told Admiral Somerville that he believed his presence at Antsirane was no longer necessary and that it was time for Ramillies to be re-deployed. In response Syfret was informed that four anti-submarine/mine-sweeping trawlers would be sent to Diego Suarez from Cape Town and that three destroyers would join Syfret on 5 June. "Though disturbed at the delay in getting Ramillies away from such a poorly protected port," Syfret was later to record, "I saw no alternative, and consequently I replied that I would comply with his proposals." As events would soon show, Syfret was right in being concerned.[5]

To replace the aircraft of *Indomitable* and *Illustrious* an Air Component was formed at Arrachart airfield with the arrival of three flights of the South African Air Force on 12 May. These three flights were amalgamated to form 20 Squadron SAAF (also known as the "Sugarcane Wing") with a strength of twenty-two machines, of which six were Martin Marylands and the rest Bristol Beauforts. Logistical support for the operational aircraft was provided by two flights (twelve aircraft) of Lockheed Lodestars and one flight of Junkers Ju 52s.[6]

Following the South African aircraft, on 29 May six Westland Lysanders were delivered by sea in crates to join the Air Component. The Lysanders were assembled at Arrachart to become 1433 Flight (Army Co-operation) RAF. The Air Component's task was to conduct reconnaissance and anti-submarine patrols, and prevent any hostile approach by enemy aircraft. Two Fleet Air Arm squadrons – 795 equipped with Fulmars and 796 with Albacores – were also stationed at Arrachart as the "Special Squadron Fleet Air Arm".[7]

Hopes of a peaceful settlement with Annet were raised when an unofficial spokesman from Tananarive arrived uninvited at Diego Suarez on 27 May. This man was an Englishman called Leslie Barnett who was the representative in Madagascar of the Standard Vacuum Oil Company of South Africa. He was also an SOE agent, code-name DZ14. Annet, as with the other senior French officials, was unwilling to treat with the British either directly or officially, so Barnett had proposed to the Governor-General, through his aide de camp Captain Fauché, that he would travel to Diego Suarez ostensibly as a representative of the business community in the capital. The businessmen wanted to normalize relationships so that they could resume trade after two years of blockade which, despite the capture of Diego Suarez, the Royal Navy still maintained upon the country's other ports.[8] This clever move by Barnett allowed him to move freely between the French and British zones.

The brief given to Barnett by Annet was to find a "basis for agreement with the British whereby French sovereignty could be safeguarded and consequent neutrality would save further bloodshed".[9] After discussions with Brigadier Lush, Barnett returned to Tananarive on 28 May with proposals for a settlement but only if Annet was prepared to discuss terms on an official footing. It appeared, as historian Martin Thomas has observed, that what had started with an "impressive" military operation would end in "shabby deal-making".[10]

However, the day following Barnett's departure, telegrams from the British government forbade Syfret and his Political Officers from negotiating with Annet officially or unofficially without reference to London. Churchill's relationship with de Gaulle had become so strained that the Prime Minister was prepared to leave Annet in place. But Eden was "up in arms" at the idea of a Vichy official being permitted to retain his authority with British approval. The Foreign Secretary wanted to "clear out the rot" and introduce a Free French governor as quickly as possible.[11]

The Foreign Office wanted Madagascar to become an active participant in the war against the Axis Powers. It did not want the island to simply be a neutral state under Vichy control. One of the reasons for this was that many of Madagascar's raw materials were needed for the munitions industry. Of these mica, rock crystal and rubber were in short supply and were urgently required. Of possibly even greater significance was the country's most valuable export – high quality graphite. Fine graphite was an important ingredient in the development of the American atomic weapons programme and there was an "acute" world shortage of this mineral.[12]

Eden's desire to install the Free French in Madagascar, and his opposition to the existing military administration, led to a bitter dispute with the War Office, which viewed Diego Suarez as little more than occupied enemy territory. The result of this wrangle was an unsatisfactory arrangement known as the "Madagascar Compromise" by which a Foreign Office official was to share the political and economic administration of the occupied zone with Brigadier Lush, who was a military appointee. That official was Laurence Grafftey-Smith, who was sent to Antsirane from the British Embassy in Cairo towards the end of May.[13]

When Barnett returned to Diego Suarez from Tananarive on 5 June 1942, nothing in the instructions he brought with him indicated that Annet was ready to accept either Allied or Free French control of the island. So no reply was sent to the Governor-General and the unsatisfactory stalemate continued. In fact Annet had relayed the British proposal – that their forces should be invited to occupy Madagascar's other key ports in return for which the regime in Tananarive would not be challenged – to Marshal Pétain, who ordered the Governor-General to reject any such offers.

However, in his memoirs, Annet claims that he was unable to negotiate openly with the British for fear of alerting the military, who still wanted to continue the fight, and of inducing civil unrest in a now deeply divided community. Though Annet was unsure of Britain's immediate intentions, he decided to try and ease tensions in the capital by ordering the reservists to stand down and return to their civilian posts.[14]

Britain's attempts at communicating with Annet and her apparent disinterest in occupying the rest of Madagascar led de Gaulle to believe that Churchill was satisfied with the existing situation. This kept Britain in possession of what was, militarily, the most important part of the island whilst the remainder was left under Vichy control. De Gaulle saw this as part of a planned dismemberment of France's empire, in which Britain would "dispose of her [France's] lands and substance fragment by fragment, perhaps even to take advantage of this dispersal to allot to themselves, here and there, parcels of her property."[15]

De Gaulle put this to Churchill and Eden on 6 June, and he again threatened to quit England and set up his Free French organization elsewhere. Four days later Churchill met the General. De Gaulle considered this to be one of the most important meetings the two men had held. It was the Prime Minister who first broached the subject of Madagascar. He admitted that his government had so far failed to form a clear policy concerning the future of the island. Yet, he told de Gaulle, "we have no ulterior motive about Madagascar. As for what we mean to do there, we have no idea as yet. The island is very large! We should like to come to some arrangement so as not to get lost in it." This, of course, did not satisfy de Gaulle, but, with the Resistance movement growing in France, the general felt that his position was becoming stronger and he was able to pressurize Churchill into making a number of promises concerning the Free French movement's participation in the administration of the French colonies. In particular, he received an assurance that Colonel Pechkoff would be allowed to go to Madagascar as the first official representative of the Free French. Churchill, however, did not say when.[16]

The War Office still believed that most of the colonists would oppose the introduction of a Free French administration. This would mean that any regime change would have to be imposed by force which, with the situation in the East far from certain, Churchill wished to avoid. So the travel ban upon Free French officials remained in place whilst the War Office continued to pray for a negotiated settlement.[17]

A few days earlier, at 22.30 hours on 29 May 1942, an unidentified aircraft had appeared over Diego Suarez and had flown off before it could be intercepted. This clearly presaged some form of attack and measures were immediately taken to prepare for a dawn raid whether by air or by sea. At 05.00 hours *Ramillies* steamed round Diego Suarez bay before anchoring in a new location. The Fleet Air Arm also flew a succession of dawn patrols across the island. The day passed seemingly without incident, though the Fleet Air Arm flew further precautionary patrols over the Bay at dusk. In fact, another aircraft had reconnoitred Diego Suarez late in the day but without being detected.[18]

Darkness descended upon Madagascar at the end of an uneventful day but at 20.25 hours a massive explosion echoed around the bay and spectacular flashes lit the sky. *Ramillies* had been hit! A torpedo from a submarine had struck the battleship in the bows and blown a hole below the waterline twenty feet wide. She settled forward in the water but remained afloat and was able to move to a shallower anchorage. Thirty minutes later there was a second explosion. This time it was the tanker SS *British Loyalty,* which had just got under way. The master of the tanker "saw the bubbling tracks of the torpedo coursing towards *Ramillies*" and "with quick thinking" he altered his course to place *British Loyalty* between the submarine and the battleship. The tanker sank almost immediately.[19]

In Antsirane there was pandemonium. Word soon spread that the Japanese were attacking the harbour and officers scurried back to their regiments whilst despatch riders rushed round the town. There was even a belated attempt to impose a blackout. It was not quite panic, remembered Sergeant Croft-Cooke, "but something uncomfortably like it".[20]

The two Flower-class corvettes were immediately put into action, spending a fruitless night searching the harbour and dropping a number of depth charges around the bay on suspect contacts. The British troops also remained at their defensive posts throughout the night, finally standing down at 11.20 hours on the morning of the 31st.[21]

At first the British believed that the attack had been the work of the French and a number of retaliatory raids were made on the French airfields in the south. Three days after the attack upon *Ramillies*, the Commandos, who were still stationed at Cap Diego, were informed by the local Malagasy that two men had been seen making their way across country some twelve miles further north. A patrol was despatched which tracked down the two men near Amponkarana Bay on the north-western coast. The men refused to give themselves up and fired upon the patrol with handguns – one even attempted to charge the Commandos with a sword. The two men were killed and buried on the spot. They were Japanese. Churchill's fears of Madagascar being used as a base for Japanese submarines had proven to be well founded. Diego Suarez had been captured only in the very nick of time.[22]

A note found on one of the men was translated by a Japanese-speaking naval officer who was flown in expressly for that reason.[23] The note indicated that they were the crew of a Japanese submarine which formed part of the 1st Division of the 8th Submarine Flotilla. The flotilla, which was commanded by Rear Admiral Ishizaki, consisted of four fleet submarines, Nos. *I-10*, *I-16*, *I-18* and *I-20*. Ishizaki's flagship, *I-10*, carried a catapult-operated aircraft, the other three submarines each carried one midget submarine. All four were veterans of Pearl Harbour. Intriguingly, a fifth submarine, *I-30*, was also included with Ishizaki's force but this boat was detached on a secret mission to France to collect "a valuable cargo". However, on her return from France I-30 struck a mine and sank. [24]

This formation, also known as the Western Advance Flotilla, was the force which Nomura had promised Admiral Fricke would be sent to operate off the African coast from May to July. It had assembled at Penang in north-western Malaya at the end of April and crossed the Indian Ocean, being refuelled at sea from two armed supply ships which accompanied the flotilla. When the flotilla arrived in African waters it launched its aircraft to reconnoitre the ports along the East African coast. At Durban they sighted up to forty Allied cargo ships at anchor but the Japanese were searching for warships. It was not until they turned their attention to Madagascar, after being informed by Vichy that a battleship and a carrier (this was before the *Illustrious* had sailed to join the Eastern Fleet) were anchored in Diego Suarez Bay, that they found suitable targets.[25]

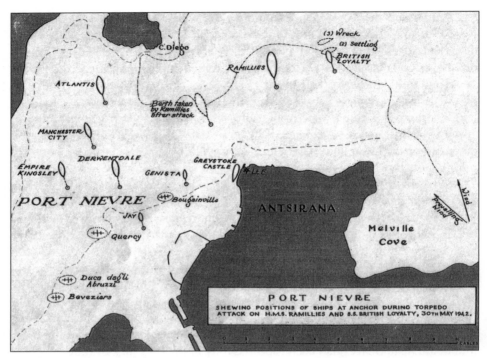

MAP 6: A map of Port Nievre, in Diego Suarez, showing the positions of the British ships at anchor during the Japanese submarine attack on HMS *Ramillies* and the supply ship SS *British Loyalty*, 30 May 1942. The positions of four Vichy French vessels sunk during the capture of Diego Suarez are also marked.

The four submarines of the flotilla converged upon Diego Suarez. On the night of 29 May, *I-16*, *I-18* and *I-20* were ordered to launch their midgets when they were about ten miles off the Orangea Peninsula. Because of the speed with which *Ironclad* had been mounted, neither an anti-submarine boom nor nets had been available and the harbour entrance was entirely open. The only anti-submarine protection at Diego Suarez consisted of the two corvettes – *Thyme* and *Genista*. At the time of the raid *Thyme* was on patrol inside the bay with *Genista* on standby. Though *I-18* was unable to release its midget submarine due to engine trouble, the other two midgets entered the harbour undetected.[26]

The two men who were shot by the commando patrol were from the midget sub of *I-20*, which had grounded on a reef near Amponkarana Bay. It was later learnt that they had ditched their craft and had been attempting to reach a pre-arranged rendezvous point where they would be met by the carrier submarines. The wreck of the midget was later spotted by a Lysander of 1433 Flight and the body of another Japanese man wearing naval uniform was also recovered from outside Diego Suarez Bay.[27]

The Japanese attack provided Smuts with the opportunity to repeat his appeal for the Allies to seize the rest of Madagascar. Offering his "sincere condolences" to Churchill on 1 June 1942, he wrote: "Attack must have been made by Vichy submarine or by Japanese submarine on Vichy information and advice. It all points to necessity of eliminating Vichy control completely from whole island as soon as possible. Appeasement is as dangerous in this case as it has proved in all others, and I trust we shall soon make a clean job of this whole business. My South African brigade group stands ready and simply awaits transport."[28]

Despite the success of the operation, the Japanese carried out no further attacks upon Diego Suarez, though the submarine flotilla continued to operate in the waters around Madagascar until the middle of July. By discharging ammunition and oil *Ramillies* was able to regain its trim and on the afternoon of 30 May the battleship, with Syfret on board, slowly made its way to Durban for repairs. *British Loyalty* was later recovered from the bottom of the bay and was also put back into service.[29]

As a footnote to this episode, there was a suggestion amongst the French that the submarine attack was concocted by the British to show the world that their capture of Diego Suarez to prevent it falling into Japanese hands was justified. The fact that the "evidence" had been removed, i.e. the two Japanese submariners had been killed and buried and the wreck of the midget recovered by the British, apparently heightened these suspicions![30]

For the next four months the Allied troops continued to strengthen the military defences of the entire area but the expected Japanese attack upon Diego Suarez failed to materialize. There was, however, a "first-class" scare when an RAF reconnaissance aircraft failed to identify a convoy approaching from the west. The troops at Diego Suarez were put into a state of alert and for ten days the newly built defences were manned in the expectation of a Japanese landing. It was a British convoy.[31]

An Intelligence report was also received which indicated that German aircraft had arrived by sea at Majunga and were being assembled by the French. Further reports claimed that German aircrews and essential parts were being flown in by seaplane from Djibouti. On 17 July, a pre-emptive raid was mounted against Majunga and Tamatave by the Arrachart Air Component. No evidence was found of any German aircraft, however, and the raid on Majunga resulted in the loss of one of the Beauforts. The plane crashed into the Betsiboka river and the crew was captured and interned at Tananarive.[32]

The only other threat to the occupying forces came from a small detachment of French troops which was still active in the north of the country. The sudden influx of thousands of men into Diego Suarez placed a great burden upon local food supplies, and the area of occupation had to be extended deeper into the country. The outposts were pushed ever further south and by June the limit of the Allied occupation in the north reached as far as Bermanja, eighty miles from Antsirane. Here the French were dug in on the other side of the River Ifany, where they appeared determined to hold their ground. This force was led by Commandant Lanneau (or Lano), a lively character who falsely claimed to have won the Victoria Cross, and who proudly sported forged ribbons of the VC and DSO on his tunic! He conducted a limited guerrilla campaign against the British outposts, punishing Malagasy villagers who had helped the invaders and, on one occasion, capturing two British soldiers.[33] Lanneau's regulars were augmented by around 100 militia. General Guillemet had issued a circular ordering the militia to attack the occupying troops "at night ... like bandits". When they could, they did.[34]

The British had supplanted the French as the administrators of Diego Suarez and they were faced with a multitude of unexpected problems. One of the first imponderables was the question of which side of the road should traffic travel? The French, and the Malagasy people, were used to driving on the right, the British on the left. It seems that an answer to this was never found and careful, or carefree, drivers simply drove down the middle.[35]

Of far greater concern to Lush's administration was the shortage of food in Antsirane. There had been a food crisis in the area even before the Allied landings and with the north now cut off from the rest of the island the situation was desperate. Another of Lush's more immediate worries was with a lack of French currency. Lush had been issued with a supply of British Military Administration sterling notes in case of just such an eventuality. Yet he felt that using Sterling would fuel Vichy propaganda claims of British colonial aggrandisement and he decided to continue with the Francs issued by the Bank of Madagascar and limit circulation by restricting withdrawals from the local banks.[36]

With the French still at the negotiating table, the complete surrender of Madagascar to the Allies appeared to be just a matter of time and it was expected that the British brigades promised to General Wavell in India would soon be released. The Chiefs of Staff had decided that the eventual garrison of Fortress Diego Suarez would consist of one mobile brigade and two garrison brigades. General Smuts offered a full brigade group – the 7th Motorized Brigade – which would be joined by two other African brigades. When these reinforcements arrived the 13th and 17th brigades would be shipped on to India.

Churchill considered Diego Suarez safe from attack, as he told Syfret on 15 May 1942: "One can hardly imagine the Japanese trying to take Diego Suarez with less than 10,000 men in transports, with battleships and carrier escort involving a very large part of their limited fleet. They have to count every ship even more carefully than we do. Therefore your problem is one of holding the place with the least subtraction from our limited resources ... The way you can help the war best is to get the 13th and 17th Brigades on to India at the earliest, and the 29th Brigade within the next two months. Everything else is subordinate to this, except of course holding Diego Suarez, which must on no account be hazarded."[37]

Field Marshal Smuts, however, still saw the situation differently and he continued to advocate a hostile advance upon Tananarive to prompt a rapid end to all French opposition. If such an operation were to take place the specialized skills of the 29th Brigade would be required.[38]

Whilst it was true that the capture of Diego Suarez, together with Kilindini, Mombassa and Colombo, had given Admiral Somerville a network of first-class ports on which to base his defence of the western Indian Ocean, the Japanese threat still remained. If a major Japanese victory in the Pacific enabled them to resume their drive westwards, Madagascar could still offer them an excellent base and, possibly, even a warm welcome.

Though Diego Suarez was securely held in Allied hands, the French retained control of two good harbours – Majunga on the west coast and Tamatave on the east – as well as a host of smaller ports where the Japanese fleet would find adequate anchorage. If the Japanese became firmly established in southern Madagascar, they would have a large number of airfields at their disposal from which they could launch attacks upon Diego Suarez. As one journalist was to observe, it might take more men to hold onto Diego Suarez than it would to seize and garrison the entire island.[39]

The Japanese threat was not imaginary. The submarine flotilla which had torpedoed *Ramillies* began to attack Allied shipping passing through the Mozambique Channel on 5 June. Over the course of the next five days, eleven merchantmen were sunk, including one, *Elysia*, which was sent to the bottom by the flotilla's supply ships. The submarines then rendezvoused with the supply ships off the south-east of Madagascar to refuel before returning to the Channel. A further thirteen ships were sunk before the flotilla made its way back to Penang at the end of July. This single formation had crippled one battleship and sunk twenty-five merchantmen totalling over 120,000 tons.[40]

Unaware of the presence of the two supply ships, the Allies assumed that the Japanese submarines were being replenished at Madagascar.[41] Though Annet refuted any suggestions that the Japanese submarines had been offered facilities in Madagascar, this was only because Admiral Ishizaki had not asked. In fact when Annet relayed to France a request for guidance should a Japanese submarine seek assistance in one of Madagascar's ports this was the answer he received: "in view of United States approval of the British operation against Diego Suarez, there would be no case for considering the Japanese as aggressors. Any request by a Japanese submarine for permission to stay in a Madagascar port longer than normal under international law should, therefore, be granted."[42]

Though the 29th Brigade had to remain on the island in case further operations were undertaken, the 13th Brigade was able to sail for India almost immediately. Little of the brigade's stores had been unloaded and it took just three days to re-embark the entire brigade and its equipment. Escorted by *Devonshire*, the 13th Brigade departed for Bombay on 20 May in *Franconia*, its stores in *Nairnbank* and *Martand*. So many of the men had contracted malaria and dengue fever that the brigade was not fit for active service for some time after it arrived in India.[43]

Three days later, four other transports, accompanied by two corvettes and two destroyers, sailed for Mombassa to collect the 4,000-strong 22nd East African Brigade, which would replace the 17th Brigade. This formation, commanded by Brigadier W.A. Dimoline, was composed of the 1st Battalion (Nyasaland) King's African Rifles (KAR); the 5th Battalion (Kenya) KAR; the 6th (Tanganyika) KAR and the 56th (Uganda) Field Battery East African Artillery.

The 17th Brigade, with hundreds of its men on the sick list, sailed for India on 12 June, leaving behind the 9th Field Regiment, which transferred to the 22nd Brigade.[44] "I must admit, we had no regrets in seeing Madagascar receding into the distance, whatever horrors of war lay ahead of us," wrote Jim Stockman. "Madagascar was certainly one of the darkest chapters in our lives, bringing back the stark reality of kill or be killed."[45]

During the third week of June the South African 7th Motorized Brigade Group also landed at Diego Suarez. The brigade was composed of the 1st City Regiment; the Pretoria Regiment; the Pretoria Highlanders; the 6th Field Regiment, South African Artillery; the 88th Field Company, South African Engineers; and 'A' Squadron, 1st Armoured Car Commando, South African Tank Corps, with twenty Marmon-Harrington armoured cars. The South Africans were moved out to the old French camp at Sakaramy where they proceeded to dig themselves in.[46]

On 25 May 1942, Lieutenan-General Platt, GOC East African Command, had been informed that Madagascar would be placed under his direct authority from the beginning of July. It would be part of the newly formed "Islands Area" along with Mauritius and the Seychelles, which would be commanded by Major-General Smallwood. To assist communications between Madagascar and the rest of Platt's command, the island of Mayotte in the Mozambique Channel, which was still held by the French, was to be captured. Mayotte, which possessed its own powerful radio station, would be used as a forward operating base for Catalinas and as a transit station for other aircraft.[47]

The small island's defensive force consisted of less than 100 armed police but, as the French Governor and his men were known Vichy supporters, it was expected that they would resist an Allied landing. It was also understood that key installations on the island had been mined and that the Governor had given instructions for these to be blown up if an invasion was attempted. The attack upon Mayotte, therefore, was planned to take place at night in order to catch the defenders off guard and so minimize the risk of casualties and of sabotage. Code-named *Throat*, the expedition would consist of the cruiser *Dauntless* (recently arrived at Diego Suarez from the Eastern Fleet), the destroyer *Active* and a military force of 30 Commandos from 121 Force with 'C' Company, 5th Battalion, King's African Rifles, supported by detachments of mortars, signals and Intelligence. It would be the KAR's first combined operation.

On 30 June 1942, the troops embarked on the two warships to make the short journey from Diego Suarez to Mayotte. At 03.00 hours on 2 July, the troops began to creep ashore at the main port, Mamudzi. They broke into the houses of the

Europeans and surprised the *Chef du District* and many of the police in their beds. The Chief of Police and a few others tried to escape by car but were stopped by roadblocks erected by the KAR. The Commandos, meanwhile, had scaled the cliffs at Dzaudzil, the off-shore administration centre. Here they captured the radio station and the Governor of the Comoros Group. The island was taken with no loss of life and no damage to the island's facilities. On the same day, the nearby island of Pamanzi was also occupied, where another airfield was established.[48]

Prior to Platt taking over at Diego Suarez he had asked Barnett to go back to Tananarive with a personal note to Annet inviting the Governor-General to send an accredited representative to Antsirane for negotiations. As the Free French were still incensed with their exclusion from Madagascar, Platt's offer could only be given verbally.[49]

Platt received no reply from Annet and it was becoming increasingly clear that the Governor-General had no desire to reach an agreement with the Allies over the future of the country. This stalemate could not be allowed to continue indefinitely, particularly as the 29th Brigade, which was sitting around doing nothing, was needed for operations in Burma. To find a solution to this problem Field Marshal Smuts called a conference on 20 June in Pretoria, attended by Generals Platt and Sturges and Brigadier Lush. The meeting gave Smuts another opportunity to explain that the occupation of Diego Suarez alone did not prevent Madagascar's other ports from being used by enemy raiders. The other men agreed and together they decided that, as Annet had shown no intention of relinquishing his authority over the rest of Madagascar willingly, he should be compelled to do so by force of arms.[50]

This view appeared to be confirmed after Monsieur Millot, President of the Planters Association, arrived in Antsirane from Tananarive on the 21st. Millot declared that most of the French in the capital wanted to reach an agreement with the British providing that the Free French were not involved. Annet, however, dare not risk a breach with Vichy by initiating such a move which meant that if Britain wanted to control the whole country force would have to be used. This, according to Millot, would allow Annet to offer a token resistance before surrendering.[51]

The plan devised by Smuts and the others, therefore, was that the ports of Majunga and Tamatave would be taken by assault and if the Governor-General still refused to accept the terms offered (that the French authorities would continue to represent the French Government and retain civil administration of the island but subject to British military control, including censorship and regulation of all external commmunications) then the Allies should advance upon Tananarive. This proposal was forwarded to London along with the recommendation that a decision on whether or not Tananarive was to be occupied had to be made very shortly if the operation was to be completed before the rainy season and before the health of the 29th Brigade deteriorated even further. Widespread malaria and dysentery, coupled with weeks of inactivity, had led to growing concerns over the physical condition of the British troops in Madagascar.[52]

Admiral Somerville added his weight to the argument in favour of occupying the whole of Madagascar when he explained to the Admiralty that by denying the enemy any possibility of a base in the western Indian Ocean more of his resources could be released to operate directly against the main Japanese forces in Burma and Malaysia. Diego Suarez would prove invaluable, he told Admiral Pound on 29 June, in relieving congestion at Durban and Colombo. "But," he emphasized, "until we have the whole of the island I shall never feel that our position is too secure."[53]

At first the Chiefs of Staff were reluctant to extend operations in Madagascar as this would require the return of the assault shipping which had been sent to India. By the middle of July, however, the situation in India had stabilized and Churchill was happy to permit further offensive operations in Madagascar. Even Alan Brooke, who had consistently argued against becoming involved in Madagascar, was now willing to consider "completing" the expedition. So, on 19 July, Churchill ordered the Chiefs of Staff to "tidy up" the island before the autumn rains put an end to operations for the year.[54]

The capture of the Malagasy capital presented considerable problems. The only road southwards down the east coast of the island from Diego Suarez travelled for just eighty miles before it lost itself in (at that time) unexplored mountains and trackless forests. Down the west side from Diego Suarez a road ran southwards through the hotter, drier and more barren western plains, but it crossed more than 300 bridges, all of which the French could destroy.

The only practical ways of reaching Tananarive were through the ports of Majunga and Tamatave. From Majunga a good road, though unmetalled, travelled directly to the capital, and Tamatave was connected to Tananarive by rail. Any further penetrations into Madagascar would, therefore, have to include more combined operations.

If the offensive was to be resumed Smuts wanted the two African brigades to be involved. But the proposed operation would include sea-borne assaults upon the defended ports of Majunga and Tamatave. So even though the assault craft used against Diego Suarez had already been sent to India to allow Wavell to begin training for amphibious operations, the 29th Brigade could not be released until the French forces in Madagascar had surrendered.

In late July, after the decision to occupy the rest of the country had been taken, word was received at Antsirane that the Manager of the Banque de Madagscar was being sent from Tananarive. Annet insisted that this individual – a Monsieur Dupont – should be received as he was "charged with important business".[55] Yet Sturges had no intention of allowing a French official to see what was happening at Diego Suarez and Dupont was permitted to travel only as far as the British outposts at Ambilobe where he was met by the Foreign Office representative, Grafftey-Smith. Dupont had been instructed to continue the talks initiated by Barnett, yet Annet still refused to enter into any official discussions. Grafftey-Smith did manage to make some good use of Dupont's visit, however, as he obtained millions of francs from the banker to relieve the financial pressure in Antsirane. Dupont only agreed to supply the notes after Grafftey-Smith pointed out that the only alternative was the introduction of Sterling.

The proposed landings at Majunga and Tamatave could only be conducted if assault ships and landing craft were made available. It was expected that operations would begin in August and continue into September and with the build-up of troops and equipment for Operation *Torch* in North Africa (planned to commence around 15th October) no more of these vessels could be released for other operations and Platt would have only those which could be released by Wavell.

The strength of the Vichy forces in central and southern Madagascar was believed to be as follows:[56]

LAND FORCES

At Majunga:	1 x 75mm gun One battalion of the *1er Régiment Mixte de Madagascar* (*RMM*) Total = 1,000 men
At Tamatave:	6 x 75mm guns One battalion of the *1er RMM* One European Company One Independent Motorised Company (Senegalese) Total = 1,500 men
At Tananarive:	4 x 75mm guns 4 x 65mm guns Two battalions of the *1er RMM* One European Company Total = 2,300 men

There were also other small detachments at Ambanja on the west coast (two companies *1er RMM*), Brickaville on the east coast (at least one company *1er RMM*) and four companies of the *Bataillon de Tirailleurs Malgaches* in the centre and far south of the island, totalling around 1,500 men. There was therefore a combined total of 6,300 men.

These troops were believed to be well supplied with 8mm Hotchkiss machine guns and 81mm Brandt mortars but short of ammunition for both the machine guns and their own rifles. It was reported that each man had only around fifty cartridges. There were also a number of Hotchkiss 13.2mm anti-aircraft guns.[57]

In addition to these regular forces, there was an unknown number of armed police, known as *Gardes Indigènes*, throughout the country.

AIR FORCES

At Ivato-Tananarive: Four Morane 406 fighters
                            Two Potez 63 bombers
                            One Potez 25 reconnaissance aircraft

NAVAL FORCES

Possibly one submarine
One sloop (carrying a floatplane)

The capture of Tananarive was to be a three-phase operation, which was code-named *Stream-Line-Jane*. The Free French were to be excluded from any involvement in the operation and de Gaulle would not be informed until 10 September, the proposed start date. As with *Ironclad*, the planners had to assume that the French would oppose in force any aggressive moves by the Allies. In fact Annet received a telegram on 5 August instructing him to try and maintain his authority over as much of the island as he could and that he should ensure "the maximum prolongation of resistance in the event of new British aggression, such as is made possible by a scorched earth policy and guerrilla-activities".[58]

The first phase of the operation – *Stream* – was the amphibious assault upon Majunga by the 29th Brigade. After the port had been secured Operation *Line* would begin. This was the landing of the 22nd East African Brigade, which would advance upon the Malagasy capital from the west. *Jane* was the re-embarkation of the 29th Brigade to sail around to the east of the island to seize the important commercial port of Tamatave. The 29th Brigade would then push up the railway line which ran between the port and the capital and link up with the East Africans at Tananarive. In support of the main operations, two diversionary attacks were also planned to confuse and distract the French. The first of these diversionary moves involved the South African Brigade. This brigade, which had assembled at Sakaramy some eighteen miles from Diego Suarez, was to push southwards in the hope of drawing forces away from the centre of the island and of mopping up any pockets of resistance which might remain in the north. At the same time a small body of commandos was to land at Morandava on the west coast of the island. The commandos were simply to land and make as much noise and fuss as they could.

A large naval force was to be made available for Operation *Stream*, part of which would remain in theatre to support the 29th Brigade's landing at Tamatave. To provide aerial support for the East African Brigade's advance from Majunga to Tananarive, the Lysanders of 1433 Flight and 20 Squadron SAAF would be transferred from Arrachart to Majunga. Losses and mechanical failure during reconnaissance patrols by 20 Squadron had reduced the South Africans to just five Marylands and seven Beauforts, but this was double the number of aircraft left available to the French.[59] RAF Catalinas of 209 Squadron operating out of

Pamanzi and Diego Suarez would provide maritime reconnaissance and close anti-submarine support to the assault forces on both coasts.[60]

To supply transport for the long drive to Tananarive, Platt had already arranged for five and a half Reserve Mechanical Transport Companies to be extracted from other areas of his East African Command. Bob Sturges was again designated Military Commander, with Garnons-Williams and Festing appointed Joint Assault Commanders for both the Majunga and Tamatave landings. Brigadier Dimoline would lead Operation *Line* whilst Platt himself would be in overall command of the entire campaign, which would eventually include seven naval and two military operations.[61]

Once again the Special Operations Executive, which had set up a local branch in Antsirane under the guise of a "Trade Office", was called upon to provide information ahead of the operation and sever communications between Majunga and key military posts further inland. For this the Mission was provided with £100,000 "to spend in securing French co-operation".[62]

Brigadier Lush had also continued to receive information from existing agents in Tananarive, including Bertha Mayer, even though she knew that her husband had been compromised and that she was under suspicion. The French were well aware that British agents were sending wireless messages from Tananarive. To try and locate the secret wireless locations they were switching off the mains electric supply in certain parts of the city without notice whilst the agents were transmitting. If the transmission stopped at the exact moment the power was cut, it would indicate that the wireless set was in that area of the city. The French were also using radio directional finding instruments.[63]

All of the British subjects in the French-controlled areas of the island were under the closest scrutiny, and three of the agents had their homes searched. One of these, DZ61, who lived several miles outside Majunga, was ordered by the police to move into the town itself so that he could be more easily watched. Barnett, meanwhile, had been formally appointed a full officer of the Mission. On his visits to Antsirane, he received training in SOE work and instructions on the Mission's specific objectives in advance of future operations.[64]

In preparation for the assault upon Majunga and Tamatave, the South African Air Force had been conducting reconnaissance flights over the central and southern areas of the island. As a result a reasonable picture of the two ports and their defences had been put together, including a 200-square-mile photographic mosaic of the Majunga area. On one of these flights a SAAF Maryland was hit by anti-aircraft fire. Though one engine was disabled the pilot, an officer called Jones, managed to keep the plane in the air until he reached Sahambave on the east coast, where he was able to land safely. His wireless was still operational and Jones made contact with his base. He was told to remain where he was until help arrived. A rescue party drawn from No.5 Commando and the Royal Engineers failed to get through by land, but Jones and his four-man crew were supplied from the air with rations and cigarettes.[65]

Meanwhile, the French discovered where the airmen were holding out and a party of forty native troops under a European officer set off to bring them in. Jones learnt that the enemy party was coming, thanks to a little trading of food (and, most probably, cigarettes) with the local Malagasy and he decided to ambush the enemy patrol.

He armed his crew with a Vickers machine gun removed from the dorsal turret of his damaged plane and hid them in a nearby bush. He then stood out in the open and waited for the French to appear. When the French party approached Jones' position, the French officer walked up to the pilot and the following conversation took place:

French officer:	"You are under arrest."
Pilot Jones:	"I am sorry. There is a misunderstanding. You are *my* prisoner. I have you covered with superior fire."
French officer:	"You make the bluff."
Pilot Jones (in Afrikaans):	"Give him a burst."
(Burst given from the machine-gun).	
French officer:	"I surrender unconditionally." [66]

The South Africans disarmed the entire party and herded them onto a small island, approximately 100 yards from the shore. Food was dropped to the prisoners by the Air Force every day until a minesweeper arrived from Diego Suarez to take off Jones, his crew and all the captives.

Other activities in advance of operations included an assault upon the island of Nosy Bé, which is some 200 miles to the north of Majunga, by two platoons of the Pretoria Highlanders and a contingent of Royal Marines. The island was known to be defended by just thirty-five reservists with four machine guns. It would be the first-ever assault landing by South African troops.

At 02.45 hours on 9 September 1942, the minelayer *Manxman* anchored off the coast of the island and "with a murderous, splitting, stab of thunder" bombarded its main town, Hellville, for fifteen minutes. There was what Private Bintliff described as a "shortlived, stuttering answer"[67] from the shore which was silenced by the infantry with mortars and machine guns. When the infantry landed there was little opposition and by noon the outlying detachments of Malagasy troops had made their way into the town to surrender. The Pretoria Highlanders remained as the garrison of the island.[68]

The nearby island of Nosy Mitsio was also occupied by a company of the First City Regiment. Here, between 4 and 9 September, the South Africans were trained in amphibious operations in anticipation of a landing in the rear of the French positions on the east coast.

The East African Brigade was relieved of its coastal duties by the 27th (Northern Rhodesia) Infantry Brigade in early August. This brigade consisted of the 2nd, 3rd and 4th Battalions of the Northern Rhodesia Regiment, attached to which was a battery of East African light artillery from Kenya. The 22nd Brigade transferred to Sakaramy, about eighteen miles from Diego Suarez, for intensive training in readiness for the coming campaign. This included learning to drive Bren gun carriers and operating with the new concept of self-contained "Fighting Groups" of infantry, artillery and armoured vehicles.[69] Also in August the Japanese submarine *I-29* began to work the waters north of Madagascar. During August and September, the submarine found and sank four Allied merchant ships. Naturally this led the Allies, and Smuts in particular, to believe that Annet was assisting the Japanese, which gave added justification for the occupation of the entire island and the removal of the Governor-General.[70]

As with *Ironclad*, secrecy was considered to be essential. Two full brigade groups preparing for active operations at Diego Suarez could not have passed unnoticed. So Platt decided to divide the force. The 29th Brigade would be the first to move, ostensibly to take part in an amphibious exercise on the African coast. Approximately a week later, the 22nd Brigade, which would not be tactically stowed, would sail from Diego Suarez, having been told that it was being shipped on to India.[71]

Chapter 9

"Before the Last Battle"

The 29th Brigade was shipped to Mombasa for the final full-scale exercise before the start of *Stream-Line-Jane* at the end of August 1942. As such an exercise could not be concealed it was carried out in a "blaze" of deliberate publicity and took the form of an amphibious assault to test Mombasa's newly completed defences, under the code-name of *Touchstone*. During this time, the REME workshop team serviced and waterproofed all vehicles for the coming campaign on the quay in Mombasa docks. Whilst at Mombasa reinforcements from the UK joined the 29th Brigade.[1]

Though the troops had not been told that further operations were imminent, the exercises and reinforcements clearly presaged some significant move, and speculation was rife. Some suggested that they were destined for Dakar, whilst others proposed an assault upon French East Africa or a landing behind Rommel's Africa Korps at El Alamein. "There were so many rumours," wrote Sergeant Lawrie of the Armoured Car Commando, "one wonders whether they were part of a policy designed to hoodwink the French or just idle speculation."[2]

The 29th Brigade and the South African Armoured Car Commando departed from Mombasa on 5 September. The naval force, designated Force M, sailed separately. That evening, as the convoy steamed southwards, the troops were officially informed of their mission. At the rendezvous point approximately ninety miles from Majunga, the ships from Mombasa joined those from Diego Suarez carrying the 22nd East African Brigade. Altogether, nearly seventy ships were assembled. To the men of the Armoured Car Commando it was a thrilling sight. "There were battleships, an aircraft carrier, cruisers, destroyers, sloops, mine-sweepers and a complete variety of merchantmen and troopships." Only then did the men realize that the impending expedition was far larger than they had ever expected.[3]

Just before midnight on 9 September, the combined convoy, led by Rear-Admiral Tennant in HMS *Birmingham*, with the aircraft carrier *Illustrious*, the Dutch cruiser *Heemskerck*, twelve destroyers and four minesweepers, anchored five miles off the western coast of Madagascar. *Illustrious*, the only carrier left with the Eastern Fleet, had thirty-six aircraft available for the operation, including eighteen Swordfish.[4]

For the assault upon Majunga the 29th Brigade was divided into two parts. The Welch Fusiliers and the East Lancs were to land at Red Beach approximately ten miles north of Majunga and attack the port from the landward side. Four hours later, at first light, the South Lancs and No.5 Commando were to make a direct amphibious assault upon Majunga, designated Green Beach.[5] The Scots Fusiliers

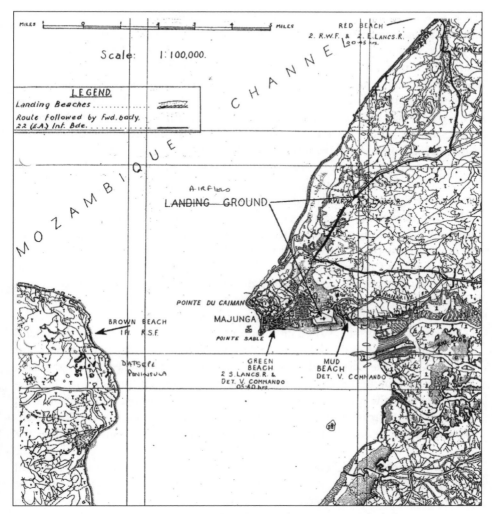

MAP 7: The assault landing beaches for the capture of Majunga on 10 September 1942.

were to remain on board ship to act as a floating reserve, apart from one company which was to land and capture the guns on the Datsepe Peninsula opposite the port. This was classified as Brown Beach. Unlike Operation *Ironclad*, there would be no advance warning before the infantry attacked.[6]

Though the skies were clear it was a dark night. "No one spoke," wrote an observer from the bridge of the destroyer *Arrow*. "Apart from the muffled splutter of their gently-running engines, the landing craft remained silent. I could not even see the troops aboard, but I knew they were there, packed like sardines, crouched over their guns."[7]

Shortly after 01.00 hours on 10 September, the first wave of the attacking force was put ashore. In the darkness the landing craft misjudged their navigation and the troops were dropped a few hundred yards south of the intended area. As a result, the landing craft returned to the convoy later than expected.

The second wave of troops clambered down the scramble nets to board the waiting landing craft. Though they had practised this manoeuvre many times there was a heavy swell and a considerable risk of being caught between the hulls of the ships and the sides of the bobbing landing craft. However, by 02.45 hours, the last of the troops had been put ashore and were following the first wave southwards.

The first wave had moved off as soon as it had disembarked. There were three roads leading southwards from the beach. One followed the coast whilst the other two ran parallel to the first but further inland. The landing beach was surrounded by jungle but the Welch Fusiliers found a track through the trees and scrub and they led the first wave southwards towards Majunga.

'B' Company of the Welch Fusiliers was instructed to take the coastal road, 'D' Company was to follow the road two miles inland and the East Lancs was to take the most distant road. The coastal road was in fact nothing more than a jungle track and Major Vaughan's company did not find it until 03.00 hours. Following the coastline beneath tall, red cliffs, Vaughan's men came upon an observation post behind Amborovy beach, four miles from Majunga. The post was taken without loss, and one French officer and sixteen men were captured.

Captain Williams' 'D' Company made more rapid progress along the inland track. Williams captured a defended position in Amborovy village, but movement was difficult in the soft, sandy soil and, with the dust knocked up by the men filling the dark night air, contact could only be maintained by each man holding onto the rifle of the one in front.[8] Further inland the East Lancs located the road and advanced towards the airfield on the outskirts of Majunga, meeting only light resistance until the battalion was held up by a strong position on the edge of the town.

Meanwhile, 'A' and 'C' companies of the Welch Fusiliers, forming the second wave of the assault force, had moved round to the south-east of Majunga to cut both the main road and the secondary road to Tananarive. Having reached the two roads leading from Majunga, the Welch Fusiliers turned north and advanced into the town against only "slight" opposition.

Earlier in Majunga, *Chef du Bataillon* Martins, the port's military commander, had been woken by an excited messenger who had told him that the British had arrived from nowhere and had landed nine miles to the north. Martins reacted exactly as predicted. He gathered together as many troops as he could and sent them to repel the invaders leaving Majunga practically undefended. Now was the time for the South Lancs and the Commandos to make their direct attack upon the weakly held port.

Accompanied by the destroyer *Blackmore*, the landing craft raced towards the harbour. As the South Lancs neared the land they were met with sporadic machine-gun fire and some men were hit, though the French gunfire ceased as the men landed. "In two minutes we were out of the boat, lining up ready to go," recalled a sergeant of the South Lancs. "That moment fire opened up – it was two machine guns, one firing from a house opposite, and one from a barge by the jetty on the left ... we turned round with our backs to the wall and opened fire with automatics, pistols, everything we'd got. They were only fifteen or twenty yards away, and we shut them up all right."

Advancing quickly the South Lancs cleared the docks area before moving into the town, encountering only small pockets of resistance. Such was the speed of the attack, eighty French soldiers were taken prisoner in the first eight minutes of the battle.[9]

At 05.40 hours, shortly after the landings in the harbour and just as dawn was breaking, Swordfish and Martlets of the Fleet Air Arm and SAAF planes based at Mayotte swarmed low over Majunga. This was a demonstration of strength rather than an aerial attack and, though the Allied aircraft strafed a few likely targets, no bombs were dropped on the town or the harbour.

Behind the assault force, the navy personnel responsible for anti–sabotage duties in the port were delayed by renewed sniping. This meant a job for the Royal Naval Commandos, who silenced the snipers with their Lewis guns and grenades.[10]

Whilst the battle continued, 2 Troop of No.5 Commando was taken by 'R' boats up the River Ikopa (a tributary of the Betsiboka) to cut off any French forces retreating from the Majunga area. "As we travelled up the river the tide began to go out and we began to run aground on sandbanks," one of the Commandos later recalled. "The river was full of crocodiles, so before we could get into the water to lighten the craft and push them off the sandbanks, hand–grenades were thrown into the river to keep the crocodiles at bay."[11] The Commandos succeeded in reaching their objective, only to learn that, by 07.00 hours, all fighting in Majunga had ceased and the French had surrendered having made no attempt to retreat.

Martins was captured by the South Lancashire Regiment and ordered to surrender. However, the French commandant needed to be assured that he had done his duty. "Did my men fight well?" Martin asked the Colonel of the South Lancs "Magnificently!" replied the British officer, somehow keeping a straight face. His honour satisfied, Martins surrendered. Two cars, each carrying a British and a French officer, then toured the town under a white flag ordering the troops to cease fire. What one journalist defined as "The Battle Before Breakfast" was over.[12]

Two hours later, after the harbour had been swept and no mines found, the first of the other British warships entered the port.[13] A number of known Vichy sympathizers were then rounded up thanks to Bishop Vernon, who, conveniently in Majunga at exactly the right time, was driven round the town in a Bren carrier pointing out the suspects.

No official casualty figures have been released for the action at Majunga. Unpublished documents indicate that just five men were killed and nine wounded, all from the 29th Brigade.[14] There were also a few civilian casualties in the town. One man, who went onto his balcony during the height of the battle wearing khaki drill, was killed and a number of others wounded.[15]

Annet had been told by Vichy that he must resist the Allies for as long as possible. This meant that he would have to withdraw from Tananarive as the

Allies approached. He would face the ignominy of becoming a fugitive in a country of which he was the Governor-General. Though Annet knew that his forces could not prevent the Allies taking control of Madagascar, he feared the political consequences of abandoning the capital at such a critical time. Upon hearing of the Majunga landing, Annet proposed to Vichy an alternative policy. He suggested that he should delegate his Secretary-General, M. Ponvienne, to run the government administration in the south whilst Annet remained in Tananarive to meet the Allies.

The reply from Vichy to this suggestion was nothing short of insulting. Annet was told that he was the French representative in Madagascar and whatever small part of the country remained unoccupied by the Allies he should continue to hold in the name of France. Vichy's orders for a prolonged resistance and for Annet to remain beyond the grasp of the Allies were, he was told, due to "reasons of general policy which may escape you, but which outweigh your arguments".

Despite the tone of this message, Annet believed the French cause would be best served by attempting to reach an advantageous settlement with the Allies whilst he still had something to bargain with. His response to Vichy was, therefore, to inform his masters on the morning of 16 September that he had contacted the British with a view to ending hostilities. He had asked Platt to receive plenipotentiaries to request "by what means we can, with honour, cease the conflict before the last battle takes place".[16]

Two envoys were selected to act on behalf of Annet and his senior military commander, General Guillemet, at talks which began in Majunga on the 17th. The Allies were represented by Laurence Grafftey-Smith, Chief Political Advisor.[17]

If Annet hoped to obtain favourable terms from the British, he was soon to be disappointed. Britain's stance remained unchanged. Madagascar could not continue as a neutral Vichy state. The island must be handed over to the Allies and become an active participant in the war against the Axis. Annet, of course, had to refuse such terms, especially as Vichy, shocked at the prospect of their Governor-General handing over the island to the British, bombarded Annet with telegrams insisting that he followed his earlier instructions.

One French historian – Robert Aron – paints quite a different picture of these events. He claims that, when the news of the Allied landings at Majunga reached Paris, Laval ordered Annet to open up official negotiations. The instruction was rescinded, however, when the Germans learnt of this move and insisted that no negotiations should take place.[18] If this was indeed the case, it meant that the Germans ordered the French to fight their former allies and that the French complied.

To coincide with the attack upon Majunga, a small party of commandos was landed from the boats of HMS *Napier* at Morondava, 380 miles further south. There were no military forces in this part of the country and the landing was unopposed. The fort at Morandava was occupied by the Commandos and the Tricolour hauled down. To the Commandos' astonishment, the Commandant's wife, seized with patriotic fervour, snatched the French flag from the soldiers and wrapped it round her body to protect it (or possibly herself) from defilement by the British!

The Commando leader, Sergeant O'Hana, was a British-Moroccan who formerly lived in Paris and who spoke fluent French. After landing, O'Hana cycled inland and took over the house of the District Commissioner, from where he telephoned Tananarive. Pretending to be the Commissioner, he told the capital that the British had landed in great numbers and that any attempt at resisting such a force was futile. Unfortunately, Annet's secretary was not convinced and he asked the "Commissioner" to name his youngest daughter. That was the end of O'Hana's charade, but it does seem that, as a precaution, some French troops were drawn away from positions facing Majunga to oppose this fictitious army. If this was true, then the diversion at Morondava must be considered a success, considering the small number of troops – just forty men of No.6 Troop – who were employed.[19]

The end of the fighting in Majunga also meant the end of the 29th Brigade's involvement and no more of its men or vehicles were sent ashore. However, there was no halt in operations. When Festing landed at 08.40 hours, he handed all the landing craft over to the East African Brigade.[20] It was vital that a number of key bridges on the road from the port to Tananarive were taken intact and speed was essential. These bridges – over the Kamaro river ninety-nine miles from Majunga and over the Betsiboka river a further thirty miles further south – were reported to be strongly defended and prepared for demolition. Platt had asked for a unit of paratroops to capture the bridges ahead of the landing at Majunga but the War Office had turned down the request, so the job of preventing the French from destroying the bridges was given to the SOE.[21]

It was expected that the French troops would not blow up the bridges unless ordered to do so from Tananarive and no air reconnaissance of the bridges had been allowed in case the defenders were panicked into premature action. It was the responsibility, therefore, of the agents in the capital to cut the telephone line from Majunga just before the landings began. There was still the possibility that the officer in charge of the bridges might destroy them on his own initiative, so a second plan was laid to send a small party of SOE operatives to capture the bridges ahead of the assault force. Both plans failed.

On the night of 7/8 September 1942, the operatives were landed on the coast to the north of Majunga from the SOE coastal freighter, *Frontier*. The first group was put ashore at the wrong point and could not find the two lorries which the local agents had waiting for them. Only one man – exhausted and overcome with malaria – made it by foot to Majunga. The second party, attempting to land in daylight, were spotted by French lookouts and had to retreat to *Frontier*.[22]

In Tananarive, the agent responsible for cutting the telephone lines acted too late and messages were sent between the port and the capital before the line was severed. Orders were therefore sent to cripple the main Betsiboka bridge. As there was no quayside at Majunga deep enough for the transport ships to approach, it would take days for the whole of the 22nd Brigade to be disembarked. So, as soon as the first troop of armoured cars and a few vehicles had landed, the forward units of the East African Brigade began the drive towards Tananarive in the hope that they could secure the bridge before the French could carry out their orders.

The East African brigade was divided into three Fighting Groups and a Forward Body:

1FG = 1/1 KAR, plus one field battery of the 9th Field Regiment RA.
2FG = 5 KAR, plus 56th (Uganda) Field Battery.
3FG = 1/6 KAR, plus a second field battery of the 9th Field Regiment.

Each Fighting Group was accompanied by a troop of three armoured cars. The Forward Body, which comprised one company, 1/1 KAR, with a mortar detachment, 145th Light Anti-Aircraft Battery, a detachment of engineers and the remainder of 'A' Squadron 1st Armoured Car Commando, set off from Majunga at 11.30 hours.[23] The Kamaro bridge was to be the East African's first objective. At 16.00 hours, after a "great dash" by the armoured cars, the Forward Body reached the bridge. Despite the fact that the French had months to plan for an Allied attack they had not prepared the bridge for demolition and the small body of *Gardes Indigènes* left guarding the bridge were quickly driven off.[24]

The next objectives were the Betsiboka bridges and this would prove a more difficult undertaking. The Betsiboka is Madagascar's largest river and the road to Tananarive was carried over the river on a series of bridges which together measured 1,600 feet. If the French had demolished the bridges the Allied advance could be held up for weeks. The bridges were more than thirty miles from the Kamaro crossing and the French were now forewarned. Speed had become even more important.

At dawn on the 11th, the Forward Body, under the command of Major Dawson, moved off. It was intended that the Forward Body would capture the bridge and then wait for the Fighting Group to arrive and consolidate the position.

The road to the Betsiboka was blocked with felled trees but the leading armoured cars approached the river at around 06.30 hours. It had taken just eighteen hours from the landing of the first troops at Majunga to reach this vital point, over 130 miles away.[25]

The largest of the bridges took the form of a steel suspension bridge with a central span of 452 feet. To everyone's dismay the French had cut the cables holding the main span earlier in the morning. But, in what a journalist who accompanied the Allies described as "a monumental piece of costly inefficiency"[26], the French engineers had done such a poor job that it had come to rest, completely intact, on the bed of the river in only three feet of water. There was a sharp descent of about thirty feet down the bank, at an angle of around forty-five degrees, and then it was an easy passage across the fallen span.

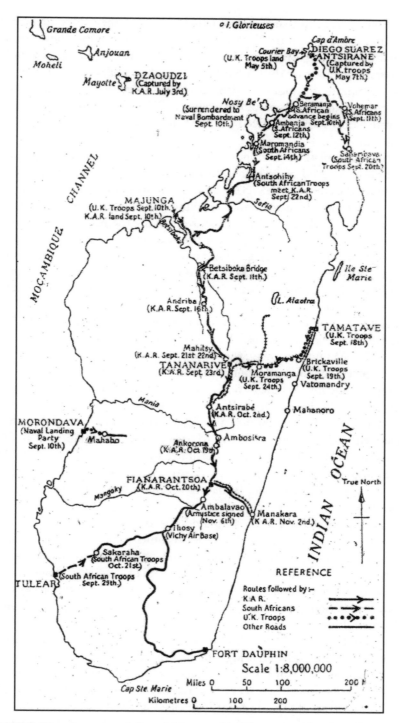

MAP 8: The advance south from Majunga to the Kamaro and Betsiboka bridges.

The French realized that they had failed to destroy the bridge adequately and, shortly after the arrival of the Forward Body, a Potez 63 bomber flew over the river and tried to finish off what the French engineers had begun. It dropped half a dozen bombs but none hit the bridge. (The French later claimed that they intended to cause the minimum amount of damage to the bridge that would delay the Allies but leave the bridge in a repairable condition. They failed on both counts, as the Allies were barely inconvenienced and the bridge had to be completely re-built on another site!)[27]

Spotting movement on the opposite side of the river, Dawson put down a barrage of mortar fire and then sent a platoon from Lieutenant King's company across the bridge under the cover of the Vickers guns of the armoured cars.[28] As soon as King reached the far bank he came under machine-gun and rifle fire. Six men were hit as King tried to climb the steep hillside overlooking the bridge. A second platoon followed across the bridge and together the two platoons cleared the enemy from their strong position. Ten Malagasy soldiers were killed, four wounded and thirty-nine taken prisoner. The Betsiboka should have been a major obstacle but it had been defended by just 80 men with 100 in reserve – most of whom had fled when the first shots were fired.

The engineers got to work on the bridge immediately. By evening of the following day the Forward Body was across the river, with the rest of No.1 Fighting Group, which had left Majunga early on the 13th, close behind.

To support the advance upon Tananarive, 20 Squadron SAAF, now re-numbered 16 Squadron, flew into Majunga North airfield early in the afternoon of 11 September. This released *Illustrious*, allowing it to return to duties with the Eastern Fleet. From Majunga the SAAF could now patrol over the whole island and the following morning two Maryland bombers undertook an offensive reconnaissance along the road from Betsiboka to the capital. The South Africans "bombed and shot up" enemy motor transport on the road and attacked Ivato airfield, though one of the Marylands was seriously damaged by anti-aircraft fire over the target.[29]

The Forward Body, now led by Captain Robertson's 'D' Company of 1/1 KAR, encountered numerous roadblocks; aerial reconnaissance reports also indicated that the French were destroying bridges and obstructing roads all the way to Tananarive. This was to be Annet's campaign plan – to slow down the British advance as much as possible in order to gain time: "Every day that passes", Annet told Vichy on 28 September 1942, "allows us to ameliorate our defences on all our axis of penetration."[30]

In this plan the *Chefs de District* were responsible for organizing the obstruction or destruction of the roads and bridges in their respective regions using local labour. It was the responsibility of the *Garde Indigènes* to cut telegraph wires, remove all means of transportation – particularly at river crossings – and to clear the line of the enemy's advance of oxen and stocks of rice.[31] Progress was therefore slow and it was not until the 16th that Robertson cleared the way through to Anjiajia on the River Mamokamita. As expected, the bridge over the river had been demolished.

The river was fordable, however, and, as Anjiajia appeared deserted, Robertson ordered Lieutenant Palmer of the Engineers to cross the river on foot with a single infantry platoon.

Nothing happened until Palmer was mounting the ridge on the southern bank. Then the enemy opened fire from concealed positions at a range of just fifty yards. Two men were wounded and Palmer took cover. Robertson immediately laid down mortar fire and sent reinforcements across. Led by Lieutenant Fraser, the men began to work round the left flank of the French position. The fighting became very confused and Fraser was killed but his sergeant, an African called Odilo, continued to press round the French flank.

At the same time Palmer, who had also been wounded, attacked the ridge frontally. One of the men involved described the action: "The Senegalese were very brave. They held their fire very late – if anything too late. By the time they opened up our platoon was committed, and there was nothing for it but to go hammer and tongs, which they did."[32] Odilo rushed the defenders from the rear, taking a key machine-gun post completely by surprise. Together, Odilo and Palmer overran then "mopped up" the entire Anjiajia position. "The askaris went mad," Corporal Purvis later wrote, "and rushed at the enemy regardless of anything but blotting them out. When they got very close they threw down their rifles, and butchered the enemy with pangas – very heavy knives with a blade about 18 inches long." Hand grenades were thrown into the trenches of those French troops that would not leave their dug outs.[33]

The KAR lost five men, with seven wounded. The defenders had fought with real determination. Vichy casualties amounted to fifty-two, of whom four Frenchmen and eighteen Senegalese were killed. Odilo was immediately awarded the Military Medal.

It took the whole of the rest of the day and the following night for No.1 Fighting Group to cross the river. The Forward Body moved on to Marotsipoy where there was a small landing ground. By the late afternoon of 18 September, aircraft were flying into Marotsipoy to form a forward base for the SAAF.[34]

Beyond Marotsipoy, excellent headway was made over the vast, desolate and uninhabited plains of the table-land. Grass fires, presumably started by the retreating French, raged on either side of the road and it appeared to the troops that the whole countryside was ablaze. From the plains, the road travelled over a steep mountain to the next defended position at the Manankazo River. For the first time in the campaign, the Bofors of 145th Light Battery were brought into action and the position was soon abandoned by the French. The narrow road through the mountainous terrain was littered with roadblocks – along one 2-mile section alone, nearly thirty roadblocks had to be removed – but, by 20 September, Brigade Headquarters had been established at Ankazobe.[35]

The KAR had travelled 300 miles from Majunga in just ten days. Tananarive was only sixty miles away but it was known that just a few miles further south at Mahitsy were the main French positions. These well-prepared defences, so skilfully concealed that aerial reconnaissance could not locate them, were some two miles wide, and held by three companies of infantry supported by six pieces of heavy artillery (including 37mm Puteaux guns taken from immobilized Renault tanks), mortars and machine-guns. Here would be fought the battle for Madagascar's capital.[36]

At approximately 12.30 hours on the 20th, the Forward Body, after passing yet another damaged bridge, was stopped by artillery and automatic fire from the first line of the Mahitsy defences. The town of Mahitsy sits at the foot of a line of wooded hills in front of which was a wide valley covered with paddy fields. The road, which was carried across the valley on a causeway, skirted round the side of the hills and was overlooked by the main French positions on the hilltops above.

The attack upon the first defensive line began with a frontal advance by 'D' Company 1/1 KAR but the Africans were soon pinned down by enemy cross-fire. The armoured cars that led the column had to drive into a cutting to shelter from the French 75s which were firing both high explosive and armour-piercing shells. The shelling ceased and the armoured cars escaped back down the road, though 'D' Company remained under cover and out of contact with the rest of the Fighting Group. Unsure of where the French guns were placed, the Group commander, Lieutenant Colonel Macnab, waited for the enemy to reveal himself.[37]

At 16.00 hours the French opened fire again and Macnab was able to determine where the enemy guns were placed. Though there were only a couple of hours of daylight remaining, Macnab sent three more companies to the centre, left and right of the French positions.

In the encroaching darkness, 'A' Company, having made a wide detour, made contact with the French left flank. After the French had been driven back for some 300 yards along the ridge, they decided to make a stand. Tracer bullets set the grass on fire and, hidden by the smoke, the French counter-attacked with hand grenades. 'A' Company fell back in some disorder. However, the fire spread along the front of the French position and when 'A' Company returned to the attack it found that the enemy had withdrawn.[38]

Major Dawson with 'B' Company, meanwhile, had manoeuvred round the French right flank to where the flash of a French 75mm gun had been seen. After clearing a small village and over-running an enemy machine-gun post, Dawson was able to move within sight of the French 75mm and direct the 25-pounders of a battery from the 9th Field Regiment onto the enemy gun position.[39] After just six rounds the 75mm was silenced.

That same day, a SAAF Maryland was tasked to reconnoitre the railway south of Tananarive. If large numbers of wagons were still to be seen on the track near the capital the South Africans were to bomb the first small bridge between Tananarive and Antsirabe to prevent the French moving supplies southwards. The plane flew off at 08.05 hours. After counting six trains and more than 100 wagons the South African fliers selected a point where the line was carried over a river, and attacked. They missed. Three Beauforts were then called up and they too bombed the bridge – and missed. After two more attacks on the 21st failed to hit the track the attempt to cut the railway line was abandoned. [40]

At daybreak on the 22nd, 'A' Company resumed its movement along the ridge. The Africans captured an old French 80mm gun and took two prisoners. Macnab by this time had been able to "pinpoint" many of the enemy positions and targets were issued to 1433 Flight. From 12.15 hours onwards two RAF Lysanders bombed and strafed the French positions from low altitude. This was too much for the defenders and sixty-eight men surrendered immediately. [41]

Having cleared the first line of the Mahitsy defences the Fighting Group was now able to advance as far as the start of the causeway. It was found that the causeway had been broken in three places, each of which was covered by an enemy post. Macnab, therefore, sent 'B' and 'C' Companies on yet another wide encircling movement – this time around the French right flank – whilst the remainder of the Fighting Group removed obstructions from the road to allow the armoured cars to get through.

This prompted the French to open fire with two 65mm guns placed near Mahitsy itself. Eleven men were wounded before the Vickers guns of the armoured cars and the artillery put the French artillery out of action. 'D' Company then pushed forwards and, after two hours of fighting, took the machine-gun positions which had been dominating the causeway. By this time the two flanking companies had forced their way into the town and, when the final frontal assault was delivered, the French defences were taken. The Battle of Mahitsy was over. This was a significant victory. The position had been held by three companies of infantry, supported by machine-guns, mortars and three field guns. Half of the Vichy artillery was now in British hands, the Malagasy troops were deserting the French and, most importantly, the road to Tananarive was open. [42]

Whilst the King's African Rifles were fighting their way towards Tananarive, the South Africans were working slowly southwards from Diego Suarez. This force, called GETCOL, consisted of a battalion of The First City Regiment, a battery of artillery, and almost a complete company of engineers, with workshops and tractors. The column was led by eight armoured cars of the Pretoria Highlanders with a motorcycle patrol out in front. [43]

It was certain that any advance southwards would be opposed by the French, as all the French officials, civilian or military, had been ordered to "impede infiltration by the British by every means available to them". [44] Commandant Lanneau's detachment of Vichy troops was still also at large in the north. But Lanneau's force was not large and serious resistance was not expected. It was the terrain that would prove to be GETCOL's most determined opponent.

The South Africans' first objective was the town of Miromandia, 230 miles from the start point at Sakaramy. Progress was good for the first eighty miles as far as Beramanja. From that point onwards the column made just fifteen miles a day on the long and arduous journey south to Miromandia, which Gandar Dower

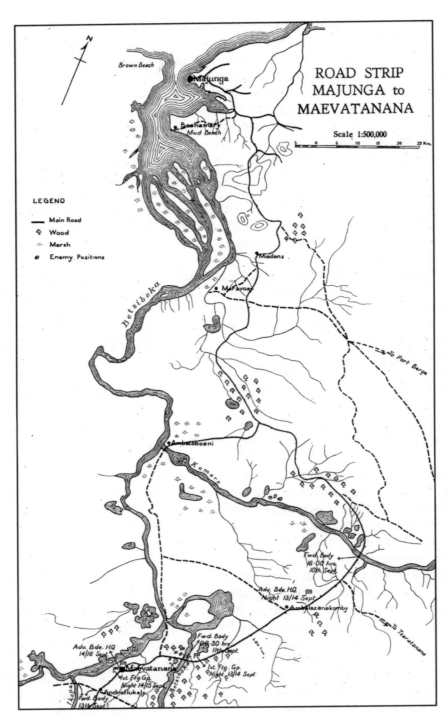

MAP 9: The main routes, landing points and salient information describing the capture of the island of Madagascar, from the Vichy French, by Allied forces.

described as "150 miles of burnt bridges, collapsing culverts, [and] clouds of mosquitoes".[45]

The mosquitoes were an immense problem. "They bite all day and at night came out by thousands," wrote GETCOL's commanding officer, Lieutenant Colonel Getcliffe in his operational summary. "All men have been bitten badly, especially those working at night." The insects were, he complained, "dreadful".[46]

The roads themselves were soft, sandy tracks through swamps, across mountains and passed the "chicken-ridden jumbles" of the Malagasy villages.[47] A four-mile stretch of the road, from Ambanja to Jangoa, was carried on a bank raised above a mangrove swamp. The weight of the passing column caused the road to break up and the last vehicles could only be towed across by coupling together two tractors.

The road between Beramanja and Madjunga crosses between 300 and 400 rivers and ravines. All the bridges capable of carrying heavy vehicles had been destroyed by the French. The other more flimsy constructions – approximately half the total number – had been left standing, but could not be used by the advancing column. At one point, where the road crossed the River Ambazoana, one 5-ton truck fell through a bridge and could not be recovered. Two 3-tonners also had to be abandoned. Each river that could not be forded had to be crossed by a temporary box-girder bridge which was laid by the engineers and taken up again after the column had passed the obstacle.

Ambazoana was the first strong French defensive position encountered. The position overlooked about 200 yards of road with mangrove swamps on either side and a tidal river with a seven-foot rise immediately in front. A determined stand by the French at this point would have been difficult to overcome but, as the position faced north and was completely open to the south, a party was landed on the coast behind the Ambazoana River and attacked the French positions from the rear. The Malagasy troops fled into the bush and the position was evacuated.

Whilst GETCOL was moving slowly southwards a second South African force was landing on the coast near Antanambo. This force, of just one detached company of the First City Regiment, was called SEACOL. It was hoped that SEACOL would cut the French communications and prevent them from retreating. However, the French withdrew more rapidly than expected and SEACOL and GETCOL met on 11 September with the enemy having slipped through the net. The next day Getcliffe made contact with the Navy and arranged for the contingent of the Pretoria Highlanders and Marines on Nosy Bé to land at Sahamalaza Bay to the south of Maromandia.

This move proved to be unnecessary, however, as the French at last decided to make a stand against the South African column. This was at Jojohely, on the fourth day of the advance to Miromandia. Here was a formidable position in very hilly and densely wooded country. The French had cut "fire lanes" through the trees where obstacles blocked the road, and the front of the position was protected by tank traps, each of which was eight feet wide and ten feet deep.

The motorcycle patrol at the head of the South African column came up against the Jojohely position on the evening of 13 September, though the leading infantry company did not arrive until dusk on the 14th. Patrols were sent out that night to probe the French defences, which were met with rifle and machine-gun fire as well as hand grenades. As the French appeared determined to hold their ground, Getcliffe decided to wait until the next day when all his force would be concentrated before attacking. The Political Officer attached to Getcliffe's headquarters drove up to the enemy positions in a civilian car and demanded that the French should surrender. "Sorry," the French commanding officer replied, "our last instructions from Tananarive were to fight to the last man."

During the night an officer of the South African Engineers made a single-handed reconnaissance of the French defences. "He took off his boots, helmet and rifle and went," reported Captain Boyle of the First City Regiment. "Ten minutes later there was a terrible explosion. No trace was ever found of him again."[48] Getcliffe now knew that the front of the French positions was heavily mined.

At 11.00 hours the next day, the British artillery reached the front and Getcliffe opened the engagement with an intense barrage in the hope this would "force a decision" without having to send his infantry against such strong defences, and into bush so thick that the men would have to cut their way through every yard.[49]

Under the cover of the barrage, the Armoured Car Squadron drove as far as the first of the roadblocks, which consisted of felled trees. The men cleared the first few trees but were stopped by machine-gun fire.

The French were well dug in and apparently unmoved by the continued shelling, so Getcliffe, reluctantly, ordered his infantry to prepare to assault the position. At 13.15 hours, however, just as the infantry were ready to attack, the white flag was raised.

The French approached Getcliffe to arrange terms but he refused to discuss their surrender unless all the French forces as far as Maromandia were included in the arrangement. If they were unable or unwilling to arrange this, Getcliffe told them, he would continue with his attack. After some debate the French agreed and they telephoned the troops at Ankaramy, who also accepted the surrender. As a result there was no further opposition from the French and GETCOL entered Maromandia on 18 September. At Jojohely, Getcliffe took twenty-three Europeans, twenty-three Creoles and eighty-nine Malagasy prisoners. A further 200 Malagasy troops took to the bush and disappeared before they could be rounded up.

By this time, the contingent from Nosy Bé had landed behind the enemy lines, at the estuary of the Andranomaraza River, in Sahamalaza Bay, on 15 September. The Highlanders and the Marines marched across country to reach Maromandia the following day ("twenty-four and a half miles we went," complained Private Bintliff, "with not a wheel of transport, nor a small cloud's respite from a wicked sun") only to be greeted with the news that the French troops had already surrendered to Getcliffe's column.[50]

Maromandia was as far as Getcliffe had been instructed to go. From there he sent a patrol southwards to make contact with a contingent of the East Africans which had been dispatched from Majunga. This East African contingent, called TWEEDOL, comprised 'D' Company 5 KAR with armoured cars, mortars and a sapper reconnaissance party. On 22 September, the two bodies met to the north of Majunga.[51]

The other southwards advance by the South Africans was down the east coast to Vohemar and Antalaha – the same route followed by Croft-Cooke in May. This column consisted of just one platoon with a mortar detachment and six armoured cars of the Pretoria Regiment, accompanied by 'C' sub-section of the Engineers. VOLCOL, as this force was called, left Beramanja on the night of 9 September. To reach the coast the column had to cross five major rivers and the Engineers were kept busy creating diversions for the column's vehicles, laying track and deploying their portable girder bridge.[52]

The town of Vohemar (now also known as Inarana) was entered on the 11th without opposition, though the *Chef du Région* was not willing to accept the authority of the South Africans and he was arrested. Five days later VOLCOL resumed its advance down the coast. Once again the Engineers, assisted by the infantry, had to repair weak or damaged bridges over four large rivers and many more smaller ones at an average of one per mile! The last river before Antalaha was crossed by pontoons found locally, which enabled the South Africans to enter the town on 24 September 1942.[53]

Chapter 10

"Death to the Traitors of Vichy"

On 13 September 1942, the 29th Brigade left Majunga for the start of Operation *Jane*, accompanied by a strong naval contingent under the command of Admiral Tennant. The importance of Tamatave to the Allies lay in its rail link with the capital. The journey by rail from Tamatave to Tananarive was little more than half of that by road from Majunga to the capital, and far faster. It would be along this railway that the Allied troops operating in the centre of the island would be supplied and reinforced.[1]

Admiral Tennant's force included three cruisers, the aircraft carrier *Illustrious* and the battleship *Warspite*, along with destroyers and minesweepers. Rather than attempt to land the troops in the heavy surf of the beaches outside the port, and in view of the light opposition met at Majunga, it had been decided that the task force would sail into Tamatave harbour in daylight and invite the town to surrender.[2] Ten Swordfish from *Illustrious*, seven armed with bombs and three with dummy parachutists, would also be in the skies above Tamatave to support the infantry assault should the French choose to resist.[3]

At 05.40 hours, on the 18th, the convoy steamed into Tamatave harbour and the cruiser *Birmingham* made radio contact with the *Chef du Région*. The French official refused to enter into negotiations with the British forces without permission from Tananarive. Nevertheless, he was informed by Admiral Tennant that representatives would be sent by boat under a white flag to arrange the British takeover of the port and, if they were fired upon, the Navy would bombard the town.[4]

"The test came at 07.35 hours, when the envoy boat left," reported James Cooper of the *Daily Express*. "Four hundred yards from the shore they found trouble. I saw tracer bullets splash near the boat, which was unarmed. The captain and the crew ducked and turned the boat around." Tennant waited a few moments for the boat to return to safety before ordering the British warships to begin the bombardment with the words, "Here we go!"[5]

A staff officer stood and watched the action from the deck of the assault ship *Dunera*: "Immediately the signal 'Fire' was run up on the *Birmingham* and every man-of-war opened up. Battle ensigns went flying up their masts and shells played on the beaches like water from a hose."[6] Each ship had been allocated a specific target ashore and though they only used their secondary armament it was more than enough. Just three minutes later Tamatave surrendered. The time was 07.55 hours.[7]

The 29th Brigade was disembarked, some by landing craft, others directly from destroyers onto the mole, without further incident. All except eighty soldiers had been left to defend Tamatave. The rest of the Vichy troops, with their artillery and machine-guns, had withdrawn the day before by train to the vital river crossing at Brickaville on the line to Tananarive.

Festing landed at 10.00 hours, by which time the town and port were securely, and peacefully, under British control. It was now a race to reach Tananarive at the same time as the East Africans. Without further delay the leading elements of the 29th Brigade began the march upon the capital.

Inevitably, the French had done all they could to obstruct the road and the troops found eight roadblocks of felled trees – some of which were sixty feet across – in only the first four miles. Yet, just before noon, a goods train with eight trucks steamed into Tamatave station! So Festing gave the South Lancs the railway whilst the Welch Fusiliers took the road. The race was on.

A party of the South Lancs, with a number of sappers, embarked on the train, which moved off at 15.00 hours. Two trucks holding French railway officials were pushed in front of the train as insurance in case the French had planned an "accident" on the line. Whenever the train arrived at a bridge which might have been mined, the foremost truck was disengaged and shoved across with Tamatave's Station Master on board.[8]

The train made good progress until it reached the River Vohitra. The bridge, of course, had been destroyed. The men had to leave their wagons and wade across the river. Continuing on foot, the South Lancs marched on into the night and it was 01.00 hours when the infantry tramped up to the bridge at Brickaville. Remarkably, this important crossing was still intact. A party of the South Lancs took off their boots and crept across the bridge. Despite the dark, they were spotted and a machine-gun opened fire. But the platoon of Malagasy troops detailed to guard the bridge surrendered after firing just a few shots.[9]

By this time the rest of the 29th Brigade had begun their disembarkation at the port. Whilst the East Lancs remained in the town, the Scots Fusiliers were moved quickly up to support the South Lancs, catching only a "passing glimpse" of Tamatave on their hurried journey to Brickaville.[10]

Earlier, the Welch Fusiliers had started along the road to Tananarive, led by 'A' Company with a mortar detachment. The advance of this company, from one of Britain's proudest regiments, must have been a sight to behold. It requisitioned bicycles, ponies and French cars; the wireless operators were in a rickshaw and the company commander was on horseback![11]

During the night the Bren gun carriers of the Welch Fusiliers were landed and, at dawn on the 19th, the remainder of the battalion was also disembarked. This force met up with the leading group, which had been brought to a halt near Marofody where they had run into the first of the demolished bridges. Though the bridge was repaired in less than five hours another demolished bridge was encountered just two miles further along the road. The battalion bivouacked for the night.

The broken bridges and the roadblocks were proving to be a major problem and Lieutenant-Colonel Stockwell devised a scheme to speed up the operation. The contingent of Royal Engineers with the battalion was divided amongst the four companies and each company was allotted a bridge to repair or an obstruction to remove. There was some risk in this as it meant that the battalion was in a highly vulnerable state, being strung out for many miles along the road. But there had not been the slightest sign of enemy opposition.

It rained almost continuously and the capes issued to the men provided little protection. The rain did nothing to deter the mosquitoes, however, and the men were attacked by the malaria-laden insects every night. The anti-mosquito cream was completely ineffective as an insect repellent but it proved to be excellent at displacing water, and it was used by the men to prevent damp getting into the electrics of the vehicles!

Whilst the Welch Fusiliers were struggling along the road, 'D' Company of the South Lancs found a number of track maintenance trolley-cars at Anivorana. By using gangs of the long-suffering Malagasy as their motive power, the platoon covered thirty miles a day for the next three days even though the railway rose through the hills to a height of 4,000 feet. However, on the 23rd, whilst at a place called Fanovana, the South Lancs learnt of the fall of Tananarive. It was the end of the race.[12]

The capital of Madagascar sits upon a 4,000-foot-high plateau amid what was described as "the best defended area of the island". Between Mahitsi and Tananarive were machine-gun posts in "resuscitated" pre-colonial forts on ridges which had been further strengthened by entrenchments. These positions, into which months of careful planning had been invested, stretched for miles. Stiff resistance was expected.[13] But Annet had no intention of defending Tananarive. Only a small force was left to delay the Allied advance near the Ivato airfield to allow the Governor-General and the remainder of his troops to withdraw from the capital. 'A' and 'B' Companies of 1/1 KAR attacked the French position which was on a ridge overlooking the airfield. In this action Sergeant Walasi's platoon surprised and captured a battery of two field-pieces before the French were able to fire a single shot. Walasi was later awarded the Military Medal.[14]

With Tananarive defenceless the *Chef du District* met Macnab and surrendered the capital of Madagascar. In the two weeks of hard marching and fighting from Majunga, No.1 Fighting Group suffered forty casualties, of which one officer and seven men had been killed. However, as Guillemet wrote on 24 September, the capture of Tananarive marked merely the end of the first phase of the colonialists' defence: "We are ready and determined to continue the fight", he told Vichy, "with all the elements that remain."[15]

After dispatching two companies to secure the main roads into the capital to prevent a counter-attack, Brigadier Dimoline and the rest of No.1 and No.3 Fighting Groups marched into Tananarive to a "tumultuous" welcome.[16] The reason for this enthusiastic greeting, it was found, was because the Malagasy now hoped that they would no longer have to pay taxes to the French!

The person most pleased to see the British troops was probably Lieutenant-Colonel Simpson Jones, who had been imprisoned in Tananarive jail for the previous seven months. Simpson Jones had joined the SOE in December 1941 and had been sent to Mauritius and then on to Vichy-held Réunion. Here he established a wireless link between Réunion and Durban and helped recruit agents to operate in Madagascar. Ironically, he had completed his mission and was returning to Mauritius when his boat capsized and he was taken prisoner. He was removed to Madagascar where he was tried and found guilty, not of espionage, Simpson Jones explained in his narrative of these events, "but something very like it". After his release he became Brigadier Lush's Personal Assistant.[17]

Platt set up his headquarters in the city and immediately issued a proclamation announcing the following:[18]

1. The establishment of military jurisdiction.
2. The British Command to be responsible for the maintenance of law and order and to respect local customs.
3. Local officials to remain at their posts under orders of the military authorities.
4. Crimes to be punished by military tribunals.
5. Local civil jurisdiction to continue, though temporarily suspended.
6. People to return to their normal occupations.
7. The French flag to continue to be flown in Tananarive.

Macnab was appointed commander of the Tananarive district and the infantry of No.1 Fighting Group formed the Tananarive garrison. A representative of the BBC was brought in to take over the running of the local radio service.

Though the stated aim of the Allies was to restore the island to France as soon as the military and political situation allowed, an interim British Military administration, headed by Lush and Grafftey-Smith, was established at Tananarive. M. Ponvienne, left in charge of the French administration in the capital, would not accept British authority and he was interned. A few of the other French officials, mostly junior post-holders, remained at their desks and carried out their usual duties, but their loyalties remained firmly with Vichy.

There were few overtly pro-German factions in the capital but there was widespread dislike of the British and almost universal suspicion of Britain's motives for occupying Madagascar.[19] Such suspicions were heightened by Britain's failure to state categorically its intentions for the future administration of the island. Churchill's reluctance to allow a Free French administration in Tananarive was due in part to advice from his Chiefs of Staff. The planning for the next major Allied offensive operation, the invasion of French North Africa, was reaching its final stages. It was thought by the Chiefs Of Staff that if the Vichyites in North Africa saw Madagascar being presented to de Gaulle it would increase their determination to resist the Allied landings.[20] Eden, on the other hand, was pressing for an early transfer of power in Madagascar to the Free French, as he feared a worsening in the already severely strained relationship with de Gaulle.[21]

There was no properly organized Free French movement in Madagascar, however, and Grafftey-Smith, who was to become Consul General at Tananarive, refused to sanction the disparate and mutually hostile groups that suddenly presented themselves as supporters of de Gaulle. A number of individuals (described by Grafftey-Smith as "men of a certain age") who saw in the political vacuum an opportunity for influence and advancement, formed themselves into a self-styled "Provisional Committee" hoping to provide the future French High Commissioner with the nucleus of a cabinet.

Though Grafftey-Smith used this group as a channel through which he could communicate to the general population, he refused to give the Provisional Committee any official recognition. This meant that the British were despised by almost all sectors of the French community. These anti-British feelings were reinforced by speeches made in radio broadcasts from Fianarantsoa by Annet and telephone calls directly to officials in the capital urging them not to co-operate with the invaders. This resulted in the French offering the British only the most "tepid" assistance.[22]

In fact, the largest Gaullist group in Tananarive was formed by a gang of youths. Some 50 children aged between fifteen and seventeen years old, including 10 girls, met openly on the outskirts of the city. Their opposition to the local authorities took the form of slogans which they daubed on buildings around the capital – "Death to the traitors of Vichy"; "Annet to the Excecution". One morning Antananarivo woke to find the Cross of Lorraine painted on most of the traffic signs in the city accompanied by the demand: "To arms, citizens". The children, though they feared reprisals against their parents, were not apprehended by Annet's police.[23]

Despite the Allied occupation of Tananarive, Annet was evidently set on continuing his stubborn resistance and, as instructed by Vichy, he had escaped to Fianarantsoa, the old southern capital. His defiant stand had already kept the 29th Brigade in Madagascar for four months and had caused the return of the assault ships and landing craft from India. There is no question that Annet delayed General Wavell's offensive against the Japanese in Burma. Wavell had planned to capture the important airfields on Akyab Island by an amphibious assault down the Arakan coast. The shortage of landing craft meant that he had to adopt a less ambitious operation with an overland advance through the Arakan supported by a limited landing from the sea.[24] Though Annet's actions were misguided, his determination to do what he saw as his duty can only be applauded. However, it must be stated that such a long campaign could possibly have been avoided if de Gaulle's plan of December 1941 – to capture Majunga and Tananarive rather than Diego Suarez – had been adopted by the Joint Planners.

If Annet was to continue his evasive tactics the campaign could last for weeks. So, on the 23rd, Platt flew back to Diego Suarez to confer with Admiral Tennant on the possibility of landing a force on the east coast which could intercept the retreating French. Tennant advised against an attempt to land troops on the poor beaches of the east coast but recommended the occupation of Tulear on the opposite coast, though this would mean a longer drive inland. On 25 September, two companies of the Pretoria Regiment, a sub-section of Engineers and three armoured cars, accompanied by a small naval force, were shipped from Diego Suarez to Tulear, the only major port on Madagascar's south-west coast. This force, which included HMS *Birmingham* with a destroyer escort, stood off Tulear (now also known as Toliara) on the 29th and called by radio for the town to be surrendered. The Vichy authorities complied and the troops landed that same day. After Tulear had been secured and the Vichy troops imprisoned, the South Africans patrolled eastwards, clearing roadblocks in preparation for an advance upon Fianarantsoa.[25]

Meanwhile, the operation to track down Annet, and drive him into the arms of the South African troops that had landed at Tulear, was entrusted to No.2 and No.3 Fighting Groups. It was known that the French still had fourteen companies in the field and that a further five were in garrison in the south.

It was understood that the French had prepared a series of defences just a few miles south of Tananarive at Behenjy, which lay besides a small river. These defences consisted of a first line north of the village, a second line which covered the bridge over the river – the bridge having already been demolished – and a third line on the road leading from Behenjy.

No.3 Fighting Group, now consisting of three companies of 1/6 KAR, three troops of armoured cars and a battery of guns, probed the Behenjy defences on the night of 25/26 September. It had been reported that Behenjy was occupied by a full battalion but it was found that only one company of local troops had been left to hold all three lines.

On the morning of the 26th, the Fighting Group commander, Lieutenant-Colonel Collins, ordered an artillery barrage of the first line. 'D' Company 1/6 KAR followed up the bombardment and found the first line abandoned. The armoured cars then led the advance towards the river but they came under fire from the village. After three hours of fighting the main Behenjy line was taken. The enemy fell back to the third line where it appeared that they might make a stand. But, after a bombardment from the artillery, the armoured cars and the infantry mortars, the defenders fled.

The drive southwards re-commenced the following day, with the sappers at the front clearing the roadblocks and creating passages around other obstructions. Where possible, local Malagasy labour was used to help move the felled trees and boulders that had been strewn across the road, but progress was painfully slow. The attitude of the Malagache has been described as "self-neutralising". They were, seemingly, as willing to co-operate with the French in building the roadblocks as they were to help the Allies remove them: "Sometimes they did not need telling," noticed Gandar Dower, "and when our men arrived we often found them happily at work pulling down the obstacles they had just put up." [26]

The roadblocks were so densely strewn that the men had to work day and night to clear a passage. The commanding officer of one of the African battalions explained how his entire battalion was occupied dismantling the obstructions:

"The whole lot never went to sleep at once. If one company was moving blocks by day, a second took on at night, and a third was rested and ready to go forward in the morning."[27]

The reason why the roadblocks were so effective was because the vegetation was so thick that it was difficult to bypass the obstructions. As well as blocking the roads, the French also tried to destroy them by blasting, though this was not a very effective measure. The road between Majunga and Tananarive, for example, was blown in ten places but none of the craters delayed the Allied advance for more than an hour. At one point mines had been laid just beyond one of the roadblocks but they were spotted, and removed by the South African engineers.[28]

The next enemy-held position was known to be at Sambaina, which the advance party – 'A' Company 1/6 KAR – reached on the 30th. As the KAR approached Sambaina a Morane fighter swept low over the road and machine-gunned the leading section but only one man was wounded. 'A' Company continued to advance upon Sambaina until it came under mortar fire from both sides of the road. One officer was killed and five men wounded. The Africans replied with their own mortars but, as darkness was falling, they pulled back a mile north of Sambaina for the night. When Captain Onslow led 'A' Company forward the next morning, he found the enemy position deserted. The French left behind three Hotchkiss guns, three mortars and much ammunition and medical equipment.

The Allied column moved on from Sambaina towards the town, and at that time the holiday resort, of Antsirabe – known as the "Vichy of Madagascar". There was a little light sniping from the retreating Frenchmen but no serious attempt at defending the town. The most serious delay to the advancing column was caused by an abandoned steamroller which had been placed across a bridge approaching the town, in a manner described by a *Times* correspondent as "typical of the childish practice of Annet's forces".[29] Crowds of relieved and excited locals "flocked" to greet the troops and followed the armoured cars, staff cars and trucks in a triumphal procession around the town.[30]

The East Africans' supply line now stretched more than 400 miles all the way back to Majunga and the French were removing all the stocks of food and petrol as they withdrew. To make matters worse, the damaged Betsiboka Bridge was breaking up and heavy rains would soon swell the river. Dimoline's extended communications were also highly vulnerable to French counter-attacks. It was known at Brigade Headquarters that an isolated French patrol of approximately one company strength was moving southwards on a parallel track with the Fighting Group. The patrol was adding to its number by rallying French units that had been scattered after the various engagements. This force clearly posed a threat to the British column. A wireless message had been intercepted which, after decoding, indicated that this patrol, led by Commandant Machefaux, would soon join the main road near Antsirabe and an ambush was planned.[31]

On the night of 3/4 October 1942, 'D' Company 1/6 KAR, supported by armoured cars and mortars, lay in wait at Betafo to the west of Antsirabe. At

01.30 hours, the advance guard of the French patrol – five men – walked into the trap. However, the French spotted one of the KAR's trucks which had been carelessly parked within view of the road. The patrol halted and then began to withdraw. The forward platoons of 'D' Company opened fire and the French replied with hand grenades. "There was a big mix up," reported Corporal Smit, "in which the armoured cars could do nothing."[32] In the confusion one man from the KAR was captured and most of Machefaux's patrol escaped. The ambush had been a failure, though the French left the ground "littered" with abandoned weapons and equipment including their wireless set and Machefaux's satchel containing his maps and code book.[33]

No.3 Fighting Group waited at Antsirabe for the rest of the brigade to join them. When the advance began again on 7 October, it was No.2 Fighting Group which took the lead.

With the capture of Tananarive, 16 Squadron was able to take over Ivato airfield. This left Ihosy as the last main airfield where there was likely to be a concentration of Vichy aircraft and, on 8 October, three Beauforts took off from Ivato to attack Ihosy. When the South Africans arrived over Ihosy, only one small single-engined plane could be seen in the hangars but five other aircraft – three Potez 25, one Potrez 63 and one Morane 406 – were spotted, partially concealed, in bushes near the airfield. The Beauforts attempted to bomb the hangars and missed completely. The South Africans then machine-gunned the hangars and attacked the aircraft in the bushes. The Morane was hit and set on fire. In the afternoon a second attack was made on Ihosy. Again the bombs were wasted, but this time all the remaining Vichy planes were hit by machine-gun fire.[34]

The destruction of the French aircraft allowed the SAAF to concentrate on providing support to the ground forces. Wherever the French made a stand the South African planes were called into action, their bombs shattering the morale of the enemy. When the supply of bombs ran short they dropped empty beer bottles, which whistled through the air with a "frightening shriek" that terrified the native troops![35]

For two days the KAR moved slowly southwards, suffering heavy casualties from French partisans concealed in the bush. The majority of the civil population, however, avoided any kind of confrontation with the British troops, despite Annet's repeated appeals for them to resist the invaders.[36]

The next defended position was at Ilaka where the road travelled through a narrow, steep-sided valley. A platoon of 'C' Company 5 KAR climbed the French position from the rear whilst 'D' Company made a frontal assault. This strong position was taken without loss and resulted in the capture of thirty French and Malagasy troops.

Continuing southwards, the KAR captured a French 65mm gun at Tsaratsotra, but only after it had damaged two vehicles. On the 13th, the advance was halted by well-prepared French defensive lines at Ambohipia and Antanjona. The enemy positions had been probed by a platoon of 5 KAR at daybreak but 5 KAR had been driven back under heavy fire. It was clear that the full strength of the Fighting Group would be required.

It took all morning for three companies of 5 KAR, supported by a troop of 56 (Uganda) Field Battery, to clear the first line of defences at Ambohipia. By late afternoon, No.3 Fighting Group had concentrated in front of the Antanjona lines. At 17.15 hours, the artillery began an intense bombardment of the French positions. Over 1,000 rounds were fired in thirty minutes and it was too much for the Malagasy troops. Many of the defenders fled into the bush or retreated southwards. As night fell, two companies of the KAR took the position without difficulty.

Over 200 French and Malagasy were captured at Antanjona yet the enemy continued to resist. Just south of Ambositra the enemy were again standing at bay.

The French had once again occupied a position on high ground overlooking the road. 'C' Company 5 KAR was ordered to advance along the road until contact was made with the enemy. This it achieved on the afternoon of 15 October, when movement was spotted on the hills above it, along what was known as the Andriamanalina Ridge. At this point the road rose between extensive, sheer-sided and rocky heights. From local information and aerial reconnaissance it was known that the road was covered by artillery, mortars and machine-guns. Though it was understood that the ground was held by only two companies of infantry, it was possible that these had been reinforced by troops from the south. As a result, Dimoline ordered patrols to find a way round these positions and he called up the rest of the brigade.

It was found that considerable trouble had been taken to prevent the position being outflanked with infantry and machine-gun posts established at the ends of both ridges. However, the KAR's patrols discovered that by making a very wide detour, the position could be turned from the west. Dimoline's plan, then, was to send 1/6 KAR to capture the posts at the end of the western ridge. 5 KAR would then attack the other fronts, driving the enemy into the arms of 1/6 KAR.

1/6 KAR moved off at 02.00 hours on 17 October. It was a difficult trek through the hills and one company was broken up to act as bearers for the rest of the battalion's mortars and other heavy equipment. With dawn came a dense mist and the leading company stumbled into a French machine-gun post. Two men were killed and another two wounded before the post was taken. For the remainder of the march 1/6 KAR encountered nothing more than the occasional bullet, but with the mist came the rain and the Africans, tired and wet, did not reach their first objective until after dark.

Early the following morning 1/6 KAR continued its trek, once again encountering French snipers. Finally, long after midnight, the battalion was in position to begin its attack. The Tanganyikans had marched for twenty-four hours, entirely on foot, carrying all their own equipment with no means of transportation – and now they had a battle to fight.[37]

5 KAR had spent the two previous days probing the other fronts of the enemy defences and moving into position on the French right flank ready for the attack,

which began at dawn on the 18th. At 04.30 hours all twenty-four guns of Dimoline's three artillery batteries opened fire. It was the first time in the campaign that there had been such a concentration of heavy ordnance.[38]

After fifteen minutes the barrage ceased and 5 KAR attacked the hills on both sides of the road. Shielded by the inevitable early morning mist, the Africans took the French by surprise. Within two hours the battle was all but over. Worse though was to follow for the French when they found their retreat blocked by 1/6 KAR advancing from the west. They were surrounded.

Until this engagement, the French had shown considerable skill in avoiding costly pitched battles. They had contrived to frustrate and delay Dimolone's men until almost the last moment before withdrawing. This changed at Andriamanalina. For the first time since the Battle of Diego Suarez the French were told that their posts must be "defended to the last". It cost them dear. In their trap the KAR snared 700 men, including 26 officers and 166 European other ranks. A large quantity of weapons, including the last two 75mm guns, mortars and machine-guns, were also taken. Remarkably, 22nd Brigade did not suffer a single casualty.[39]

The sudden collapse of such a strong position and the capture of almost all the defending troops prompted Colonel Metras, who commanded all the French defences from north of Tananarive to south of Ambositra, to surrender. Since the start of the campaign on 10 September, the French had lost, either killed, captured or dispersed, the equivalent of three battalions. Annet was now left with just eight companies of men, including garrison troops, and all his heavy artillery had been taken.[40]

Yet the French Governor-General would not give up despite the obvious futility of his endeavours. Vichy applauded Annet's actions, reporting daily to the German Armistice Commission on the "heroic resistance of the French troops which had in their disfavour only their weakness in numbers and matériel."[41] The determination of the French to fight to the very end was displayed by the remnants of their air force. On 21 October, the *Groupe Aérien Mixte* was officially disbanded. Yet its sole surviving machine (a *Phrygane*, which was a light, three-seater passenger aircraft that had been pressed into service) attempted to fly a final sortie on the following day from Ihosy. Only when the airfield at Ihosy was bombed for a second time was the French aerial threat finally eliminated.[42] The message was clear – the French were not beaten yet.

So, on 20 October, the long march south was taken up once more, this time with 1/6 KAR in the lead. For the next four days the Africans encountered only light opposition but the roadblocks were more numerous than ever before. With the help of local labour, No.3 Fighting Group was able to clear the road as far as Ambohimahasoa. A few miles to the south of this village the road forked, with the main road passing through another strong French position at Mandalahy. The other road, which branched to the east through Vohiparara, took a longer route but it bypassed the Mandalahy position and was not as powerfully defended.

Dimoline despatched the whole of No.2 Fighting Group on the longer route through Vohiparara, and advanced directly upon Mandalahy with the rest of the brigade. According to Moyse-Bartlett, the French saw the brigade divide into two parts but they either failed to appreciate the significance of the move, or they were unable to change their dispositions to meet the threat from both directions.[43] This meant that the route through Vohiparara remained inadequately protected.

Throughout the 27th, the Africans pushed on in the pouring rain along the two roads. There were far fewer roadblocks on the Vohiparara road and the bridges, though they had been prepared for demolition, remained intact. It was an entirely different situation on the main Mandalahy road, where all the bridges were down and heavily blocked. Whilst waiting for two of the bridges to be repaired, two companies of 1/6 KAR patrolled southwards and took a deserter from the forces defending Mandalahy. From his interrogation and the aerial reports already received, Dimoline now had a very clear picture of the Mandalahy defences.

The French had dug themselves in on a series of high and steep ridges which they had cleared of vegetation to avoid fires. The road passed between these positions, which were held by two companies of infantry to the east and one company to the west. Dimoline's plan was to deliver a feint attack, including an aerial bombardment, against the western ridge and then assault the eastern heights with 1/6 KAR supported by massed artillery.

On the morning of 28 October, 'B' Company, 1/6 KAR opened fire against the eastern heights with every weapon it had got. 'B' Company then returned to re-join the rest of the battalion for the main attack which began at dawn on the 29th.

The Africans moved into their forming-up position for the attack at 03.00 hours. At 04.35 hours the artillery barrage began upon located targets, under the cover of which 1/6 KAR took the defenders on the western ridge completely by surprise. The defenders, it seemed, were "completely bemused and paralysed" by the artillery bombardment which had been "devastatingly" accurate.[44] It took the Africans until midday to clear all the positions and marshal all the prisoners. Large numbers of Malagasy troops fled southwards or disappeared into the bush, with the result that only thirty-one Europeans and sixty-five natives were captured.

Just before 1/6 KAR had begun its attack upon Mandalahy, the flanking force of No.2 Fighting Group had moved through Vohiparara behind the French positions and, at dawn, captured Colonel Tricoire and his staff in their command post at Alakamisy. Though Tricoire was cut off from his men at Mandalahy he refused to surrender the position without permission from his commanding officer at Fianarantsoa.[45]

The old southern capital, to where Annet had retreated following the fall of Tananarive, was the next objective of 22nd East African Brigade. Advance Brigade Headquarters reached Fianarantsoa in the afternoon of the 29th and the town was surrendered to Dimoline without any resistance from the French. Between Mandalahy and Fianarantsoa almost 800 prisoners were picked up and it was clear that Annet had very few troops left. The Malagasy troops were deserting in large numbers: "We are not interested in fighting," one of them explained. "The French shoot us if we run away in battle, so best to desert before."[46] Still, however, there was no sign of any general capitulation and the Governor-General had continued his withdrawal and was now at Ihosy, some 100 miles further south.

Aerial reconnaissance along the road to Ihosy had discovered that some of the remaining French had established themselves in yet another strong position at Vatoavo and they were in the process of blocking the road with trees. So, when No. 2 Fighting Group moved off from Fianarantsoa on 2 November, the men knew that they still faced more hard work and fighting before the campaign was won.

Towards midday, the Forward Body encountered a defensive position at a village called Antanandava, though the French were cutting trees when the Africans approached and were taken by surprise. The French rallied quickly and they managed to hold off the Africans as they withdrew.

Later that day the headquarters staff of the French artillery, which no longer had any artillery left to command, surrendered at the Talata-Ampana monastery. Throughout the following day, in pouring rain, the KAR cleared the road as far as Vatoavo in preparation for yet another battle in this seemingly endless campaign. However, the situation was about to change.

The South African troops who had landed at Tulear had begun to move northwards. This advance began on 3 November and, as with the other expeditions, progress was hampered by weak or damaged bridges and yet more roadblocks. As well as the usual trees, some of the roadblocks were formed by "colossal" rocks blown onto the road, many of which had to be blasted aside by the South African Engineers. Nevertheless, by 6 November, the convoy was just sixty miles from Ihosy. At last, Annet was trapped.[47]

On the morning of 4 November, 'C' Company 5 KAR climbed the heights in front of Vatoavo village. The French responded with mortar and machine-gun fire. This revealed their positions and gave the Allied artillery a target to aim at. After a short bombardment, and before the KAR reached the French entrenchments, white flags appeared along the enemy line.

The Vatoavo position was regarded as being the most formidable yet encountered but *Capitaine* Mayer, who commanded 278 men, had received a telephone call ordering him to surrender. At last, after fighting its way through 660 miles of roadblocks, broken bridges and strong defensive positions, the East African Brigade's campaign was over.

On 5 November, Annet's representative – a Norwegian clergyman from Ihosy – arrived at Dimoline's headquarters to request terms of surrender. Hostilities ceased at 14.00 hours. The terms offered to Annet were, of course, those he had rejected six months earlier. Now he was willing to accept. He had done all he could to defend the country entrusted to him.[48]

Annet was represented by a *Capitaine* Fauché. Though Fauché had nothing to bargain with, he managed to extract seven concessions in the wording of the settlement document (the Ambalavao Convention) and he prolonged the discussions until one minute after midnight on 6 November. The significance of this was that the French troops had been under arms for six months since the attack upon Diego Suarez and that entitled them to a campaign medal and "privileged emoluments".[49] Churchill announced the end of the campaign to the House of Commons on 10 November, declaring that the Armistice had been signed and that "everything is proceeding smoothly".[50]

Of far greater significance than the terms of the armistice was the agreement on the future administration of the island which finally had been reached in London between Britain and the French National Committee. The travel restrictions placed on de Gaulle had been relaxed and the General was touring French Equatorial Africa when he was contacted by his London office with the news that Britain was to occupy the rest of Madagascar. De Gaulle was told that after the completion of the British operation, Fighting France would be invited to administer the island and that Eden wanted to re-open negotiations on the subject. This was enough to tempt de Gaulle back to the UK, and talks with Eden and Churchill began on 30 September. The first meeting broke up in acrimony and it took until 10 December before the issue was settled.[51]

Though the individual chosen by de Gaulle to represent the Free French – General Legentilhomme – would have most of the powers and responsibilities previously held by the Governor-General, Madagascar continued, for all military purposes, to fall under Platt's East African Command and, in naval terms, under the authority of the Commander-in-Chief, Eastern Fleet. All air forces based on the island were under the strategic authority of the RAF's Middle Eastern Command.

The French and colonial military forces on the island were to be re-organized, both for the defence of the country and, if necessary, for deployment overseas in aid of the Allied cause. Fortress Diego Suarez remained a separate military zone under direct British control and subject to special security restrictions. This agreement remained in force for the duration of the war, with Diego Suarez continuing to be used as a convoy assembly point and refuelling station.[52]

General Legentilhomme (who had previously served in Madagascar) flew to Nairobi on 16 December 1942 and from there was taken to Tamatave on the FFS *Léopard*. On 8 January 1943, Platt formally handed over the administration of the island to Legentilhomme, who became High Commissioner of Madagascar and its Dependencies.[53] Though the British Military Administration ceased immediately, military and civil liaison officers were retained in Tananarive. Legentilhomme stayed in Madagascar for just four months, being succeeded by Pierre de Saint-Mart in May 1943, who was granted the re-designated post of Governor-General.[54] The wheel of Madagascar's fortunes turned full circle when the former Governor, Marcel de Coppet, ousted by Pétain in 1940, returned to his post in May 1946.

The achievements of Dimoline's men were considerable. As the KAR's historian, Moyse-Bartlett wrote, in the face of an enemy force about double their number, fighting in familiar country from positions of their own choosing, they took nearly 3,500 prisoners, 16 field guns, more than 50 heavy machine-guns and numerous light machine-guns, mortars and rifles. It cost them just 27 men killed and eighty-two wounded.[55]

According to Dimoline, the French General Staff "believed that they could hold out for at least 3 months and they attempted with great obstinacy to delay each mile of the advance by all conceivable methods of obstruction and demolition, and to make use of every weapon and unit at their disposal."[56] Yet, as one commentator wrote shortly after the end of the conflict, it had been a "strange" campaign. "Frequently it had been a war of spades rather than of rifles, with the local natives working hard for both sides ... In different phases the campaign had been characterized by stages of unopposed progress or of mere token resistance, by brief and unexpected battles, by sudden and dramatic capitulations."[57]

The correspondent, Gandar Dower, who followed the troops as far as Tananarive, believed that the French had made a number of "serious military blunders" during the campaign. But what he defined as "the root cause" of the French collapse was a failure of morale brought about by their policy of, "Resist as long and as fiercely as you can without any loss of life."[58]

A British Government-sponsored historian of this conflict, Christopher Buckley, writing in 1954, also drew the conclusion that Annet's delaying tactics proved "fatal" to the morale of his own troops. It is certainly true that large numbers of Malagasy soldiers did abandon the Vichy cause during the retreat. Their personal commitment to the French, however, must have been suspect and many Malagasy fled only after being engaged by the British forces. Nor does Buckley offer any alternative policy. If Annet had dug in before Tananarive with all his forces and fought a major battle, he could not have influenced the final result and the campaign would have ended much sooner.[59]

Moyse-Bartlett took an opposing view to Buckley. He believed that "much thought" had been given to the plan of defence and that the French showed "considerable military skill" in preparing their many positions. However, Moyse-Bartlett was critical of the French tactics in defence of these positions which he saw as "curiously" inflexible. "They were repeatedly taken by surprise; often bewildered by the speed of the KAR attack, and appeared quite unable to adjust their dispositions to meet unexpected outflanking movements." Moyse-Barlett also pointed out that whilst the French positions were usually well built, they were often sited along the slopes and crests of bare hillsides where they offered excellent targets for the British aircraft and artillery.[60]

Brigadier Dimoline saw the conflict in far simpler terms. Though the French had more troops in total, he wrote, "the success of the fighting was due to the greater number of forces at our disposal in any one engagement [combined with] air superiority and artillery superiority."[61]

Another reason given for the French collapse was the effectiveness of the propaganda broadcasts from the radio station in Mauritius. "We can now reveal", reported *The Daily Sketch*, "that Radio Propaganda played a big part in the quick surrender of Madagascar. For weeks before the attack the British and South African Radios poured out, in French and also in Malagache, the facts about Axis pressure, Japanese atrocities and Laval's prospective surrender of the island. The result was that native troops deserted the French, the native population accepted the British as deliverers and the French defenders were too disheartened to carry on. This is believed to have been the most successful British Propaganda of the war."[62]

One French historian of the Vichy era, Robert Aron, has entirely mis-represented the campaign in Madagascar. Not only does he state that the French had only two men killed in the *Stream-Line-Jane* operations but he actually claims that: "The British warned the French of where they were going to attack and the latter politely gave way"! [63]

Allied casualties for the entire *Stream-Line-Jane* offensive were light, totalling 142 killed or wounded. It was malaria which, as was expected, took the greatest toll of the troops. In the Armoured Car Commando, half of all the men contracted the disease, whereas casualties from all other causes amongst the South African Commando amounted to just six.[64]

It was a similar story with the 29th Brigade. In the South Lancs, for example, almost 500 men found themselves in hospital, mainly because of malaria and dysentery, and at one stage more than 200 cases of malaria were reported in a single week in this battalion alone. Only the askaris of the East African Brigade appeared to be immune to the disease.[65]

One of the great successes of the campaign was the effectiveness of the South African armoured cars. Surprisingly, after the destruction of the British tanks at Antsirane, the light armour plating on the Marmon-Harringtons proved extremely resilient. It provided complete protection against small-arms fire, including armour-piercing rounds, and even direct hits by the high-explosive shells of the 75mm and 65mm field guns did no more than cause small splits in the armour. In fact, during the early stages of the campaign, the French actually reported that they had been attacked by British tanks![66]

To facilitate the military administration of Madagascar, the 'Islands Area' of East Africa Command was created, with Major-General Smallwood as GOC Islands Area HQ was at Tananarive until July 1943 when it relocated to Diego Suarez. The South African Motorised Brigade returned to Africa in December but the 27th Northern Rhodesian Brigade continued to garrison Fortress Diego Suarez whilst the 22nd East African Brigade was distributed around the island. With its headquarters at Antsirabe, the 22nd Brigade had battalions at Tananarive, Ambositra and Fianarantsoa, plus detached companies at Manakara, Ihosy and Tuelar. A further field battalion of the King's African Rifles (1/3) was shipped to Madagascar and was posted to Tananarive, whilst KAR garrison battalions were sent from Africa to occupy Tamatave and Majunga.[67]

The only time that any of these troops were called into action after Annet's surrender was in November 1943, when elements of the 1st, 3rd, 5th and 6th KAR had to suppress a mutiny by the 1st Battalion the Mauritius Regiment. This battalion had been sent to Madagascar to be "toughened up" before going to Burma and it had been placed in camp near Diego Suarez. A number of factors caused the Mauritians to rebel against their officers – not the least being that the men had only enlisted for home defence – and it was the KAR that had to go into the camp to restore order.[68]

Though some Free French forces were permitted to contribute to the administration and defence of the island, there were still 1,800 British and 12,000 African troops equipped for mobile warfare in Madagascar at the end of 1943. The KAR returned to Africa in May 1944, followed a month later by the 27th Rhodesian Brigade. British forces remained at Diego Suarez until the end of the war and in 1945 a regular BOAC service between Mombasa and Diego Suarez was established using Short Sunderland seaplanes tended by RAF personnel.[69]

Chapter 11

"Incalculable Consequences"

L ittle more than forty-eight hours after Armand Annet had surrendered Madagascar, British and American troops landed in French North Africa. The Free French were not involved and, once again, de Gaulle was not informed of the operation in advance.

At first the landings were opposed and Hitler insisted that the French should accept German military assistance and allow German troops into the colony. But, after just three days of fighting, the whole of France's North African possessions were surrendered to the Allies.

Hitler's response was immediate and on the night of 8–9 November 1942, German troops crossed the demarcation line and began to occupy the Vichy-controlled areas of metropolitan France. Events, however, were spinning out of Hitler's control.

On 23 November, following a proclamation from Algiers announcing North Africa's independence and its commitment to join the Allies in the war against Germany, French West Africa followed suit. Vichy had finally lost its empire.[1]

With the loss of its colonies, the only weapon left in the hands of the disintegrating Vichy government was the Fleet. A large part of the French Navy was anchored at Toulon and a German force attempted to capture the warships with a surprise attack upon the port. The last significant act of Pétain's feeble administration was to order the destruction of the ships which, two years earlier, the Marshal could have preserved for France by handing them over to the Allies.

Darlan had never wavered from his pledge to Churchill that the French Fleet would not fall into the hands of the Germans. On the morning of 27 November 1942 that promise was fulfilled when the fleet at Toulon was scuttled before the Germans could intervene. This sad, though vital action, showed Churchill, and indeed the rest of the world, that the attack at Mers-el-Kébir had been entirely unnecessary. Churchill had misjudged the determination of his allies and with that one misconceived act – described by Admiral Sommerville as "the biggest political blunder of modern times"[2] – he had turned them into enemies.

At the same time that Hitler attempted to seize the Toulon fleet, the small French army which had been permitted under the 1940 Armistice was disarmed by German soldiers. It was, effectively, the end of the Vichy regime.

The demise of Pétain's government lent an increased legitimacy to de Gaulle's French National Committee and it spurred the Free French forces to move against Réunion. Towards the end of November, the super-cruiser *Léopard* arrived off St Denis. The Governor, Aubert, refused to acknowledge de Gaulle's authority and with a band of 400 die-hard supporters, he retreated to the mountains. However, after what was described as the "persuasive effect" of 200 shells fired from *Léopard*, Aubert accepted the terms he was offered and Réunion joined the Allies. Madagascar's tiny neighbour was the last Vichy territory to fall in the Second World War.[3]

"The Madagascar episode was in its secrecy of planning and precision of tactical execution a model for amphibious descents," Churchill was later to write,[4] and the significance of the operation was not lost on the participants. "It was a brilliant experiment in combined operations," wrote Gandar Dower in 1943, "that knitting of land, sea and air power, which will play so vital a part in the later stages of the war." Brigadier Festing considered that it had been "a privilege" to have assisted "in a combined operation which may be described as a complete entity, comprising as it did a planning period, a long sea voyage and the successful capture of a defended fleet base. I understand that this is not an exaggeration to say that an operation of this nature and at this range has not taken place since the period of the Napoleonic Wars."[5]

Though the British celebrated their success, their forced occupation of Madagascar had far-reaching, and, in some cases, long-lasting consequences. Possibly the most immediate consequence of Britain's capture of Madagascar was that the country soon became an important source of raw materials for use in the munitions industry.

Experts and officials were sent from Britain and the USA to assess the quantity and quality of the available materials and to organize their collection and shipment. The speed with which these individuals were dispatched to Madagascar, very shortly after Annet's surrender, indicates how important the items must have been. The country was able to provide large quantities of rubber and quartz, both of which were in short supply, and the highest grades of amber mica used in the manufacture of spark plugs in aero-engines. But it was graphite which received the most attention.

Before the war Madagascar had been the world's largest exporter of graphite, which was quarried by the London-based company Morgan Crucible. With the outbreak of hostilities, its representative at Tamatave had been interned and a freighter loaded with graphite was prevented from leaving the port. This graphite was one of the first purchases made by the British administrators when they took over Tananarive and by 15 December 1942, just five weeks after the French surrender, its shipment had been arranged to the UK and the USA.

To help with the future extraction of the mineral, 40,000 heavy-duty bags were sought from as far afield as Europe, Africa and America.[6] The first nuclear chain-reacting pile built in the US, towards the end of 1942, contained 400 tons of graphite. The second one was built in the spring of 1943 after the first graphite shipment from Madagascar.[7]

The years of Free French rule brought much hardship to the people of Madagascar with great demands being made upon the island's resources in support of the Allied cause. The Malagasy economy had suffered severely during the two years of blockade by the Royal Navy and, before the Allies could take full advantage of the island's raw materials, large quantities of manufactured goods had to be imported from the West. The destruction of the 12 million-franc Betsiboka Bridge and the "appalling and wanton damage" caused by the French troops in their long withdrawal through the country further delayed the country's economic development.[8]

The much-feared Japanese attack in the Indian Ocean failed to materialize. After the destruction of its carrier fleet by the US Navy at the Battle of Midway, in June 1942, Japan was no longer capable of large-scale offensive action. Axis raiders, however, continued to prowl the shipping lanes that passed Madagascar. Because the Royal Navy was concentrating its efforts on protecting the vital North Atlantic convoys, many Allied merchant ships were sent through the Indian Ocean without naval escort. It was these lone vessels that the German and Japanese submarines preyed on and, between the time of Pearl Harbor in December 1941 and February 1945, 271 merchantmen were sunk in the Indian Ocean.[9]

To help combat the submarines Madagascar, as well as Mayotte, became a base for reconnaissance aircraft which escorted the passing convoys and undertook anti-submarine patrols. An 8,000-foot-long, hard-earth runway was formed at Cap Diego on the Andrakaka Peninsula to accommodate long-range Liberator bombers. Though Liberators did not land at Cap Diego – Catalina flying boats which landed in the bay were deployed instead – the runway was used by cargo planes bringing supplies to Fortress Diego Suarez from Africa.[10]

On 20 August 1943, two RAF Catalina flying-boats sank a German U-boat which had been operating out of the Japanese base at Penang. *U-197* was first spotted some 250 miles to the south-west of Madagascar, off Cap Sainte Marie (Tanjona Vohimena). After an intermittent running battle which lasted over four hours, the submarine was struck by depth charges and sank with the loss of all its sixty-seven crew. The Catalinas returned and landed at Tulear.[11]

Possibly the most serious long-term consequence of the invasion of Madagascar was the "lasting" effect it had upon de Gaulle's relationship with Britain and America. The entire Madagascar episode was, as Martin Thomas of the University of the West of England saw it, a "humiliating" experience for de Gaulle, which exposed his weakness and his utter dependence upon Britain and her resources at that time.[12] De Gaulle had no love for France's traditional enemy, England, and he would never trust her, nor would he ever forget the way he had been intentionally misled by the British Government.

A month following *Ironclad*, and before being deceived yet again over *Stream-Line-Jane*, he warned Churchill of this: "If you want to maintain Franco-British friendship for later on, you must, as from now, take care to avoid what might trouble it in a lasting way … There exists no colony, however fine, that would be worth the friendship of France to Great Britain."[13] After the war de Gaulle was quite willing to collaborate with France's former enemies, Germany and Italy, in the development of the European Common Market. Yet when Britain applied to join the Common Market in the 1960s de Gaulle repeatedly blocked the application. Only after de Gaulle died in 1970 would Britain be accepted into the European Community. The consequences of that decision by de Gaulle still affects Britain and its people.

De Gaulle also led France away from military ties with the US–dominated North Atlantic Treaty Organisation (NATO). Unwilling to trust in an alliance with Britain and the US, de Gaulle maintained a policy of military independence. This included the building of France's own nuclear weapons, which were kept outside the NATO command structure.

De Gaulle's anger at being excluded from Operation *Ironclad* was entirely understandable. The colonials fought tenaciously at Diego Suarez and Annet continued to resist for a further six months. They could scarcely have done more to oppose the Allies even if the Free French had been involved. De Gaulle was quite correct when, in a meeting with Churchill on 28 July 1942, he told the Prime Minister: "As for Madagascar, if you had let us land at Majunga while you operated at Diego Suarez, the affair would have been over long ago. We would have marched on Tananarive and everything would have been settled. Instead you wasted your time negotiating with the representative of Vichy."[14]

Churchill of course had genuine concerns about security. It would have been impossible to move thousands of Free French troops out of Britain without attracting attention and, with Madagascar frequently in the headlines, their destination would have been obvious. There was also the increasing friction between the Free French and the British authorities in the Levant which demonstrated just how difficult it would be to work with the ever-prickly de Gaulle in Madagascar. Furthermore, as almost everyone in Madagascar, both civil and military, detested the Free French it was felt that a prolonged period of British administration was necessary in Tananarive to ensure tranquillity and stability throughout the island.[15]

De Gaulle as an individual (rather than the Free French movement in general) was also seen by Allied leaders, particularly Roosevelt, as a political liability ahead of the landings in North Africa. De Gaulle would be no more welcome in Morocco, Algeria or Tunisia than he was in Madagascar. Churchill and Roosevelt hoped that following the Allied occupation of France's most important colonial block a more senior, and more respected, military figure would emerge to take over the leadership of the Free French. "It is quite possible", Churchill told Eden on 22 September 1942, "that as a result of 'Torch' we may be in relation with a French anti-German organisation very much wider in its basis than that presided over by de Gaulle. It would be wise to keep options in our hands as long as possible."[16] With this in mind, de Gaulle was kept out of Madagascar until the political situation in North Africa had been resolved.

But if de Gaulle had been involved in the planning of the operation and a few selected Free French representatives included in Sturges' staff, all the subsequent difficulties with de Gaulle could have been avoided. It might also have sent out the signal that Britain was not intent upon territorial aggrandisement and therefore lessened the impact of Vichy propaganda.

There is no doubt that Madagascar marked a turning point in Anglo–French relations generally. The attack upon Syria was against German air bases and to stop the supply of weapons to an active enemy. Its occupation was completely justified on both moral and military grounds. None of that could be said about Madagascar. Vichy had repeatedly denied that it would allow the Japanese into Madagascar and the air and sea forces present in the country had never threatened Allied shipping which passed the island almost every day. It is also a fact that the British did not give the colonials a chance to surrender until after they had torpedoed the French ships and bombed their aircraft. After such unprovoked aggression the French could hardly have been expected not to fight back.

De Gaulle did eventually travel to Madagascar. In a pre–election tour of France's African colonies, de Gaulle visited the island in the summer of 1958. He won the election, becoming President of France in December of that year.

For his determination to do what he considered to be his duty, Governor-General Annet was interned in South Africa and later transferred to North Africa. After a further twenty-one months in Fresnes prison he was sent for trial at the High Court at Versailles in March 1947. He was condemned to "National Degradation", which was one of the sentences meted out to those who had collaborated with the Germans. This punishment meant the removal of the right to vote and the right to stand for election, as well as being rendered ineligible to practice certain professions or hold public office. This judgement was harsh on Annet.

In his defence of Madagascar, Annet resisted the attacks of an aggressor upon French sovereign territory. Even a senior British official acknowledged that Annet's conscience could bear "no shadow of guilt" concerning his actions in Madagascar. Annet had only done what his government had demanded of him.

Three of Annet's generals, including General Guillemet, also stood trial for their part in the defence of Madagascar but all were acquitted. *Colonel* Claerebout, promoted by Pétain to *Général de Brigade*, was demoted by de Gaulle to his former rank. Most of the other French prisoners taken at Antsirane were interned in the UK until January 1943. They were then released to form the *Régiment Blindé des Fusiliers Marins*, which took part in the liberation of France with the Allies in 1944.[17] *Capitaine* Maerten, on the other hand, though disillusioned with the Vichy regime, was unwilling to side with de Gaulle, and he asked if he could join the British armed forces. He subsequently became a member of the SOE for whom he served with distinction and well-maintained secrecy, his files remaining closed to the public for many decades after the war.[18]

Such, indeed, was the secrecy surrounding the SOE's activities that Syfret was not fully aware of the part played by *Lindi* and her crew. As a result the Admiral did not mention any of these men in his list of recommendations for the award of medals in his report of June 1942. It was not until March 1943 that the skipper of *Lindi*, Lieutenant Booker, was rewarded for his "gallantry and endurance under difficult conditions" with the award of the DSC[19]

Despite the subsequent failings at Majunga, the SOE's operations in Madagascar were a considerable success. This was due, almost entirely, to Percy Mayer. This exceptional individual continued in the service of the SOE, being parachuted into France in March 1944, where he organized and trained the resistance groups in the Limoges area. According to his personal SOE file, Mayer specialized in guerrilla warfare and his forces created "havoc" amongst the German lines of communication. Major Mayer was awarded the Military Cross but was unable to receive his medal at a normal investiture due to security concerns. Mayer was eventually decorated by King George at a specially arranged secret reception.[20]

Bishop Vernon's suspected involvement in the SOE operations was never forgotten by the French and it put a great strain on his relationship with the local authorities. He retired to Britain soon after the war.[21]

After the capture of Tananarive, the 29th Brigade was shipped to South Africa for an extended period of recuperation. Every battalion was "riddled" with malaria and it was three months before the brigade was able to follow the 17th and 13th Brigades to India.[22] The 29th Brigade became part of the 36th Division, which was commanded by Festing, recently promoted to the rank of Major-General. It was intended that the 29th Brigade would form, as Churchill put it "the steel tip to the lance"[23] which was to be thrust into Burma in the long offensive to re-capture the country from the Japanese. For twelve months the 29th Brigade continued to train in amphibious and jungle warfare in preparation for a sea-borne attack against the Arakan coast. But the competition for landing craft and assault ships for the Italian campaign and the final invasion of Europe led to this plan being cancelled. The 29th Brigade's specialist skills were not called upon again.[24]

Francis Festing went on to achieve the highest military rank of Field Marshal, in which capacity he became Chief of the Imperial General Staff. Hugh Stockwell of the Welch Fusiliers took over the 29th Brigade from Festing. Promoted to Lieutenant-General, Stockwell commanded the British troops during the infamous Suez Crisis of 1956. He retired a full General, his final appointment being Deputy Supreme Allied Commander Europe.

Britain's capture of Diego Suarez spelt the effective end of Hitler's Madagascar Plan, even though the subject was still being discussed by leading Nazis as late as 24 July 1942.[25] One of the stated aims of the Plan (as expressed by Franz Rademacher on 3 July 1940) was that: "This arrangement would prevent the possible establishment in Palestine by the Jews of a Vatican State of their own, and the opportunity for them to exploit for their own purposes the symbolic importance which Jerusalem has for the Christian and Mohammedan parts of the world". In 1948, the independent state of Israel was founded in Palestine, just as the Nazis had feared.

After the war the Madagascar independence movement was revived with renewed vigour, leading to a widespread insurrection in 1947 which was only suppressed after months of bitter fighting that resulted in approximately 60–80,000 casualties. In 1958, the government of President de Gaulle sanctioned a referendum on the question of independence for Madagascar, the consequence of which was that the island finally became an autonomous sovereign republic in 1960.[26] Diego Suarez, however, continued to be used by the French navy until 1972.

Today Madagascar is a deeply divided country. Ethnic and political conflicts have driven this already poor country into desperate poverty. Disputed elections in December 2001 led to strikes, outbursts of violence and a blockade of Antananarivo which paralysed the county. For many months internal communications were severed and air travel to and from Madagascar was irregular and uncertain. A degree of stability returned to the country in 2002 but a *coup d'état* in March 2009 ousted the government. Malaria and cholera continue to be rampant and medical supplies scarce. The latest statistics indicate that 90 per cent of its 22 million people live on less than two dollars a day; its economic prospects remain poor.

So, were the operations to seize and occupy Madagascar a vital and timely intervention at a critical stage in Britain's war of survival, or were they a poor use of severely limited resources? In order to answer this question, we must remind ourselves of the military situation in the Eastern theatre at the beginning of 1942.

In the first two weeks of April, the Japanese First Air Fleet (the formation which had attacked Pearl Harbour) bombed Colombo and Trincomalee in Ceylon, then sunk two heavy cruisers and the aircraft carrier *Hermes*. Another Japanese naval force sank 92,000 tons of shipping in the Indian Ocean during the same few days. The Indian mainland was also bombed and a further 32,000 tons of shipping was sent to the bottom of the sub-continent's west coast.

On land, Wavell was compelled to cable London on 12 April 1942 with a desperate appeal that "unless effort is made to supply our essential needs … I must warn you that we shall never regain control of the Indian Ocean and Bay of Bengal and run risk of losing India". Three days later Churchill told Roosevelt: "With so much of the weight of Japan thrown upon us we have more than we can bear."[27]

When the Chiefs of Staff sat to evaluate Britain's position in the Far East, they concluded that if Wavell was not reinforced there was a "real danger of losing our Indian Empire – with incalculable consequences to the future conduct of the war". But to use troops ear-marked for India against Madagascar was "sheer madness" according to Wavell. "Unless War Cabinet considers 'Ironclad' of greater strategical importance than Ceylon they are taking very grave risks indeed in diverting so large a proportion of meagre resources in [the] East to it."

Yet Churchill simply could not run the risk of Japanese raiders cutting Britain's communications with India. The occupation of Diego Suarez was therefore, as one of the official historians of Second World War explained, "an insurance against a risk which seemed very real during the months of March and April when a Japanese fleet was free to prowl about the Indian Ocean and play havoc with our shipping."[28]

The German viewpoint, as expressed by Admiral Raeder in his talks with Hitler, was summarized by official South African historians as follows: "He [Raeder] sketched the rapid Japanese advance in Burma and the Indonesian islands, and predicted the early capture of Ceylon, which would have sweeping effects on

British sea-power in the Indian Ocean and on oil supplies from Persia. Only Alexandria, Durban and Simonstown would be available for the repair of large British warships, and an early German-Italian attack on the British key positions of Suez would have a decisive influence on the outcome of the war."[29]

This was part of the *Oberkommando der Wehmacht*'s "Great Plan" for "the conquest of Egypt and Persia and joining of hands with the Japanese on the shores of the Indian Ocean". Though the Japanese were unenthusiastic about such close co-operation, this event was seen by the Government historian Christopher Buckley as a "disastrous possibility".[30]

There certainly seems to be little doubt that, at the time, the balance of informed opinion was that politically, as well as strategically, Britain's seizure of Madagascar was a "necessity". To the military historian P. Kemp, "the whole strategical concept of the war depended at that moment" on denying the Japanese a base in the western Indian Ocean.[31]

In nearby Mauritius, the occupation of Madagascar by the Japanese was considered to be "inevitable", whilst in neighbouring South Africa it was thought "likely" and when Colonel Pechkoff arrived in Cape Town he found that "everybody is talking about it".[32] Even the French *Secretariat d'Etat à la Marine Cabinet* reported on 12 February 1942 that Madagascar was: "the next major object of the Japanese". [33]

Andre Wessels of the University of the Orange Free State stated unequivocally that "the campaign *undoubtedly* contributed towards the eventual Allied success in the Far East, as well as in the Middle East and Mediterranean".[34] Prime Minister Smuts was even more emphatic. "There is an area which we cannot afford to lose, without the greatest danger to our future victory. That is the Indian Ocean and the lands bordering on it, from the Middle East through Iran and Iraq to India and Celyon. Their loss would put us in such an unfavourable position for defence and eventual offensive and the enemy in such a powerful position for the future, that we dare not risk such a loss."[35] Yet not everybody, then or since, has agreed.

On 23 April 1942, less than two weeks before the landings at Courrier Bay, the JPS submitted its observations on the mounting of Operation *Ironclad* to the Chiefs of Staff. This was a balanced report, outlining both the advantages and disadvantages of the impending operation. Under the heading "Reasons which led to mounting 'Ironclad'", were listed the following:

1. The Eastern Fleet was virtually unformed.
2. Singapore and Rangoon had fallen.
3. The defences of Ceylon were altogether inadequate.
4. Diego Suarez appeared to offer the best alternative base.
5. In enemy hands it [Diego Suarez] would constitute a danger to our sea communications, particularly the Middle East reinforcement route.
6. In these circumstances we felt it advisable to insure against possible Japanese action by organizing W.S.17 in such a way as to enable the operation to be carried out.

The nine-page report found only two disadvantages in undertaking the operation, which it identified as "COST". "The cost of undertaking operation 'Ironclad' will be:

1. On a short-term view, the withholding of forces urgently required in the India–Ceylon theatre.
2. On a long-term view the likelihood of a substantial commitment ... which with our other commitments we may be unable to meet."

The recommendation of the Joint Planners was that, if possible, the operation should be postponed until the intentions of the Japanese in the Indian Ocean had been revealed.[36] Two days later, at the request of the Chiefs of Staff, the Joint Intelligence Sub-Committee produced an appraisal of Japan's likely intentions and objectives: "Japan's object is to secure for herself exclusive control of the whole of the East Asiatic area. Within that area she will, when she has developed the resources, be substantially self-sufficient on a wartime economy. Because of the distance separating this area from the Allies' bases, attack on Japanese communications would necessarily be limited to submarine warfare and air attacks. Japan has seen the comparative failure of the formidable U-boat effort made by Germany against Britain and is therefore unlikely to fear that submarine warfare could vitally affect her, in her enclosed waters and with her multiplicity of air bases.

"The forces of the United Nations are building up and by the end of 1942 will have attained proportions which will seriously threaten Japan. It must be her aim therefore to consolidate her gains this year and achieve as far as possible an unassailable position. She may then think it worth her while to offer peace.

"Japan aims at occupying Burma and possibly pushing beyond the frontier into parts of Bengal and Assam. By propaganda and subversion, coupled probably with air and sea raids she will try to break our control in India ... in any event she will go far enough into Burma to cut effective communications with China. With China isolated, she would hope to force Chiang Kai-Shek to make peace or to weaken and discredit him sufficiently to end organized Chinese resistance.

"Sea and air raids on bases and ports in Ceylon and East India will no doubt continue and be intensified. Japan will continue to harass our shipping routes in the Indian Ocean, and interfere as much as possible with our supply routes serving Australia, India and the Middle East. A fuelling base in Madagascar would be of great value to Japan for this purpose."

The Joint Intelligence Sub-Committee concluded that: "with the connivance of the French, she may try to establish a base there", and that such a base was therefore one of Japan's "immediate" aims.[37] Six days later the Chiefs Of Staff, despite all their reservations, sanctioned Operation *Ironclad*.

E. Harrison, in one of the most recent commentaries on the campaigns in Madagascar, saw the occupation of Diego Suarez as "the best strategic move" for

Japan. With Diego Suarez in their hands, Harrison has written, "the Japanese would have split the British Empire in two. Even the mere presence of large Japanese naval forces in the west of the Indian Ocean would have put Britain's communications under intolerable strain and raised the spectre of a disaster in the Middle East even greater than that in South-East Asia." Harrison quotes the words of two historians who questioned the value of Operation *Ironclad*. The first of these is Woodburn Kirby, who wrote that: "the occupation of Madagascar was never considered by the Japanese". The second is J. Butler, who asked, "Was Ironclad necessary?" and then stated that "the Japanese had no intention of using Diego Suarez themselves". As Harrison points out, neither of these offer any evidence to support such unguarded statements.[38]

Harrison's view is reinforced by Gerhard Weinberg, who stated that: "The leadership in both Germany and Japan, especially that of the two navies, saw quite clearly that control of the Indian Ocean was essential to Axis victory".[39] H.P. Wilmot saw the Indian Ocean as "a pivotal area of global strategy" and to M. Simpson "that vast sea was a crucial strategic area for the British Empire."[40]

As we know, even after the British capture of Antsirane, the Germans were still pressing the Japanese to move into the western Indian Ocean. On 13 May 1942 Admirals Fricke and Nomura met again to consider the situation in Madagascar. Fricke urged the Japanese to mount an immediate counter-attack upon Diego Suarez before the British could consolidate their position. The subject was then discussed a number of times in both Berlin and Tokyo, until the successes in the Pacific by the United States ended any possibility of the Japanese extending their operations further west.[41]

There was further justification for the Allied occupation of Madagascar in Laval's own declaration that France's overseas territories would be offered to Germany as a source of raw materials and for military bases. It is also known that in April 1942 Laval proposed to discuss the use of Madagascar by the Japanese navy with Admiral Mitami.[42]

Yet Madagascar is far enough away from Europe for de Coppet and his successors to have resisted attempts by Vichy to impose its will upon the distant colony should they have so desired.[43] A part of this debate, therefore, must be the question of whether or not the Allies could have achieved their objectives in Madagascar by peaceful means. We know that Roosevelt was contemplating a trade agreement with Madagascar. This, no doubt, would have enabled the United States to obtain the much-desired quantities of graphite considerably sooner than it eventually did in December 1942. Such a deal with the States would have been of great benefit to Madagascar, whose economy had declined severely during the two years of blockade. It is hard to see how any Governor-General would have jeopardized an agreement with the US by permitting the Japanese free access to the island's military facilities.

On the other hand, after the capture of Diego Suarez, Annet had every opportunity to come to terms with the Allies. Though he knew that Britain's actions had full US approval, the Governor-General failed to make a single genuine attempt at achieving a settlement with the Allies. Regardless of his subsequent protestations, none of Annet's words or deeds, nor indeed those of his predecessor, Cayla, gave the slightest indication that he would have welcomed any formal approach by the Allies.

Churchill certainly had no doubt that Operation *Ironclad* had been a worthwhile enterprise, as he revealed in Volume IV of his history of the war: "The news [of the capture of Diego Suarez] arrived at a time when we sorely needed success. It was in fact for long months the only sign of good and efficient war direction of which the British public were conscious." Without question it seemed at the time that the Allies had at last seized the initiative and just five days after the completion of *Ironclad*, *The New York Times* felt able to declare that "the tide of the war is at last on the turn".[44]

As it transpired, though Britain's military planners were unaware of it at the time, the Japanese had reached the limit of their westward advance before *Ironclad* was undertaken. There was, therefore, no possibility of Japan occupying Madagascar with a large military force. We also know that little more than a month after authorizing *Ironclad*, Churchill himself had dismissed the likelihood of Japan mounting a large-scale operation against Madagascar. As he explained to Wavell on 18 April 1942, if the Japanese could defeat Chiang Kai-shek in China then they would be able to release up to twenty divisions for the invasion of India. The Japanese, Churchill reasoned (in contradiction to the Joint Intelligence Sub-Committee's assessment), were more likely therefore to drive north into China than west across the Indian Ocean.[45]

Finally, the destruction of the Japanese carrier fleet by the US Navy at the Battle of Midway Island in the first week of June effectively ended Japan's capacity for offensive action. If Churchill had waited another month before launching *Ironclad*, as indeed the Chiefs of Staff had recommended, the changed circumstances might have rendered the entire Madagascar enterprise unnecessary. However, the highly successful operations of the Japanese submarine flotilla in the Mozambique Channel in the summer of 1942 indicate what even a small force based in Madagascar could have achieved over an extended period of time. Indeed, Japan's failure to exploit Britain's weakness in the East by occupying the islands of the Indian Ocean was seen by the historian Nicholas Rogers as "one of the great might-have-beens of history".[46]

We know that General Alan Brooke opposed Operation *Ironclad* on military grounds as did General Wavell, who protested "strongly" at the delay to his offensive in Burma caused by the Madagascar expedition.[47] Indeed, Wavell had planned to capture the Burmese port of Akyab by amphibious assault but the landing craft he had been promised were diverted to Madagascar. Wavell consequently attempted to take Akyab by land, which resulted in the defeat of all six British brigades involved in the operation. This important port remained in Japanese hands for a further two years.

The Admiralty had also opposed any action against Madagascar. As early as June 1941, the difficulties and expense of maintaining the blockade of Madagascar prompted the commander of the Eastern Fleet to recommend the occupation of the island. This was rejected by the Admiralty's Directorate of Plans, who feared that such an act would spark a renewal of the naval conflict with Vichy in the Mediterranean.[48]

Many others condemned the hostile invasion of Madagascar as a serious political error. The author Richard Overy regarded the occupation of Madagascar as a politically inspired move. Overy explained that, in 1942, after a series of military defeats, the Allies needed a "solid" victory. An invasion of Europe to confront their main enemy, Germany, was beyond their means so a softer target was found in the isolated, Vichy-held island. "The choice of Madagascar", Overy declared, "was an admission of weakness, not strength." It would be unkind, Overy has written, "to argue that Ironclad was the best the Allies could do in the summer of 1942, but it was not far short."[49]

It is certainly true that Churchill felt the weight of failure on his shoulders. Just three days after W.S.17 had left the Clyde, Churchill had to confess to the Conservative Party Central Committee that in the previous twelve months he had presided over "an almost unbroken series of military misfortunes". Four days later he opened his heart to Eden: "No man", Churchill told the Foreign Secretary, "has had to bear such disasters as I have."[50]

Desmond Dinan therefore saw Churchill's decision to attack Madagascar as being motivated by his desire for a victory in the East rather than an "objective strategic assessment" of the operation's merits. Dinan also saw the resulting breach with de Gaulle as an "inordinate political price" which Britain had to pay for a "questionable" strategic gain. Furthermore, Dinan blamed Churchill for allowing the Madagascar affair to drift on for months. "He had advocated the original invasion of the island," Dinan observed, "lost interest soon afterwards at a time when decisive leadership was needed, and exacerbated the conflict with de Gaulle."[51]

Conversely, Churchill was able to use the promise of the future installation of a Free French Governor in Tananarive as a "bargaining chip" to keep de Gaulle in check during the crucial weeks leading up to Operation Torch. As Martin Thomas explained, Churchill would play this chip whenever de Gaulle raised objections to British policy towards the Levant or French North Africa. Thomas believed that far from neglecting the Madagascar question Churchill used it both as a carrot and a stick to "strengthen his hand" with Carlton Gardens at a time when de Gaulle was proving difficult to control.[52]

It was the rift which the capture of Madagascar created in Anglo-French relations that also caused the great soldier-historian Basil Liddell Hart to consider the operation a mistake. Because of the large numbers involved in Ironclad he saw it as an "expensive" diversion of force based merely on an assumption that the Japanese would intervene. The resources directly employed in Ironclad – around 13,000 men, 46 ships and 118 aircraft, in addition to the entire Eastern Fleet deployed indirectly in support – were certainly very considerable, and probably more than was necessary. The loss of the battleship Ramillies for several months at a critical stage in the war at sea added to the costs of the operation. As Liddell Hart concluded, "fear proved in the long-term a bad counsellor."[53] He was probably right.

The French have never accepted Britain's stated reasons for occupying Madagascar. Shortly after the war Adrienne Hytier wrote that the British "did not really believe in their pretext"[54] for attacking Diego Suarez, and this view is still being repeated in the twenty-first century. As recently as May 2000, an article on Operation *Ironclad* in a French naval magazine opened with these words: "If anyone can find strategic justifications for certain British operations that were carried out against the French in 1940–42, at Mers-el-Kébir or in the Levant [Syria], there seems to be even less justification for Ironclad, the conquest of Diego Suarez in Madagascar." The author of this piece continues to promote the standard Vichy argument that the island would never have been handed over to the Japanese and that Britain was merely looking to acquire new territory to offset its losses in the Far East.[55] "Diego Suarez", the French Rear-Admiral Paul Auphan concluded, "promised an easy training ground and an easy victory."[56] It was neither.

Chapter 12

Exploring the battlegrounds of
Operation *Ironclad*

Antsirane, now Antsiranana, but still usually referred to as Diego Suarez (or simply Diego) is Madagascar's fifth largest town with a population of about 80,000. The old colonial names linger on throughout Madagascar, despite "political" attempts to localize many place-names. Antsiranana is still a major military and naval base and the Malagasy armed forces maintain a significant presence in and around the town.

Overlooking Port Nievre, along the Boulevard Millitaire, the former Defence Headquarters and the adjacent Malagasy Barracks are now occupied by a regiment of Marines. The Artillery Commander's house and the Artillery Depot now hold a regiment of infantry. There is a military hospital here as well as the depots of other military units. Along the front of the barracks is a long line of bomb casings linked together with anchor chain (circa 1942). In the harbour, accessible from the Rue des Quais, is the dry dock in which the *Wartenfels* was scuttled. Small naval vessels can be seen tied up here by the entrance to the dock. The jetty onto which the Royal Marines disembarked is still there at the extreme western end of the commercial harbour.

To the east of the harbour, on the north-eastern extremity of the Antsiranana peninsula, are the remains of a single concrete machine-gun emplacement. It overhangs the bay at the Ponte du Corail, and is found by following the track along the right-hand side of the civilian hospital. At the top of the emplacement is a memorial to the two Japanese crewmen of the midget submarine killed by Commandos after the attack upon HMS *Ramillies*. Part of the wreckage of their boat is incorporated within the memorial. It is in perfect condition and was visited by a Japanese delegation in 2003.

On the outskirts of Antsiranana, on the road to Arrachart airport, is the British cemetery. It is maintained in excellent order by the Commonwealth War Graves Commission and is one of the few places in Diego Suarez which is sign-posted. The French cemetery is nearby, clearly identifiable by the red, white and blue roundels either side of an impressive white arch.

At the airport, the shell of the large hangar destroyed by the Fleet Air Arm remains empty and abandoned at the end of the modern runway. The original airfield entrance, with the French Air Force insignia carved in stone above the portal, is still used today.

The great natural rock monolith that is Windsor Castle is visible for many miles around in almost every direction and can be seen clearly from Antsiranana. The road to Windsor Castle is a ninety-minute rollercoaster ride over ramshackle bridges, down stony ravines, across dry plains and through the collection of wooden and tin huts that is Anamakia village where the captured French naval officer was handed Syfret's letter. About five miles from Antsiranana the road rises gently over the Col de Bonne Nouvelle. The position is marked by a concrete machine-gun emplacement and the outlines of earthen trenches. At Ampasindava the road turns north away from the track to Mangorky and Ambararata Bay, and a short distance further on branches left towards Windsor Castle. This deeply rutted and boulder-strewn road can only be used by vehicles with four-wheel drive, and then only in the dry season. In the rainy season the road is utterly impassable.

The trek across country to Windsor Castle begins about a mile from Courrier Bay. It is a long and arduous climb over difficult terrain but always ahead is the magnificent rock formation which dominates the skyline. A stone stairway, cut out of the rock by the French, runs from the foot of the rock to the infantry post on the flat summit of the monolith. The stairway is in reasonably good condition in parts but this is another hard and steep climb. As the British discovered, the position was virtually impregnable.

The infantry post is on two levels with the garrison's living quarters set on a small plateau below the summit. Some twenty feet above is the actual infantry and observation post. The views from the top are spectacular. The whole of Courrier Bay can be seen reaching out into the Mozambique Channel, as can the entire countryside as far as Antsiranana.

The long, white line of the former military airstrip on Cap Diego can also be seen from here. It is still available for civilian aircraft as an emergency landing ground. Also at Cap Diego is the former French *Camp des Tirailleurs*, until recently used as a training area by the Malagasy military, and the remains of a coastal battery which held two 75mm naval guns.

The road to Courrier Bay was actually constructed by the French to supply the Cisteaux coastal battery situated towards the northern end of the bay which was captured by the Commandos ahead of the main landings. Halfway up the hill at the very end of this road sit two ruined machine-gun positions built, no doubt, to defend the battery. The battery itself, which consists of four gun emplacements linked by a deep communications trench, all in stone and concrete, commands the entire bay. If this battery had gone into action in 1942, it would have created immense difficulties for Syfret and his ships. On the reverse slope of the hill is a complex of buildings used by the garrison. These are becoming absorbed into the bush and have the appearance of a lost city.

The mangrove swamps referred to in the battalion War Diaries of the 29th Brigade are fast disappearing. The mangroves are being cut by the Malagasy for fencing posts. However, both Anamakia village and the rest of the countryside between Courrier Bay and Antsiranana appears untouched by time.

The meat factory of La Scama no longer exists, though it is possible that the local brewery occupies at least some of the factory's former site. The crumbling relic of the cairn erected by the Royal Scots Fusiliers in 1942 sits forlornly by the side of the road on the outskirts of Antsiranana, but not in its original position. It was moved some years ago, the plaque also having been damaged. A new bronze plaque was sent from Scotland in 1999 and this was placed in Antsiranana cathedral.

Also at the side of the road, but a little nearer to the town centre, is the pillbox which inflicted such damage upon the attacking forces. The position actually consists of two pillboxes. The one on the right-hand side held a machine gun to help defend the other pillbox, which housed one of the 75mm cannon. Locals say that in one of the pillboxes was the entrance to a tunnel which ran along the Joffre Line, now, sadly, filled with debris.

The Orangea Peninsula, which forms the south-eastern arm of the entrance to Diego Suarez Bay, was of the utmost importance to the French and was powerfully defended. This became apparent to Sturges when he examined captured French plans and, sensibly, he declined to attack. The road from Antsiranana to Orangea skirts the eastern edge of the bay, passing below Fort Bellevue at the end of the Joffre Line. As the road winds around the bay it penetrates a narrow defile, a little beyond which is the starting point for the climb up to the Montagne d'Francais. Named after the French and their Malagasy troops killed during the conflict, the track is marked at points by white crosses, supposedly to represent Christ's journey to Calgary. At the top of the mountain is Fort d'Ankorike. As with Windsor Castle, it was built on two levels with an observation post at the very summit. The fort completely commands the road below, including the defile. From the observation post the whole of the bay and the town can be seen clearly. The defenders would have been able to watch the battle unfold below them in comparative safety, though, no doubt, with some trepidation.

Continuing around the bay, the road leads to the Orangea military zone. Formerly a large military camp (known in 1942 as Camp d'Ankorike), it is now an abandoned complex of barracks and offices with just a handful of men to guard the decaying remains. A permit to enter the camp must be purchased from the sentry at the roadblock and a means of identification (i.e. passport) is usually requested. The road stops at the end of the camp, from where a track runs to the batteries at the Cap Miné that guard the Orangea Pass. The track twists its way through sand-dunes and bush before reaching the first of the battery's buildings and the civilian lighthouse. Another permit must be purchased from the guard who lives with his family in one of the old French buildings.

There were five batteries at Orangea and the entire complex extends right around the headland. Built along conventional nineteenth century designs, the main armament consisted of four large-calibre (320) guns in masonry emplacements underneath which were the supply magazines and casemates. All of this is in surprisingly good condition, apart from the four, now dismounted, cannon. Ahead of this battery are three, more modern, gun emplacements and built on the cliff edge are positions for smaller ordnance or machine guns. Constructed below ground level is the main magazine, now occupied by a small herd of goats.

The most impressive battery is at Le Point de Vue, far to the south in the centre of the Orangea Peninsula, some 240 metres above sea level. It consists of four comparatively modern guns and a large armoured optical range-finder. The guns could fire three rounds a minute to a distance of nineteen miles.

Across the narrow harbour entrance the position of the searchlight can just be identified on the northern arm, where white breakers indicate the proximity of dangerous reefs just outside the harbour entrance. The charge of *Anthony* past these reefs and through the harbour entrance at full speed and in complete darkness was a remarkable piece of seamanship.

Adjacent to the grounds of the Université du Nord, overlooking Diego Suarez Bay, is Coastal Defence Battery No.6 at Lazaret Point. This is very similar in design to the principle battery at Cap Miné with the interesting addition of an extended sunken gallery to permit the safe transfer of men and ammunition from the magazine to the gun positions. Whereas the magazine at Orangea was occupied by goats, this one is the home to a colony of pigs.

Finally, onto the Joffre (or G-H) Line. The population of Antsiranana has more than doubled since 1942 and urban development has engulfed most of the fortifications. Both Fort Caimans and Fort Bellevue are now surrounded by houses. The grounds of the former have become a banana field; the main gun position of the latter is a public toilet!

Both were built with an elevated central gun emplacement enclosed within a masonry perimeter wall which was itself protected by a spike-topped iron fence. The design is very similar in principle to a medieval motte-and-bailey castle. Apart from these structures and the pillbox on the Anamakia road, the Joffre Line has gone. But the Marshal's statue at the end of the Rue Joffre still stares proudly out to sea above the port his fortifications once defended.

Appendices

Operation *Ironclad*

Combined Commander-in-Chief: Rear-Admiral E.N. Syfret
Military Commander, 121 Force: Major-General R.G. Sturges
Naval Assault Commander: Captain G.A. Garnons-Williams
Military Assault Commander: Brigadier F.W. Festing
Chief Political Officer: Brigadier M.S. Lush

HM Ships employed

Force F

Battleship
Ramillies (8 x 15-inch guns)   Flag, Rear-Admiral E.N. Syfret

Aircraft Carriers
Indomitable (16 x 4.6-inch guns)   Flag, Rear-Admiral D.W. Boyd
   800 Squadron (8 Fairey Fulmars)
   806 Squadron (4 Fairey Albacores)
   827 & 831 Squadrons (24 Albacores)
   880 Sqaudron (9 Hawker Sea Hurricanes)

Illustrious (16 x 4.6-inch guns)
   810 & 829 Squadrons (20 Fairey Swordfish)
   881 Squadron (12 Grumman Martlets)
   882 Squadron (8 Martlets and 1 Fulmar)

Cruisers
Devonshire (8 x 8-inch guns)
Hermione (10 x 5.25-inch guns)

Destroyers
Pakenham (4 x 4-inch high-angle (HA) guns)
Laforey (6 x 4.7-inch guns)
Lightning (6 x 4.7-inch guns)
Lookout (6 x 4.7-inch guns)
Javelin (6 x 4.7-inch guns)

Inconstant (4 x 4.7-inch guns)
Active (4 x 4.7-inch guns)
Anthony (4 x 4.7-inch guns)
Duncan (4 x 4.7-inch guns)
Paladin (4 x 4-inch HA guns)
Panther (4 x 4-inch HA guns)

Corvettes
Freesia (1 x 4-inch gun)
Fritillary (1 x 4-inch gun)
Genista (1 x 4-inch gun)

Cyclamen (1 x 54-inch gun)
Thyme (1 x 4-inch gun)
Jasmine (1 x 4-inch gun)

Minesweepers
Cromer (1 x 3-inch HA gun)
Poole (1 x 3-inch HA gun)
Auricula (1 x 4-inch gun)
Nigella (1 x 4-inch gun)
Romney (1 x 3-inch HA gun)
Cromarty (1 x 3-inch HA gun)

Assault Ships
Keren
Karanja
Royal Ulsterman
Winchester Castle
Sobieski

Personnel Ships
Oransay

Duchess of Atholl
Franconia

Motor Transport Ships
City of Hong Kong
Mahout
Thalatta
Empire Kingsley
Nairn Bank
Martand

Tank Landing Ship
Bachaquero

Fleet Auxiliaries
Easedale (oiler)
Derwentdale (motor landing craft)

Hospital Ship
Atlantis

In addition, the SS *Greystoke Castle* arrived at Diego Suarez on 7 May with stores and ammo from Durban, consisting of:

1,000 x 250lb bombs
500 x 500lb bombs
250,000 tracer rounds
2,000,000 rounds of machine–gun ammunition
2 W/T vehicles
500 tons of high–octane aviation fuel

South African Air Force units
(deploying to Kenya on 5 May 1942)

32 Coastal Reconnaissance Flight (5 Martin Marylands)
36 Coastal Reconnaissance Flight (5 Bristol Beauforts)
37 Coastal Reconnaissance Flight (5 Beauforts and 1 Maryland)
50 Transport Flight (6 Junkers Ju 52s)
53 Transport Flight (6 Lockheed Lodestars)
54 Transport Flight (6 Lodestars)

(Details taken from *Battle Summaries* No.16, pp.58–59)

Operation *Ironclad* – 121 Force

Headquarters 121 Force

Royal Engineers detachment 121 Force
Signals Section 121 Force
Royal Army Service Corps 121 Force
Royal Army Medical Corps 121 Force
Royal Army Ordnance Corps 121 Force
Pay Corps detachment
Provost detachment
Pioneer detachment

29th Independent Infantry Brigade Group

HQ 29 Infantry Brigade
Defence Platoon
Brigade Signals Section
1st Battalion Royal Scots Fusiliers
2nd Battalion Royal Welch Fusiliers
2nd Battalion East Lancashire Regiment
2nd Battalion South Lancashire Regiment
'B' Special Service Squadron, Royal Armoured Corps
455 Light Battery, Royal Artillery
145 Light Anti-Aircraft Troop, Royal Artillery
236 Field Company, Royal Engineers (less one Section)

17th Infantry Brigade Group

HQ 17 Infantry Brigade
Defence Platoon
Brigade Signals Section
Light Aid Detachment
2nd Battalion Royal Scots Fusiliers
2nd Battalion Northamptonshire Regiment
6th Battalion Seaforth Highlanders
9 Field Regiment, Royal Artillery
38 Field Company, Royal Engineers
141 Field Ambulance, Royal Army Medical Corps

13th Infantry Brigade Group
91st Field Regiment, Royal Artillery
252 Field Company, Royal Engineers
2nd Battalion The Cameronians
2nd Battalion Inniskilling Fusiliers
2nd BattalionWiltshire Regiment
13th Infantry Brigade Company, Royal Army Service Corps
164 Field Ambulance, Royal Army Medical Corps

No. 5 Army Commando
(Details taken from *Battle Summaries* No.16, p.16, and H. Joslen, *Orders of Battle*, vol.1, pp.276–7)

French Forces
Diego Suarez/Antsirane April–May 1942

Fortress Commander, Diego Suarez: Colonel Claerebout
Naval Commander, Diego Suarez: *Capitaine* Maerten
Detachment commander, *Groupe Aérien Mixte*: *Capitaine* Bache

Garrison, Fortress Diego Suarez
2me Regiment Mixte de Madagascar (*RMM*) (Col. Rouvés)
  1er Bataillon (Major Viennot)
    1er Compagnie (Senegalese)
    2me Compagnie (Senegalese)
    3me Compagnie (Comorien)
  2me Bataillon (Malagache)
    5me Compagnie
    6me Compagnie
    7me Compagnie
  3me Bataillon (*Malagache*: *Capitaine* Thomas)
    8me Compagnie
    9me Compangnie
    10me Compagnie

Détachment de reconnaissance motorisé (DRM)

Groupe Campagne et Montagne [Field and Mountain Artillery Group] (Major Charles)
Coastal Artillery (Lieutenant-Colonel Pichon)
Anti-Aircraft Artillery

Deployment of French forces at Diego Suarez 5 May 1942

Lanivato (Baie de Rigny)

Four-man outpost, with radio:	Camp d'Ambre
8th & 10th Companies *3/2 RMM*:	Camp du Sakaramy
One 75mm field battery:	Arrachart Airfield
9th Company *3/2 RMM*:	Orangéa Peninsula
5th Company *2/2 RMM*:	Camp d'Ankorika
Two 80mm field guns:	Fort d'Ankorika

Two 80mm field guns:	Mamelon Vert
One 164mm coastal battery:	Le Point de Vue
One 100mm coastal battery:	Poste Optique/Sémaphore d'Orangéa
One 320mm coastal battery:	Cap Miné
Three 47mm naval guns:	Plage d'Orangéa

Antsirane
6th Company *2/2 RMM*
One 75mm field battery
One 75mm mobile field section
One 65mm mobile anti-tank section
One 75mm coastal gun (at lighthouse)
Two 90mm AA guns
One 13.2mm AA section

Antanambao (and Joffre Line)
1/2 RMM (all three companies)
Four 75mm anti-tank guns

Cap Diego Peninsula
7th Company *2/2 RMM*:	Camp des Tirailleurs
One 65mm anti-tank section:	Andrakaka Isthmus
One 240mm coastal battery:	Andrahompotsy
Two 75mm naval guns:	Cap Diego

Windsor Castle/Courrier Bay
One combat group with one 60mm mortar:	Windsor Castle
One 138mm coastal battery:	WSW of Windsor Castle
One infantry section:	WSW of Windsor Castle

Ampasindava
One outpost, with one infantry section

(Details extracted from "Afrique Orientale Française" component of État-Major des Colonies (1er Bureau), *Situation des effectifs aux Colonies a la date du 1er Avril 1942*, dated 11 June 1942 in SHAT 8H83 dossier 6)

French Naval Assets

Diego Suarez anchorage
  Bougainville (auxiliary cruiser)
  Bévéziers (submarine)
  D'Entrecasteaux (colonial sloop)

Majunga
  Glorieux (submarine)

At sea
  D'Iberville
  Le Héros (submarine)
  Le Monge (submarine)

Detachment *Groupe Aérien Mixte* (Diego–Arrachart)
  3 Potez 63
  5 Morane 406
  2 Potez 25

(Details extracted from "Afrique Orientale Française" component of État-Major des Colonies (1er Bureau), *Situation des effectifs aux Colonies a la date du 1er Avril 1942*, dated 11 June 1942 in SHAT 8H83 dossier 6)

Appendix V

Letter to the Governor of Diego Suarez
(Translation)

On board the British Flagship
3 May 1942

Your Excellency,

The strategic position of Diego Suarez requires that it should not fall into the hands of the Japanese and that the territory should be available for those forces which are fighting to restore freedom in the world and secure the liberation of France and French territory. It cannot be allowed to suffer the fate of Indo-China.

I therefore request that in order that bloodshed may be avoided you will surrender the territory under your control to me unconditionally and instruct your officials and armed forces to obey the orders which I shall issue.

The action which I am now taking on the instruction of H.M. Government has the full approval of the Government of the United States.

In order to assist you in reaching a favourable decision, I have been instructed by H.M. Government to inform you of the following:

(1) Diego Suarez is French and will remain French, and will be restored to France after the war. H.M. Government have repeatedly made it clear that they do not covet an inch of French territory. I repeat this assurance.

(2) Funds will be made available to meet the salaries and pensions of all personnel, civil and military, who elect to co-operate with the United Nations.

(3) If any civil and military employees do not wish to co-operate, they will, provided they can claim the right to residence in Metropolitan France, be repatriated as and when shipping becomes available.

(4) The trade of Diego Suarez with the United Nations will be restored. H.M. Government will extend to Diego Suarez all the economic benefits accepted to French territories which have already joined the United Nations.

(5) There must be no destruction of civil and military installations, W/T stations, war stores, etc. Those responsible for any such sabotage will not benefit by conditions (2) and (3) above.

Your reply to this communication should be sent to me immediately in plain language by radio on 500 kc/s (600 metres), using call sign GBXZ. Alternatively, it should be sent by the hand of an officer under flag of truce, to the Officer Commanding Occupying Troops.

I am, Your Excellency,
(Sgd.) *E. N. Syfret.*
Rear Admiral and Commander-in-Chief British Forces.

Operation *Stream-Line-Jane*

Forces employed

Rear-Admiral W.G. Tennant & Major-General R.G. Sturges, R.M., Joint Commanders

Naval Force M

Cruisers
Birmingham (Flag)
Dauntless
Gambia
Caradoc

Battleship (for Operation 'Jane' only)
Warspite

Anti-Aircraft ship (ex-Light Cruiser)
HMNS *Heemskerck*

Aircraft carrier
Illustrious

Monitor
Erebus

Headquarters ship
Albatross

Fast Minelayer
Manxman

Destroyers
1st Division (carrier screen)
HMNS *Van Galen*
HMNS *Tjerk Hiddes*

2nd Division (anti-submarine)
Norman
Nizam
Foxhound
Hotspur

3rd Division (anti-submarine)
Arrow
Blackmore
Active
Inconstant

4th Division (battleship screen)
Fortune
Nepal

Detached to Morondava
HMAS *Napier*

Minesweepers (14th Flotilla):	*Cromer; Cromarty; Romney; Freesia*
Anti-submarine Whalers:	*Sigfar; Lurcher; Mastiff*
Netlayer (Stream only):	*Brittany*
Assault Ships (29th Brigade):	*Empire Pride; Dunera; Dilwara*
Motor Transport Ship (29th Brigade):	Ocean Viking
Personnel Ships (22nd Brigade):	*Empire Woodlark; Abosso; Khedive-Ismail; Llandaff Castle*
Motor Transport ships (22nd Brigade)	*Ocean Vesper; Empire Squire; Delius; Wanderer*

Maintenance Convoy

Motor Transport ships:	*Gascony; Advisor* *Charlton Hall; Ross*
Personnel ship:	*Empire Trooper*

Oilers:	*British Energy; Easedale*
	Eaglesdale; Doryssa
Petrol tanker:	*Kola*
Hospital ships:	*Vasna; Dorsetshire*

Air Component

Ship-borne aircraft (HMS *Illustrious*):
6 Fairey Fulmars
18 Fairey Swordfish
21 Grumman Martlets

Long-range, shore-based aircraft:
6 Martin Marylands
8 Bristol Beauforts
5 Westland Lysanders
6 Fairey Albacores
6 Fairey Fulmars
8 Supermarine Walrus (6 for Operation *Stream*)
7 Consolidated Catalinas

Land Forces

29th Independent Infantry Brigade Group
  (see Operation *Ironclad*, above)
No.5 Army Commando
145th Light Anti-Aircraft Troop, Royal Artillery
'A' Squadron, 1st Armoured Car Commando, South African Tank Corps

22nd (East Africa) Infantry Brigade Group
  1/1 Battalion (Nyasaland), King's African Rifles
  5th Battalion (Kenya), King's African Rifles
  1/6 Battalion (Tanganyika), King's African Rifles
  56th (Uganda) Field Battery, East African Artillery
  9th Field Regiment, Royal Artillery
  60th Field Company, East African Engineers
  5th (Kenya) Field Ambulance

(Details taken from TNA CB 3303 (3) *Naval Staff History*, vol. III, Appendix A, and H.F. Joslen, *Orders of Battle*, vol.II, pp.421–2)

French Order of Battle
September–November 1942

Commanding Officer: *Général de brigade* Guillemet

Unit & Commander	Coy.	Place & date engaged
1er Regiment Mixte de Madagascar (*RMM*)		
1er Bataillon de Marche	14	Part Ambohidratimo; 23 September
(Cmdt. Brunot, captured 19 Oct)		Part with Machefaux; 4 October
	15	Sambaina; 30 September
	16	Sambaina; 30 September
	22	Behenjy; 26 September
2me Bataillon de Marche	17	Mandalahy; 29 October
(Lt.-Col. Tricoire captured 29 Oct.)	18	Mandalahy; 29 October
	19	Vatoavo; 4 November
	20	Mandalahy; 29 October
3me Bataillon de Marche	2	Amnositra; 19 October
(Cmdt. Peytauin, captured 13 Oct)	3	Mahitsy; 22 September
	13	Mahitsy; 22 September
	21	Mahitsy; 22 September
Détachment de reconnaissance motorisé		
(Lt. Fiaggianelli captured 16 Sept)	1	Anjiajia; 16 September
2me Bataillon 1er RMM	5	Majunga; 10 September
(Cmdt. Martin, captured 10 Sept)	6	(and in *Esme* operations)
	7	Majunga; 10 September
	8	Majunga; 10 September
3me Bataillon 1er RMM	9	Antanjona; 13 October
(Lt.-Col. Pensereau, capt. 13 Oct)	10	Antanjona; 13 October
	11	Antanjona; 13 October
	12	Antanjona; 13 October

Bataillon de Tirailleurs Malagaches
(Capt. Darcis)

	1	Fianarantsoa; 29 October
	2	Tulear; 29 September
	3	Vatoavo; 4 November
	4	*Training Coy. only*
	5	Ilaka; 10 October

Artillery
(Col. Gilberteau, captured 2 Nov)

	4 x 80mm	2 at Mahitsy; 22 September
		2 at Ambohidratimo; 23 September
	4 x 75mm	2 at Mahitsy; 22 September
		2 at Ivato; 19 October
	4 x 65mm	2 at Mahitsy; 22 September
		1 at Tsarasaotra; 12 October
		1 at Ambositra; 16 October
	4 x 37mm	Captured at isolated points

Aircraft

	3 Potez 25	*All destroyed by No.16 Squadron*
	1 Morane 406	*SAAF on the ground at Ihosy,*
	1 Potez 63	*between 8 October and 12 October*

(Details taken from W.A. Dimoline, *An Account of 22 E.A. Infantry Brigade, 10th September–6th November 1942*)

Notes

Chapter 1: "Age-Long Enemies"

1. The operation for which the Marines and the 29th Brigade were practising for was Operation *Hardboiled*, which was an amphibious assault upon Stavanger on the Norwegian coast. In fact this was an entirely fictitious operation invented by the Future Operations Planning Section of the Joint Planning Staff to throw the Germans onto the defensive, M. Howard, *British Intelligence in the Second World War*, vol. Five, p.23; J. Kemp, *The Royal Scots Fusiliers*, pp.61–3.
2. E. Spears, *Assignment to Catastrophe*, pp.236–336.
3. R. Aron, *The Vichy Regime, 1940–44*, p.65.
4. Aron, p.9; Spears, p.510.
5. C. Ponting, *Churchill*, p.453; E. Gates, *End of the Affair*, pp.118 & 487.
6. L. Grafftey-Smith, *Hands to Play*, p.30; I. Ousby, *Occupation*, p.44.
7. A. Hytier, *Two Years of French Foreign Policy*, p.39.
8. G. Warner, *Iraq and Syria 1941*, p.32; A. Marder, *Operation Menace*, p.10.
9. Hytier, pp.54–60; R. Lamb, *Churchill as War Leader*, pp.63–73. Actual French casualties at Mers-el-Kébir were 1,297 killed and 351 wounded. E. Gates, *End of the Affair*, p.359.
10. Marder, p.3.
11. The most notable raid occurred on the night of 3–4 March 1942, against the Renault works. Though the factory was supplying war material to the Germans, the bombing resulted in around 2,500 French civilians being killed or wounded, L. Woodward, *British Foreign Policy*, p.291; Hytier, p.345.
12. Lamb, pp.69–71; Hytier, pp.82–4; J. Néré, *The Foreign Policy of France*, pp.253–4.
13. Dakar was protected by eight 9.4-inch guns, submarine patrols and the new battleship *Richelieu*, Marder, p.12.
14. J. Williams, *The Guns of Dakar*, p.9.
15. Hytier, p.96.
16. One hundred German aircraft, twenty-two Iraqi aircraft and four trainloads of munitions passed through Syria, Aron, pp.312–3.
17. Warner, pp.59–63. The seizure of Syria and Iraq, followed by the occupation of Persia in August 1941, gave Britain continuous land access all the way from the Persian Gulf to the Caucasus. This allowed an alternative supply route to Russia, which avoided the perilous route through the Arctic. C. Buckley, *Five Ventures*, p.165.
18. Hytier, pp.278–9.
19. C. Shores, *Dust Clouds in the Middle East*, pp.200–1.
20. C. Buckley, pp.137–8.
21. Aron, p.310.
22. S. Roskill, *War at Sea*, vol. II, p.185.
23. A. Jackson, *War and Empire in Mauritius and the Indian Ocean*, pp.34–5.

24. *The Daily Telegraph*, May 6 1942.
25. W. Churchill, *The Hinge of Fate*, pp.107 & 201.
26. Buckley, p.167.
27. TNA PREM 3/265/11; M. Thomas, "Imperial Backwater or Strategic Outpost? The British Takeover of Vichy Madagascar 1942", *The Historical Journal*, 39, 4 (1996), p.52; Lamb, pp.147–54. It has been stated that the Germans had already "earmarked" Diego Suarez as a suitable submarine base. J. Slader, *The Fourth Service*, p.169.
28. TNA CAB 121/622, COS (40) 1017 (JP) and JP (40) 740; Jackson, p.53.
29. TNA CAB 121/622, COS (41) 399th (1).
30. TNA CAB 121/622, JP (41) 1043. Considering the intense fighting that later ensued, it is interesting to note that the Joint Planners recorded the following opinion: "In view of the fairly low state of morale of the garrison and the small number of European troops it is quite possible that the appearance of a capital ship and the threat of bombardment would cause Diego Suarez to capitulate without resistance", JP (41) 1015.
31. TNA DEFE 2/108, proposal submitted to Mountbatten by Lieutenant-Commander Costobadie and Major Parks, 3 January 1942. Mountbatten actually supported this scheme and he sent it on to the Force Commanders of Operation *Bonus* with his recommendation!
32. TNA CAB 121/622, COS (41) 402nd (4) and JP (41) 1015.
33. TNA CAB 121/622, COS (41) 427th (8) and JP (41) 1070.
34. TNA CAB 121/622, COS (41) 49th (0).
35. De Gaulle, *The Call to Honour*, Vol.1, pp.329–30.
36. TNA PREM 3/265/1, Note to Churchill, 17 February 1941.
37. TNA FO 371/31897; De Gaulle, p.240.
38. Lamb, p.118. Churchill, *Hinge of Fate*, p.199.
39. R. Croft-Cooke, *The Blood-Red Island*, pp.45–6.
40. P. Bell, *France and Britain 1940–1994*, p.44.
41. Hytier, pp.145–6 & 152.
42. Hytier, pp.156 & 205.
43. TNA CAB 84/43, JP (42) 291. The Joint Planning Staff had only a few French and Admiralty charts, all of which were forty years old, and the details of defensive armament available to them dated back to 1923, TNA ADM 203/60, Lecture by G. Butler, *Operation Ironclad*. Colonel Sam Bassett also explained in J. Leasor's *War at the Top*, pp.132–3, how a number of pre-war reports compiled on Madagascar were given away for salvage by the Admiralty.
44. M. Brown, *History of Madagascar*, p.202.
45. In its efforts to protect Egypt and the Nile, Britain sought to establish a protectorate over Zanzibar. Germany was a major Power in that part of east Africa at that time and a deal was struck which allowed Britain to move into Zanzibar in return for which Germany would receive Heligoland. However, this arrangement contravened an earlier convention which guaranteed Zanzibar's independence. France protested at this diplomatic breach which led the British Prime Minister, Lord Salisbury, to hand Madagascar to the French, Brown, pp.215–6.
46. Brown, pp.224–31. The lack of development in Madagascar was to some degree intentional, as a former king, Radana I, explained: "If I make roads, the white man will come and take my country. I have two allies – forest and fever", H. Bradt, *Madagascar*, p.109.
47. Collected papers of Bishop Lang, vol.184, ff 72–3; Jackson, p.52.
48. M. Philippon made this statement on 18 January 1941; see Gandar Dower, *Into Madagascar*, p.89.

49. By the time of the Allied invasion of Madagascar, exports had decreased to just twenty-two per cent of its pre-war level, M. Thomas, *The French Empire at War*, pp.142–3.

50. De Gaulle, p.241; Brown, p.255.

51. J. Suret-Canale, *French Colonialism in Tropical Africa*, p.464.

52. De Gaulle, p.239.

53. The report's description of Annet was: "He does not seem to be a man of great personality. He lacks initiative and seems to be incapable of taking the smallest decision without first referring to Vichy, to whom he is apparently completely subservient. Of weak character, he is unlikely to take strong action at any time." PRO WO 208/1519.

54. D. Dilks, *The Diaries of Sir Alexander Cadogan*, 19/9/42, p.478.

55. Of even greater concern to the colonialists was the shortage of chemicals for the water-treatment plants with the consequential risk of a major typhoid outbreak; Lang Papers, vol.184, ff. 72–3.

56. Jackson, pp.140–4.

57. TNA CAB 121/622, COS(41) 432nd Mtg.

58. Brown, pp.249–55; Bradt, *Madagascar*, p.8.

59. Brown, p.148.

60. S. Rigge, *World War II: War in the Outposts*, 101; J. Ladd, *By Sea, By Land*, p.107.

61. TNA ADM 203/60, Lecture by G. Butler, *Operation Ironclad*.

62. B. Fergusson, *The Watery Maze*, pp.157–8.

63. J. Thompson, *The Royal Marines*, p.294. The number of aircraft was actually reduced from fifteen to just five Lysanders. Sturges, understandably, saw this as "a little peculiar", yet he was assured by the Chief of the Air Staff that this was "perfectly adequate", Supplement to *The London Gazette*, 4 March 1948, p.1605.

64. De Gaulle, p.241.

65. Churchill, *The Hinge of Fate*, pp.198–9.

66. De Gaulle, pp.330–1.

67. TNA CAB 121/622, COS (41) 417th (7) JP (41) 1043, 11 December 1941.

68. TNA CAB 121/622, COS (41) 404th (5) to COS (42) 5th Meeting (0), 31 January 1942.

69. TNA FO 371/31897.

70. R. Breitman, *The Architect of Genocide*, p.6; Brown, p.44. In the summer of 1940 an SS-*Obersturmfuhrer*, Theodor Dannecker, was sent to Paris to head the *Judenreferat*, or Jewish Affairs Bureau. Dannecker was chosen for this post because he was an "expert" on the Madagascar Plan, P. Webster, *Pétain's Crime*, p.107.

71. Breitman, pp.61 & 97; D. Goldhagen, *Hitler's Willing Executioners*, p.146.

72. M. Marrus, *The Holocaust in History*, p.32.

73. P. Neville, *The Holocaust*, p.44. The American Jewish Committee published a booklet in 1941 which gave the following verdict on the Madagascar Plan: "The terrible risks involved in a mass settlement of white people in an isolated, backward, disease-ridden tropical wilderness are evident. They cannot be disregarded except by men who are completely devoid of human feeling. The forced deportation of Jews en masse to the island of Madagascar must be resisted."

74. L. Dawidowicz, *The War against the Jews*, p.157.

75. P. Allen, *Madagascar*, p.44; Breitman, p.121; A. Farmer, *Anti-Semitism and the Holocaust*, pp.55–6, 72 & 114. It is possible that definite plans for the extermination of the Jews were not finalized until January 1942, at the now notorious Wannsee Conference, Marrus, p.32.

Chapter 2: "A Considerable Gamble"

1. P. Kemp, *The Red Dragon*, p.98.
2. Lamb, p.147.
3. It was one of Britain's greatest fears that Japanese and German forces would join hands in the Middle East – "under the shadow of Sinai", as the Ministry of Information was to declare; HMSO *Combined Operations*, p.97.
4. G. Weinberg, *A World at Arms*, p.307; J. Brown, *Eagles Strike*, p.383; Jackson, p.32; The agreement between Germany and Japan was included in the Tripartite Pact of December 1941, Roskill, *War at Sea*, vol. II, p.184. The boundary between the Japanese and the German operational spheres was longitude 70 degrees East with the proviso that "in the Indian Ocean operations may be carried out beyond the agreed boundary if the situation requires", Turner, Gordon-Cummings & Betzler, *War in the Southern Oceans*, p.115.
5. War Diary of Naval Attaché, Tokyo, Admiralty Reel 482, NHB, quoted in A. Marder *et al*, *Old Friends New Enemies*, p.155–6.
6. Attention was also drawn in the report to the political significance of such a move by the Japanese as it would call into question France's relationship with the Allied Powers. Allowing the Japanese into Madagascar might be a step further down the road of collaboration than the French wanted to travel and Hitler did not believe France would give her consent to such an arrangement. The likelihood was that the French garrison in Madagascar would oppose any take-over of the island either by Allied or Axis forces. *Brassey's Naval Annual*, 1948 edition, p.267. Churchill, *The Hinge of Fate*, p.200.
7. W. Kimball, *Forged in War*, pp.76 & 170; TNA WO 208/1528, "Reports concerning MADAGASCAR appearing in BJs", 22 March 1942; E. Harrison, "British Subversion in French East Africa, 1941–42: SOE's Todd Mission", *English Historical Review*, April 1999, p.359.
8. TNA WO 208/1528, MI3 Summary of Political Intelligence Reports, No.174.
9. TNA WO 208/929 & 1493; Aston Papers, *Field Security Orders – IRONCLAD*.
10. Telegram to Secretary of State for Dominion Affairs, 16 January 42, TNA FO 371/31897.
11. De Gaulle, pp.332–3.
12. Churchill, *The Hinge of Fate*, p.198.
13. M. Simpson & J. Somerville, *The Somerville Papers*, p.356; L. Turner, *War in the Southern Oceans*, pp.114–5.
14. A. Danchev & D. Todman, *Alanbrooke Diaries*, p.212.
15. TNA CAB 121/622, COS (42) 81st (10); COS (42) 7th Mtg. (0); TNA CAB 120/122, Memo to the Prime Minister from Ismay, 13 March 1942; A. Bryant, *The Turn of the Tide*, pp.339–40 & 365. In a memo to Churchill on 13 March, Ismay also pointed out that if the Royal Navy was driven from Ceylon, Diego Suarez would be of "very great value", TNA CAB 120/122.
16. TNA CAB 121/622, p.18. Eden's minute to and Churchill's reply, 2 Feb 42.
17. Kimball, *Churchill & Roosevelt*, vol.1, C-25, p.350 & R-102, p.353; TNA FO 371/31897.
18. TNA CAB 121/622 COS (42) 69 (0) & COS (42) 92nd (11).
19. Report of General Sturges, *The London Gazette*, 4 March 1948, pp.1606–7.
20. TNA ADM 202/396.
21. Churchill to Roosevelt, 14 March 1942, Churchill, *Hinge of Fate*, p.201.
22. J. Ladd, *By Sea, By Land*, p.107.
23. TNA CAB 121/622, COS (42) 83rd Mtg/8th Mtg (0), dated 13/3/42; it was understood that the 29th Brigade could be kept in Madagascar for two months, whereas the 17th

Brigade was to continue to India as soon as Diego Suarez had been captured, M. Page, *King's African Rifles*, p.115.

24. By coincidence, a relative of Admiral Syfret, Lieutenant-Colonel W.M. Syfret, had commanded a battalion of the RSF in 1940, J. Kemp, p.63.

25. J. Bright, *The 9th Queen's Royal Lancers*, pp.338–9.

26. B. Kennett & J. Tatman, *The Craftsmen of the Army*, p.113.

27. Buckley, *Five Ventures*, p.168.

28. C. Durtnell, *The Fifth British Division*, pp.58–9.

29. Thompson, *The Royal Marines*, p.293.

30. Report of General Sturges, *The London Gazette*, 4 March 1948 p.1607. *Keren*, a former P & O vessel, was later designated a Landing Ship Head Quarters (LHSQ). Slader, *The Fourth Service*, p.169; The *Sobieski* was in mid-Atlantic in 1939 when Germany invaded Poland and she sailed directly to the UK.

31. W. Kimball, *Churchill & Roosevelt*, vol.1, C-44, p.404.

32. Kimball, vol.1, R-119–20, pp.406–7.

33. The six were: the defence of Ceylon and Madagascar, the defence of the coast of Egypt and Libya against invasion, air patrols in home waters and the Bay of Biscay, increased security against invasion across the Channel and the bombing offensive against Germany, M. Gilbert, *Road To Victory*, p.77.

34. W. Tute, *The Reluctant Enemies*, p.207.

35. TNA CAB 121/622, COS (42) 69 (0), 18 March 1942; *Naval Staff History, vol. III, War with Japan*, p.1; Ministry of Information, *The Royal Marines*, p.50.

36. TNA ADM 223/550, 15/3/42, to C-in-C Mediterranean.

37. *Battle Summaries* No.16, Naval Operations at the Capture of Diego Suarez, pp.31–2.

38. TNA CAB 121/622, 158A & 137A. It was reported by the Americans that the ships had actually set sail and they were accompanied by two French cruisers.

39. Churchill, *Hinge of Fate*, vol. IV, pp.201–2. De Gaulle, p.241; TNA CAB 121/622, 164 A.

40. De Gaulle, pp.240–1 & p.341.

41. Annotation by PM on minute Eden to PM dated 5 March 1942.

42. TNA ADM 199/1277 Halifax to Eden, 5 March 1942.

43. Ponting, *Churchill*, p.479.

44. J. Harvey, *The War Diaries of Oliver Harvey*, p.121. Whitehall also believed that the Free French might intentionally leak the news of an impending Allied move against Madagascar in order to undermine Vichy's claim to supremacy in French Africa, M. Thomas, *The French Empire at War*, p.141.

45. Churchill to Ismay, 30/3/42, in M. Lush, *A Life of Service*, p.139.

46. TNA CAB 121/622, 161A, 168C, 168E.

47. TNA HS 3/21.

48. M. Thomas, *The Historical Journal*, 39, 4, pp.1055 & 1058.

49. S. Clark, *The Man who is France*, p.153.

50. Quoted by D. Dinan, *The Politics of Persuasion*, p.219.

51. According to a Reuters report in *The Evening Standard* of 14 March, the Vichy Government stated that it would not willingly allow Madagascar to be occupied by the Japanese. This prompted the US to seek clarification of what "willingly" meant! The *Evening Standard*, London 14, 18, 23 and 24 March 1942.

52. The *Evening Standard*, 24 March 1942.

53. *War Illustrated*, 2 April 1942, vol.5, p.586.

54. R. James, *Winston S. Churchill, His Complete Speeches*, vol.VI, pp.6633–4.
55. TNA CAB 121/622, 127B, Proposals by Colonel Stanley, Operation Ironclad, Note on Cover, 17 March 1942.
56. D. Wheatley, *The Deception Planners*, pp.45–8; Testimony of Sgt. F.H. Thomas, RAF. There is a contradictory account of the cover plan in M. Howard, *British Intelligence in the Second World War*, Vol. Five, p.23. Howard states that the cover plan for *Ironclad* was for an operation against the Italian-occupied Dodecanese Islands in the eastern Mediterranean.
57. TNA ADM 203/60, G. Butler, *Operation* Ironclad.
58. NLR-MR-FDRWSA-1942–17B and 18S Churchill to Roosevelt, 27 March 1942 and 28 April.
59. Churchill, *Hinge of Fate*, p.204; TNA CAB 120/169D, PM's personal telegram No.T.530/2, 3 April 1942, No.131.
60. W. Jervois, *History of the Northamptonshire Regiment*, p.98.
61. J. Pendlebury, *History of the East Lancashire Regiment*, p.242; P. Kemp, *The Red Dragon*, p.99; J. Stockman, "Madagascar 1942", *British Army Review*, April 1986, p.75. TNA CAB 121/622, COS (42) 8th Meeting (0) Annex II. Convoy W.S. 17 consisted of twenty-five vessels plus the escort of twenty-six warships, R. Manners, *My War Years, 1942*; The list of ships in W.S. 17 can be found in *A Book of Thanks to the South African Women's Auxiliary Service*, pp.80–4. The "Winston Specials" – fast convoys with vital reinforcements or equipment – sailed every month round the Cape. Originally these convoys only sailed to Egypt but after Pearl Harbour the W.S. code-name was also given to urgent convoys to Singapore, Australia and India, A. Marder, *Old Friends New Enemies*, p.161.
62. Durtnell, p.59.
63. *A Book of Thanks to the South African Women's Auxiliary Service*, p.80.
64. J. Kemp, p.60.
65. TNA CAB 106/674.
66. ADM 223/550, Naval Cypher 1305B/16/4/42 to Syfret. General Sturges was notified about the inclusion of 13 Brigade on 17 April, *The London Gazette*, 4 March 1948, p.1608. See also TNA CAB 121/622, 155, 170 & 170 A and 170 B.
67. *A Book of Thanks to the South African Women's Auxiliary Service*, pp.80–4. *Battle Summaries No.16*, p.33.
68. This was one of Churchill's pet ideas, which he had first raised with Prime Minister Lloyd George during the First World War, when Churchill was Minister of Munitions, see Churchill, *Hinge of Fate*, pp.297–300.
69. Altogether *Bachaquero* carried fifty-four vehicles and guns, Sturges' report, *The London Gazette* 4 March 1948, p.1612.
70. B. Macdermott, *Ships Without Names*, pp.17–18.
71. Kimball, C-42, p.438.
72. *Battle Summaries No.16*, p.32. The cruisers were *Leygues*, *Gloire*, and *Montcalm*. L. Woodward, *British Foreign Policy*, vol. II, p.295.
73. The tropical uniforms, along with anachronistic pith helmets, were issued on 2 April; Durtnell, p.59.
74. Diego Suarez is 9,877 miles by sea from the UK, TNA CAB 121/622 JP (40) 740.
75. J. Kemp, pp.63–4. It was a similar story for the men of the 17th Brigade who "cursed swore and moaned" as they were repeatedly marched from the bottom of the ship to the top and then all round it. J. Stockman "Madagascar 1942", p.77. Testimony of F. Thomas.
76. R. Neillands, *The Raiders*, p.120; Crofte-Cooke, p.42.

Chapter 3: "Let's Risk Something"

1. Testimony of Sergeant Clegg, *The Royal Hussars Journal*, pp.155–6.
2. Sturges' Report, *Supplement to The London Gazette*, 4 March 1948, p.1608.
3. R. Manners, *My War Years*, May 1941–Mar 1942.
4. Jervois, p.99; D. Helm, memoir; J. Stockman, "Madagascar 1942", *British Army Review* No.82, p76–7.
5. Turner, Gordon-Cummings & Betzler, pp.115–6.
6. Simpson, *The Somerville Papers*, p.355; Kimball, *Churchill & Roosevelt*, pp.452–3.
7. L.C.F. Turner, *War in the Southern Oceans*, p.117.
8. TNA ADM 223/550, Naval Cypher 1639B 13/4/42; M. Howard, *British Intelligence in the Second World War, Volume Five*, p.24. None of the personal narratives examined in the compilation of this work make any reference to the changed cover story.
9. *Battle Summaries* No.16, p.33.
10. Churchill, *Hinge of Fate*, p.205.
11. TNA CAB 121/623 Telegram No.1730B to the Senior Office Force F 29/4/42.
12. B. Mullaly, *Regimental History of the South Lancashire Regiment*, p.381.
13. *War Illustrated*, vol.10, No.232, p.31. Those responsible for "strategic deception" under Colonel Oliver Stanley's Future Operational Planning Section did such a good job with Operation *Ironclad* that no two accounts agree on the exact nature, or timing, of the various leaks, rumours and cover stories that were circulated. One officer stated that the cover story he had been given, and which he was told to "refer to" was that the convoy's next port of call was Mombasa, H. Emerton, *Unfeignedly Thankful*, p.14.
14. *Battle Summaries* No.16, p.34; S. Woodburn Kirby, *History of the Second World War*, vol. 2, p.134–5.
15. Kennett & Tatman, p.114.
16. *Battle Summaries* No.16, p.32.
17. Testimony of Sergeant Arthur Lowe of the Royal Engineers Postal Service; Aston Papers, *Field Security Orders*.
18. A. Annet, *Aux heures troublées de l'Afrique française*, p.121.
19. TNA HS 3/21, DZ report No.92 of 20/4/42.
20. Report of General Sturges, *The London Gazette*, 4 March 1948, pp.1607–8. AIR 23/6587, Narrative of South African Air Force Operations in Madagascar, pp.3–6.
21. Report of R.W. Roberts, Acting Commodore, SS *Oronsay*, CAB 106/749; Jervois, p.99; The final decision to proceed with *Ironclad* was not taken until 24 April and Syfret was not informed until 1 May. If the operation had to be cancelled the Chiefs of Staff decided that the 29th Brigade would be held at Mombasa, pending re-deployment elsewhere, and the naval force would assemble at Ile des Roches in the Seychelles, TNA CAB 121/623 JP (42) 322. In 121 Force Operational Order No.1, Antsirane was code-named Arbroath, Diego Suarez North was Berwick, Andrakaka was Kintyre, Mangorky was Montrose and so on.
22. Croft-Cooke, pp.236–7; The decision not to include the US leaflets and to burn them can be found in TNA CAB 121/623 JP (42) 374. Various versions of the leaflets, and their translation, are in CAB 120/209A, B, C & D.
23. TNA CAB 81/107 JIC (42) 140 (0) *French Reactions to Operation "Ironclad"*.
24. TNA CAB 121/623, JP (42) 435, Annex 1.
25. Woodward, p.326.
26. D. Dilkes, *The Diaries of Sir Alexander Cadogan*, p.449.

27. The PWE originally recommended that 5,000,000 leaflets should be dropped in Unoccupied France and 2,000,000 on "defined urban targets" in Occupied France, D. Garnett, *Political Warfare Activities*, pp.212–13.

28. A. Bryant, *The Turn of the Tide*, pp.365–6.

29. Danchev & Todman, pp.252 & 254–5.

30. Woodward, p.296.

31. Churchill, *Hinge of Fate*, p.197.

32. TNA CAB 81/107, JIC (42)152, *Enemy Intentions*.

33. Harvey diaries, p.125.

34. TNA CAB 121/623, COS (42) 134th (5) & JP (42) 452; TNA AIR 8/1135; the counter-measures against possible French retaliation were forwarded to the COS by the Chief of the Air Staff and they were: a) The mining of the ports of Toulon and Marseilles; b) Retaliatory bombing of French towns, including Vichy; c) Attacks against French naval units in ports; d) Reconnaissance of French naval bases, TNA COS (42) 123 (0); *Roosevelt's Correspondence* Churchill to Roosevelt (NLR-MR-FDRWSC-1942–17B).

35. Kimball, *Churchill & Roosevelt*, p.477; Woodward, p.327.

36. Cited in C. Williams, *The Last Great Frenchman*, p.178.

37. TNA CAB 102/650, W. Mackenzie, *History of the Special Operations Executive*, vol.II, pp.498–9.

38. SOE Reports to the Cabinet HQ file 50, *An Account of S.O.E. Operations in Madagascar*.

39. E. Harrison, "British Subversion in French East Africa", p.340; Maerten had commanded the supercruiser *Mogador*, P.Auphan, *French Navy in World War II*, p.133; Annet, p.94.

40. E. Harrison, pp.345–6.

41. There were DZs up to the number 67 and other named individuals, TNA HS 3/23. The Anglican Bishop at Tananarive, the Right Reverend Gerald Vernon, was able to move around the country without arousing suspicion. His presence at both Diego Suarez and Majunga at the same time as the British landings, however, led the French to suspect that, as Vernon himself put it, he was "part of the plot". Later, he was to acknowledge that "no French official could believe that I was anything but a paid agent of the British Government", Fisher Papers, Vol.73, ff.342 & 348. There was a surprisingly large Anglican population of 23,054 in 1941, the result, no doubt, of the activities of the missionaries of the 18th and early 19th centuries. There were, however, only three English clergymen, the rest were natives, *Crockford's Clerical Directory, 1941*, pp.2025–5.

42. TNA HS 3/23, Report of DZ6. H. Legg, *The Turn of the Tide*, pp.8–9.

43. TNA HS 3/23, HQ Report, SOE Durban.

44. Legg, pp.8–9.

45. Report of DZ6, TNA HS 3/23.

46. TNA CAB 106/749, Report by Captain Roberts, Master, S.S. *Oransay*. The official history of the Royal Scots Fusiliers states that the troops were informed of their destination "as soon as the ships had left the quay", J. Kemp, p.65.

47. The slow convoy was designated Convoy "Y" and it consisted of *Empire Kingsley, Bachaquero, Easedale, Derwentdale, Martand, Mahout, Nairnbank* and *Thalatta*, escorted by *Devonshire, Active, Duncan, Freesia, Fritillary, Thyme, Jasmine, Cromer, Poole, Auricula, Nigella, Romney* and *Cromarty*. *City of Hong Kong*, which had not arrived in time, followed the next day, escorted by *Gemista* and *Cyclamen*. The fast convoy, "Z", consisted of the *Oronsay, Keren, Karanja, Royal Ulsterman, Winchester Castle, Sobieski, Duchess of Atholl* and *Franconia*, whilst the destroyers were *Lightning, Lookout, Javelin* and *Inconstant*. *Battle Summaries*, p.37.

48. TNA ADM 203/60, Butler, *Operation* Ironclad, A Lecture, p.2.
49. Bryant, *Turn of the Tide*, p.366.
50. TNA HS3/21; Churchill, *Hinge of Fate*, p.205.

Chapter 4: "Ironclad Begun"
1. Pépin-Lehalleur, "Ironclad", *Historia magazine*, No.39, p.1085; *Crockford's Clerical Directory, 1941*, p.2024; J. Hammerton, *The Second Great War*, vol.6, p.2239; TNA CAB 121/622, JP (41) 1070; Penrith, J & D, *Madagascar*, pp.18–22; Bradt, *Madagascar*, p.287.
2. Bradt; TNA WO 208/1519, IS(0) Intelligence Notes, Madagascar, 22 February 1942.
3. TNA HS 3/21, *Information required by Force Commander from Todd Mission*, Report no.80 of 31/12041.
4. H. Darrieus & J. Quéguiner, *Historique de la Marine francaise*, p.283; Lord Rennell of Rodd, *British Military Administration of Occupied Territories in Africa*, p.210; Y. Buffetout, "Opération Ironclad", *Marines & Forces navales*, No.66, p.55; The Senegalese arrived on the auxiliary cruiser *Bougainville*, Aston Papers, *Report on Interrogation of German and Italian Prisoners*.
5. *Etude sur la Défense de Madagascar*, S.H.A.T. 1 P 34 – dossier 6.
6. Shores, p.277. C. J. Ehrengardt & C. Shores, *L'aviation de Vichy au Combat, les Campagnes Oubliées*, vol.1; M. Thomas, *The Historical Journal*, p.1053; S.H.A.T. 8 H 82 – dossier 4, pp.1–4.
7. S.H.A.T. 8H 85 d2.
8. Buckley, p.169.
9. *Operation Bonus: Appreciation & Outline Plan*, TNA CAB 121/622, JP (41) 1070.
10. TNA HS 3/21, *Information required by Force Commander*, Report no.70 of 24/3/42; A. Jones, *No Easy Choices*, p.189. S.H.A.T. 8H 105 d 1, *Bataille de Diégo-Suarez*.
11. S.H.M. TTD 772.
12. TNA WO 208/1519; J. Kemp, p.91; TNA CAB 121/622, JP (41) 1043 & 1070: S.H.A.T. 8H 105 d 1.
13. H. Darrieus & J. Quéguiner, p.283; J. Williams, *The Guns of Dakar*, pp.153–4. The auxilliary cruiser *Bougainville* was a converted banana ship, P. Auphan, *The French Navy in World War II*, p.205; TNA HS 3/21.
14. TNA HS 3/21, *Information required by Force Commander*, Report no. 78 of 30/12/41 and no.61 of 17/8/42. The Italian freighter was the M.V. *Duca Degli Abruzzi* and the passenger ship was the M.V. *Somalia*. It seems that the German and Italian crews generally remained on board their ships as contact with the French in Diego Suarez sometimes led to "incidents", Annet, pp.127–8. The two Greek ships were the *Yanis* and the *Yenoje*, Annet, p.128; see also Pépin-Lehalleur, *Historia* magazine, p.1090.
15. There is also evidence that the Governor-General received orders to "accept" the presence of Japanese submarines but to resist any British force, R. Paxton, *Vichy France*, p.313.
16. Harrison, p.353.
17. TNA CAB 121/622, Prime Minister's personal memo serial no. D.75/2 169A.
18. *Battle Summaries* No.16, pp.34–5.
19. TNA ADM 202/397, *121 Force Operational Instruction No. 2*, 23 April 1942.
20. TNA ADM 202/395, *Orders for Diversionary Operation off Ambodi-Vahibe*.
21. TNA ADM 202/397, *121 Force Operational Instruction No.3*; TNA WO 106/3611, "*Notes from Theatres of War: No.9 Madagascar, May 1942*"; TNA HS 3/23.
22. TNA CAB 121/622, JP (41) 1070.
23. Festing's Report in TNA ADM 199/937.

24. 1, 2 & 3 Troops of No.5 Commando were to land at Red Beach North and 4, 5 and 6 Troops were to take Red Beach South, TNA DEFE 2/319, p.535.
25. TNA ADM 203/60, G. Butler, *Operation* Ironclad, A Lecture.
26. Buckley, p.171; Woodburn Kirby, p.137. TNA ADM 202/397, *Operation* Ironclad *121 Force Operations Order No.1*. C. Durtnell, *The Fifth Division*, p.63. Because it was necessary to land all the 17th and 29th Brigades, equipment and transport before any elements of the 13th Brigade could be disembarked, this last brigade would not be available to participate in the operation until day seventeen, TNA CAB 121/622 COS (42) 92nd (11).
27. TNA COS (W) 166; J.Stockman, *"Madagascar 1942"*, Part 2, p.65; J. Kemp, p.65. TNA WO 174/30, *Account of Activities of 'C' Company 2nd Btn. East Lancs. during Operation Ironclad*, p.2.
28. Pendlebury, p.242.
29. C. Buckley, p.171; TNA CAB 121/623, COS (42) 34th Mtg. (0).
30. Croft-Cooke, pp.13, 19, 54–5.
31. TNA ADM 202/397, *121 Force Operational Instructions*.
32. Garnett, *Political Warfare*, p.215.
33. TNA ADM 202/395, *Operation "Ironclad" Air Operation Order No.1*.
34. TNA ADM 202/395.
35. Kimball, *Churchill & Roosevelt*, p.481; TNA ADM 202/395 *Operation "Ironclad" Communications Orders*; A number of Force F's own aircraft were also held in readiness in case of a Japanese attack, *Naval Staff History, vol. III*, p.2; as it transpired, the only "interference" from the Japanese was from a Kawanishi H6K *"Mavis"* flying boat, which flew a reconnaissance patrol from its base in the Andaman Islands, Shores, pp.278–9; L. Woodward, *British Foreign* Policy, vol.II, p.286; *Battle Summaries* No.16, p.37.
36. TNA ADM 223/550 Naval Cypher 1617B 20/4/42; despite these precautions, Sommerville doubted that his reconnaissance aircraft would have been able to detect the Japanese if they did attempt to intervene, A. Marder, *Old Friends New Enemies*, p.156.
37. Tute, p.203.
38. *Battle Summaries* No.16, p.39.
39. TNA CAB 106/749, *Report by Captain R.W. Roberts*.
40. According to the letter recommending the captain of *Lindi*, Lieutenant A.G. Booker, for an award, if the error in the charts had remained unnoticed it "might have led to the most serious consequences", TNA ADM 14315.
41. Legg, pp.22–3.
42. TNA CAB 120/220, Admiralty message No.1958B to S.O. Force F.
43. *Battle Summaries* No.16, Plan 5.
44. TNA ADM 223/550, Naval Cypher 17429/4.
45. H. Emerton, *Unfeignedly Thankful*, p.15.
46. TNA HS 3/23, Report of DZ5.
47. The error by the landing craft heading for Red Beach South caused 4, 5 & 6 Troops to be forty minutes late reaching their objective, and one of the LCAs had to be abandoned; TNA DEFE 2/319, *Operations in Madagascar 20th March to 20th October 1942 No.5 Commando*, pp.535–6.
48. Jervois, p.99; Roskill, p.189; *Battle Summaries* No.16, pp.39–40.
49. R. Neillands, *The Raiders*, pp.120–1; *The Daily Telegraph*, 25 May 1942. Captured French orders stated: "Tir de nuit n'est pas envisagé, l'accès de la Baie étant considéré comme impossible de nuit", TNA ADM 203/60, G. Butler, *Operation* Ironclad.
50. TNA HS 3/23, Report from DZ5, p.1; W. Knight, *Memories*, p.32; Legg, p.24.

51. *War Illustrated*, vol.10, No.232, p.31; TNA DEFE 2/319, p.535.

52. Buckley, p.175.

53. TNA DEFE 2/319, *Operations in Madagascar*, p.536.

54. The men with automatic weapons were carrying Thompson submachine guns, TNA DEFE 2/319, p.536. By this stage, a total of 23 Europeans and 200 natives had been made prisoner, Buckley, p.175.

55. J. Kemp, p.73.

56. Buckley, p.176; TNA ADM 202/395, *Operation "Ironclad" Orders for Diversionary Operations off Ambodi-Vahibe*.

57. *Naval Staff History*, p.4; S.H.A.T. 8 H 82 – dossier 4, *Opérations de Diégo-Suarez*, p.6.

58. *Battle Summaries* No.16, p.41.

59. HMSO, *Fleet Air Arm*, p.114.

60. R. Sturtivant, *The Swordfish Story*, p.117; Annet, p.127; *Diary of Jean Hanlon*, TNA ADM 199/937. It is possible that some of the torpedoes may have struck the sloop but failed to explode, TNA ADM 207/11, War Diary of 810 Squadron.

61. Darrieus and Quéguiner, p.283. HMSO *Fleet Air Arm*, p.114; Sturtivant, p.117.

62. Y. Buffetout, "Opération Ironclad" *Marines & Forces navales*, No.66, pp.54–55; Annet, p.129.

63. S.H.A.T. 2P 12 D5.

64. Buckley, p.176.

65. Sturtivant, pp.117 & 120.

66. Annet, p.129; Syfret's Report in TNA HS 3/23.

67. TNA ADM 207/37, War Diary of No.880 Squadron.

68. Shores, p.279.

69. The telephone line from Windsor Castle passed through the Ciseaux Battery and when the Windsor Castle guard tried to telephone Antsirane it was a British voice that answered! *Diary of Jean Hanlon*, TNA ADM 199/937.

70. The Swordfish were supposed to have two Martlets with them to provide fighter protection but the Swordfish arrived over the target too late, and the Martlets had return to their carrier, Sturtivant, p.117.

71. *Hermione* was later replaced by the more heavily armed *Devonshire*, J. Moulins, "Diego-Suarez, 5–8 mai, 1942, Operation Ironclad", *Magazine 39–45*, No.214, p.20.

72. S.H.A.T 8 H 82 – dossier 4, p.9; TNA ADM 202/363; *Diary of Jean Hanlon*.

73. *The Daily Telegraph*, Tuesday, 19 May 1942.

74. *The London Gazette*, 4 March 1948, p.1611.

75. TNA WO 174/30, Account of Activities of 'D' Company 2nd Btn., E. Lancs., during Operation Ironclad, p.1.

76. The words are those of Lieutenant-Commander A.H. Ballard, who was Joint Principal Beach Master, *War Illustrated*, vol.10, No.232, p.31.

77. Pendlebury, p.242.

78. Buckley, p.176; War Diary 'C' Company 2nd East Lancs., TNA WO 170/30.

79. Approximately thirty-five of the mines were found by the minesweepers in the operation, TNA ADM 203/60, G. Butler, *Operation* Ironclad.

80. B. Macdermott, *Ships Without Names*, p.18.

81. Supplement to *The London Gazette* 4 March 1948, p.1600; W. Knight, *Memories*, p.34; *Battle Summaries* No.16, Appendix G.

82. Shores, p.280; TNA ADM 207/11.; *Diary of Jean Hanlon*, TNA ADM 199/937.

83. *Notes from Theatre of War*, vol. III, p.31.
84. Macdermott, p.18.
85. *Ibid*, p.19.

Chapter 5: "The Crack of the Shells"

1. J. Kemp, p.68.
2. Testimony of Corporal E. Butterfield, TNA ADM 202/307.
3. J. Kemp, p.69; *The London Gazette* 4 March 1948, p.1610.
4. *Combined Operations*, p.101; J. Kemp, p.69.
5. Croft-Cooke, p.23.
6. P. Kemp, *The Red Dragon, The Story of the Royal Welch Fusiliers*, p.103; Croft-Cooke, pp.23–4.
7. See Appendix IV; Buckley, p.171.
8. J. Kemp, p.70. Y. Buffetout, "Opération Ironclad", p.55; *Historia* magazine, p.1090.
9. Sturges also later questioned the wisdom of the diversionary attack by the *Hermione*. The landing at Courrier Bay had been so successful that the French at Antsirane may have been taken completely by surprise, but the bombardment by *Hermione* put the entire garrison on the alert, *The London Gazette*, 2 March 1948, p.1610.
10. Moulins, *Magazine 39–45*, No.214, p.20.
11. *Historia* magazine.
12. Buckley, p.178.
13. *The London Gazette* 4 March 1948, p.1611.
14. Croft-Cooke, p.25.
15. J. Bright, *The 9th Queen's Royal Lancers*, p.340; Emerton, *Unfeignedly Thankful*, p.17.
16. P. Kemp, *Red Dragon*, p.103.
17. *Battle Summaries* No.16, p.42.
18. Mullaly, p.382.
19. TNA WO 174/24, Appendix A to War Diary, 455th Independent Light Battery R.A.
20. Moulins, p.21; TNA CAB 106/674, Report of Clarebout, Maerten, Rous and Bache.
21. *The London Gazette*, 4 March 1948, p.1611; TNA WO 174/24, War Diary, 1st Btn. RSF, Sheet 2.
22. *Notes from Theatres of War*, No.9, p.31.
23. D. Fletcher, "The Flying Tank", *Military Illustrated*, September 1996, pp.21–4.
24. *The Royal Hussars Journal*, p.158; J. Bright, p.340.
25. Sgt. Grimes was awarded the DCM, TNA WO 373/29 3596.
26. Report of Captain R.D. Oliver, *The London Gazette*, 4 March 1948, p.1597; Shores, pp.279–80; Annet, p.130, claimed in his memoirs that he ordered General Guillemet to send all available aircraft against the attackers but that the instruction was misunderstood.
27. J. Kemp, p.70.
28. *The Royal Hussars Journal*, p.159. Clegg was actually a member of the 11th Hussars though he was serving with the 10th Hussars in the Special Service Squadron.
29. *The Royal Hussars Journal*, pp.159–60.
30. Testimony of E. Butterfield Signals Platoon HQ Company, 1st Btn RSF.
31. TNA WO 373/29 *Honours & Awards* No. 3589.
32. R. Manners, *My War Years*, May 1942.
33. Mullaly, pp.382–3.
34. Testimony of B. Grehan; TNA CAB 106/674, p.30.

35. *Notes from Theatres of War*, No.9, p.37. There is evidence that the confusion was so great that units of the 29th Brigade fired upon each other. According to the Account of the Activities of 'C' Company 2nd Btn. East Lancs, p.4, one of its platoons was shot at during the night from a nearby wood. In the morning it was found that the wood was occupied by a stray section of the RSF.
36. J. Kemp, p.72.
37. Buckley, p.178.
38. *The Royal Hussars Journal*, p.159.
39. Legg, p.32.
40. J.H. Patterson memoir.
41. P. Kemp, *Red Dragon*, p.105; In TNA WO 208/1519, Fort Caimans – the principle fieldwork was described as, "A permanent work with five concrete faces, the top of the work being 16 feet above the interior. A spiked railing 12 feet high runs round the rear of the work ... There are emplacements for two guns."
42. *Combined Operations*, p.101; Annet, p.129; S.H.A.T. 8H 105 d1. Despite the evident strength of the G-H Line one of the defenders described the trenches as being "too narrow, and not deep enough, without a firestep and without communication trenches", *Diary of Jean Hanlon*, TNA ADM 199/137.
43. *The Royal Hussars Journal*, p.158; Corporal Butterfield of the RSF stated that one of the 75mm guns near the road was on rails, Testimony of E. Butterfield; J.Kemp, p.74; Durtell, p.64.
44. *The London Gazette*, 4 March 1948, p.1613.
45. Emerton, p.18.
46. *The London Gazette*, 4 March 1948, p.1611–12.
47. J. Stockman, *Seaforth Highlanders 1939–45*, p.87.
48. *The London Gazette*, 4 March 1948, p.1612.
49. TNA ADM 203/60, G. Butler, *Operation* Ironclad, A Lecture; Stockman, "Madagascar 1942", p.69.
50. J. Kemp, p.74.

Chapter 6: "Savage Hearts"

1. Pendlebury, p.244.
2. P. Kemp, *Red Dragon*, p.104; J. Kemp, pp.75–6.
3. War Diary, 9th Field Regiment TNA WO 174/19; War Diary 455th Light Battery, TNA WO 174/24.
4. *The London Gazette*, 4 March 1948, p.1614; Buckley, p.179.
5. Quoted in A. Banks, *The Wings of the Dawning*, p.71.
6. Buckley, p.176; HMSO *Fleet Air Arm*, p.114; *Battle Summaries* No.16, Appendix G; Annet, p.127.
7. DEFE 2/319, p.536; TNA HS 3/23, Report from DZ5, p.2 (this agent accompanied No.5 Commando throughout the entire operation, acting as a guide and translator); Report of *Capitaine* Simon, S.H.M. TTD 772.
8. Pendlebury, p.244.
9. Mulally, p.383.
10. Mulally, pp.383–4; TNA WO 373/29, Honours and Awards, 3599.
11. Mulally, p.384.
12. A number of different reasons have been given for the breakdown in wireless communication. In the Chiefs of the General Staff report, *Notes from Theatres of War*, No.9, p.32, it is stated

that the problem was caused because of the difficult nature of the ground, which did not permit a serviceable wireless set to be carried.

13. *Daily Mail*, 19 May 1942.
14. TNA ADM 207/37, Diary of No.880 Squadron.
15. Sturtivant, *The Swordfish Story*, p.118.
16. Pépin-Lehalleur, p.1091.
17. Pépin-Lehalleur, p.1090.
18. J. Kemp, p.77; TNA WO 174/30, Account of the Activities of 'D' Company, 2nd East Lancs during Operation *Ironclad*, p.2.
19. Stockman, *Seaforth Highlanders*, p.95.
20. TNA WO 174/30, Account of the Activities of 'B' Company, 2nd East Lancashire Regiment; J. Pendlebury, p.244.
21. Ward received the MM, TNA WO 373/29 3605.
22. J. Kemp, pp.78–80. The French officer was Lieutenant Bande of the *2me RMM*.
23. Mulally, p.385; Sturges' Report, *The London Gazette*, 2 March 1948, p.1613; War Diary 2nd Btn. South Lancs., TNA WO 174/31.
24. C. Buckley, pp.182–3; War Diary 2nd Btn. South Lancs.
25. HMSO, *Combined Operations*, p.102.
26. Brandon was recommended for the MC but his actions were considered to be "not up to standard", TNA WO 373/29 3587.
27. Buckley, p.183. TNA WO 174/24. Appendix 'A' to War Diary, 455th Independent Light Battery R.A.
28. In his lecture *Operation* Ironclad, G. Butler stated that the French actually did mount a counter-attack; P. Kemp, *Red Dragon*, p.105.
29. Letter to Mountbatten, 6 May 1942, quoted in P. Warner and S. Seno, *The Coffin Boats*, p.141.
30. The *Evening Standard*, London, 7 May 1942.
31. R. Overy, in *Why the Allies Won*, p.135, states that the ships had "almost run out of fuel and water by 7 May"; Report of General Sturges, *The London Gazette*, 2 March, 1948, p.1613.
32. Hammerton, p.2240; Grafftey-Smith, p.53.
33. S. Clark, *The Man who is France*, p.155; L. Woodward, p.364.
34. J. Kemp, p.80. A poster from the *Administrateur-Marie* of Diego-Suarez ordering the call-up of the reservists can be found in the Royal Welch Fusiliers Museum.
35. TNA CAB 121/623, 321B, memo from Eden to Churchill, 18 May 1942.
36. Sturges' Report, *The London Gazette*, 4 March 1948, p.1611.
37. TNA HS 3/21; *Notes from Theatres of War*, p.32.
38. *The Daily Mail*, 19 May 1942.
39. HMSO *Fleet Air Arm*, p.114.
40. TNA WO 174/30, Account of the Activities of 'C' Company, 2nd East Lancs during Operation *Ironclad*, p.4.
41. J. Kemp, p.81.
42. TNA WO 174/30, Account of the Activities of 'B' Company, 2nd East Lancs during Operation *Ironclad*.
43. J. Kemp, p.81.
44. War Diary, 1st Btn. RSF, TNA WO 174/24; Sturges' report, p.1611.
45. *Battle Summaries* No.16, p.46.
46. Buckley, p.182; *The Royal Marines*, pp.50–1 & 55; Sturges' Report, p.1614; Syfret's Report, TNA HS 3/23.

47. Syfret's Report, *ibid.*
48. *Battle Summaries* No.16; J. Ladd, *By Land, By Sea*, p.108. *The Times*, 16 May 1942.
49. No.881 Squadron Diary, entry for 6 May 1942.
50. The official report recorded that the Commandos had been able to find only one rowing boat at Diego Suarez and it was considered impractical to attempt the crossing, TNA DEFE 2/319, p.536. By contrast. Captain J.H. Patterson refers to the official view in his unpublished memoirs but states that he and his fellow officers "knew better".
51. *The Royal Marines*, pp.52–3.
52. Ladd, *ibid.*
53. According to Powell, Mayer said that his nom de guerre, or code-name, was "Casson". TNA ADM 202/363.
54. *Notes from Theatres of War*, No. 9, p.33; *War Illustrated*, vol.5, No.130.
55. *Combined Operations*, p.103; TNA ADM 202/363, Report of General Sturges.
56. R. Morton, *Memoirs*, p.9.
57. Durtnell, p.65.
58. Jervois, p.102.
59. Jervois, pp.102–3.
60. Buckley, p.185.
61. In fact only two French guns had been disabled by the British bombardment, P. Moulins, *Magazine 39–45*, No.214, p.23.
62. Morton, p.10.
63. *Notes from Theatres of War*, No. 9, p.33; J. Kemp, pp.85–6; Sgt. O.R. Jones was awarded the DCM, P. Kemp, *Red Dragon*, p.106; Jervois, pp.104–5; TNA WO 373/29 3598.
64. Stockman, *Seaforth Highlanders*, p.92.
65. Stockman, "Madagascar 1942", pp.69–71. The official accounts by Buckley, p.185 and HMSO *Combined Operations*, p.103, give the false impression that the 17th Brigade passed through the French defences without opposition.
66. Stockman, *Seaforth Highlanders*, pp.94–99.
67. J. Kemp, pp.86–7.
68. Mulally, p.386.
69. Croft-Cooke, pp.44–6.
70. War Diary for 6 May 1942, 9th Field Regiment, TNA WO 174/10; Roskill, p.185.
71. Syfret's Report, TNA HS 3/23.
72. *The London Gazette*, 4 March 1948, p.1615.
73. Jervois, p.106.
74. *Battle Summaries* No.16, Appendix E and G.
75. TNA CAB 106/674, Appendix B; Syfret was also promoted to Acting Vice-Admiral, Hammerton, p.2239.
76. French casualty figures were approximately 150 killed and 500 wounded, Buckley, p.187. The medal for which most of the French combatants received recommendations was the Colonial Medal with the inscription "Déigo-Suarez", S.H.M. TTD 772; J. Moulins, *Magazine 39–45*, No.214, p.26.
77. Churchill, *Hinge of Fate*, p.208.

Chapter 7: "End of an Era"

1. TNA ADM 203/60, G. Butler, *Operation* Ironclad.
2. Stockman "Madagascar 1942" Part 1, p.78; Others felt the same. D. Helm, a Despatch Rider with the 2nd Btn. RSF, wrote in his memoir: "As they marched in what seemed

a never ending line we stood in awe at what we would have had to face." It is interesting to note that, though the British combatants frequently referred to the black troops they encountered as Senegalese, they constituted only a small part of the garrison. This is revealed in the list of prisoners, in which the Senegalese numbered just 266 whereas the Malagasy troops captured exceeded 3,000, S.H.A.T. 8H 105 d1.

3. Croft-Cooke, p.56; J. Sym, *Seaforth Highlanders*, p.245.
4. The wounded arrived at Durban on 19 May, *The Times*, 19 May 1942.
5. TNA CAB 121/623, p.38, Telegram No.2355C; S.H.A.T. 8H 105 d1.
6. TNA HS 3/23, Commanding Officer's Report, p.10.
7. P. Kemp, *Red Dragon*, p.107; Croft-Cooke, pp.46, 54 & 64; L. Grafftey-Smith, *Hands to Play*, p.35.
8. Croft-Cooke, pp.47 & 54–124.
9. Croft-Cooke, pp.44–6.
10. TNA WO 208/1519, IS (0) Intelligence Notes Madagascar. At Daker were two battleships, four 6-inch cruisers, six large destroyers, four other destroyers and twenty-one submarines.
11. *Historia* magazine, p.1091. The cargo ship was diverted to the Comoros Islands.
12. Alexander later received the DSC, Sturtivant, *The Swordfish Story*, pp.118–9.
13. *The London Gazette*, 4 March 1948, pp.1593 & 1604.
14. Tute, *Reluctant Enemies*, pp.205–6; Darrieus & Quéguiner, pp.282–3; Annet, p.127.
15. The Martlets' section leader was missing for two days and believed lost. He had, however, swam ashore and had been taken on board another ship, HMSO, *Fleet Air Arm*, pp.114–5; Shores, pp.281–2.
16. Shores, pp.278–9; as it transpired a severe gale in the Indian Ocean had prevented Somerville's planes from flying any reconnaissance patrols during the period of the battle, Squadron Diary of No.888 Squadron, May 1942.
17. TNA CAB 80/65 COS (42) 329 & 331. In WO 208/1519 the Intelligence report did not consider it likely that the Japanese would mount a full-scale combined operation against Diego Suarez as long as the Eastern Fleet remained in being. What was thought more probable was a "tip and run" raid with a maximum attacking force of four cruisers and an aircraft carrier, possibly supported by submarines.
18. Turner, Gordon-Cummings & Betzler, pp.141–2.
19. J. Kemp, p.91.
20. TNA HS 3/23, Commanding Officer's Report, p.12.
21. The REME Force Ordnance Workshop consisted of fifty all ranks with just one machinery lorry, two store trucks and a 30 cwt breakdown truck, but they were able to use the heavy tools in the French arsenal. B. Kennett & J. Tatman, *Craftsmen of the Army*, pp.114–15. See also TNA HS 3/23, Commanding Officer's Report, p.12.
22. Simpson & Somerville, pp.418–20; *Naval Staff History*, vol.3, p.5.
23. M. Page, *History of the King's African Rifles*, pp.130–1; TNA HS 3/23.
24. TNA ADM 223/551, Naval Cypher No.0438C/11 May.
25. Croft-Cooke, p.41.
26. S. Rigge, *World War II: War in the Outposts*, p.102.
27. Croft-Cooke, p.53; TNA CAB 121/623, Telegram No.2317C.
28. Grafftey-Smith, p.36.
29. *Evening Standard*, London 5 May 1942.
30. Inevitably, Tokyo declared that they never had any designs upon Madagascar, Hammerton, *The Second Great War*, vol.6, p.2240.
31. *The Daily Telegraph*, 8 May 1942.

32. *The Times*, 6 May 1942.
33. *Evening Standard*, London, 5 May 1942.
34. S. Clark, *The Man who is France*, p.155.
35. De Gaulle, pp.344–8.
36. James, *Churchill's Speeches*, vol. VI, p.6628
37. The full text of the statement can be found in Hammerton, p.2240.
38. James, p.6633–4.
39. De Gaulle, pp.242–3; Williams, p.179; Woodward, p.329.
40. De Gaulle, pp.242–3.
41. *ibid.*
42. De Gaulle told General Leclerc in Brazzaville that the forces he would be required to send to Diego Suarez were likely to be: One HQ Staff; three battalions of light infantry (tirailleurs); one tank company; one artillery battery; one transport company; and support services, De Gaulle, pp.348–9.
43. Simpson & Somerville, p.420.
44. Danchev & Todman, pp.258, 261–63 & 278.
45. Letter to Beirut, Brazzaville and Noumea, De Gaulle, pp.353–4; F. Kersaudy, *Churchill and De Gaulle*, p.187.
46. TNA PREM 3/120/7, 11 April & 30 May 1942.
47. Jackson, pp.55–6.
48. TNA ADM 203/60, G. Butler, *Operation* Ironclad.
49. TNA CAB 106/674, An account of Operation 'Ironclad', p.18.
50. *Battle Summaries* No.16, pp.53–4; Macdermott, *Ships Without Names*, p.19.
51. D. Lee, *Beachead Assault*, pp.39–40.
52. TNA HS 3/23.
53. Kennett & Tatman, p.115.
54. Moulins, *Magazine 39–45*, No.214, p.19.

Chapter 8: "Shabby Deal-Making"

1. Churchill, *Hinge of Fate*, pp.208–9.
2. TNA CAB 121/622 COS (42) 69 (O), 18 May 1942; TNA CAB 121/624 *Situation in Madagascar May–June 1942*; Syfret's original instructions had actually requested him to seek a *causa belli* with the local French authorities. The admiral had requested verification of this, which resulted in his instructions being amended to read *modus vivendi* instead. When the staff officer in London responsible for the error was asked for an explanation, he replied: "Why the hell should I be expected to know French?" Quoted in Kersaudy, p.185.
3. *The Pioneer*, No.1, Wednesday 20 May, 1942.
4. Buckley, p.188.
5. Syfret's Report in TNA HS 3/23.
6. TNA AIR 23/6587.
7. Shores, p.285; R. Nesbit, "The Majunga Raid" *Aeroplane Monthly*, March 1995, p.43; W. Platt, "Operations of East Africa Command 12th July, 1941 to 8th January, 1943"; *The London Gazette*, 17 July 1946, pp.3719. Code-named *Operation Sugarcane*, it had been arranged that the South African aircraft would return to Cape Town and Durban as soon as the Lysanders were operational. But the failure to reach a *modus vivendi* with Annet meant that further operations were likely and the South African Wing remained in Madagascar until the end of hostilities, TNA AIR 23/6587, pp.8–9.
8. Grafftey-Smith, p.38; Annet, p.151.

9. M. Lush, *A Life of Service*, p.143.

10. M. Thomas, *The Historical Journal*, 39,4 (1996), p.1063.

11. J. Harvey, pp.124–5.

12. Grafftey-Smith, pp.69–70.

13. Dinan, *The Politics of Persuasion*, pp.224–5; Grafftey-Smith, pp.36–7.

14. J. Moulins, *Magazine 39–45*, No.214, p.24; Annet, p.144.

15. De Gaulle, p.245.

16. De Gaulle, pp.244–6.

17. M. Thomas, *The French Empire at War*, pp.146–7.

18. *Naval Staff History, Vol. III, War With Japan*, p.7.

19. Marder *et al*, *Old Friends New Enemies*, p.158; Legg, p.38.

20. Croft-Cooke, p.82.

21. Jervois, p.106.

22. Neillands, pp.120–1. The Commando patrol covered forty-three miles in seventeen hours to track down the two men. The Commandos remained at Cap Diego for three weeks after the French surrender before moving to Antsirane, TNA DEFE 2/319, *Operations in Madagascar*, p.538.

23. P. Kemp, *Underwater Warriors*, p.90; TNA ADM 199/3527, 2 June 1942.

24. The Japanese aircraft that was flown from *I-10* was a Yokosuka E14Y1 *Glen*. The wings and floats of this plane could be detached and the tail-plane and struts folded to allow the plane to be stored in a cylindrical hanger inside the submarine, Nesbit, p.44; On her return trip to Penang, I-30 struck a British mine off Singapore, Turner, Gordon-Cummings & Betzler, pp.139–40.

25. The supply ships which accompanied the submarine flotilla were the auxiliary cruisers *Hokoku Maru* and *Aikoku Maru*, Roskill, p.185; Marder, *Old Friends New Enemies*, p.160; Warner & Seno, p.134. Interestingly, the Admiralty only admitted to the inclusion of a battleship with Force F after *Ramillies* had been hit and its presence could no longer be kept a secret, Hammerton, pp.2239–40.

26. An anti-submarine net-laying craft was due to secure Diego Suarez harbour in August after laying nets at Kilindini and the Seychelles, Marder *et al*, *Old Friends New Enemies* p.59; A. Jones, *No Easy Choices*, p.192.

27. Nesbit, "The Majunga Raid", *Aeroplane Monthly*, March 1995, p.43; Kemp, *Underwater Warriors*, p.88.

28. Churchill, *Hinge of Fate*, p.210.

29. The oil from the *British Loyalty* was recovered by being pumped into the tanks of the MV *Derwentdale* which, despite having been modified to carry landing craft, was itself a tanker, *The Bulldozer*, No.9, Autumn 2003. The unfortunate *British Loyalty* was sunk a second time, in 1944, by a Japanese submarine in the Addu Attol lagoon, and once again it was salved and returned to service as a refuelling hulk, J. Rohwer, *Axis Submarine Success of WW2*.

30. M. Brown, p.258.

31. P. Kemp, *The Red Dragon*, p.107; W. Breldford, *The Story of the Northern Rhodesia Regiment*, p.87.

32. Nesbit, pp.45–6.

33. Buckley, p.188; UWH 126, 1698. Stockman also relates in *Seaforth Highlanders*, p.97, that even as far north as the Orangea Peninsular there was "sporadic resistance and sniping"; E. Nativel, "La `guérilla' des troupes vichystes à Madagascar", *Revue Historique des Armée*, No.210, p.56; Thomas *The Historical Journal*, 39, 4, p.1070.

34. Nativel, p.58.
35. Croft-Cooke, pp.42 and 125.
36. Lord Rennell of Rodd, *British Military Administration of Occupied Territories in Africa*, p.210.
37. Churchill, *Hinge of Fate*, p.208.
38. TNA CAB 121/623, p.40, Telegram No.2317C and p.37, Telegram No.812.
39. Gandar Dower, p.12.
40. For a detailed description of the Royal Navy's response to these attacks (which was accomplished by only three of the four submarines, as *I-18* had engine trouble) see *Naval Staff History, vol. III*, pp.7–11.
41. R. Osborne, *World War II in Colonial Africa*, p.238.
42. Grafftey-Smith, *Hands to Play*, p.32.
43. TNA HS 3/23 Commanding Officer's Report, p.12.
44. Buckley, pp.188–9; Page, p.117. The Seaforth Highlanders alone had more than 220 men suffering from "Madagascaritis", Stockman, *Seaforth Highlanders*, p.97.
45. Stockman, *Seaforth Highlanders*, p.98.
46. The Mk. III Marmon-Harrington was armed with two Vickers .303-inch machine guns, mounted front and rear. UWH vol.126, p.1698; A. Wessels, "South Africa and the War against Japan", p.8.
47. Platt, "Operations of East Africa Command", pp.3715–6; *Naval Staff History, vol. III*, p.9.
48. Page, p.118. Mamudzi is now known as Mamoudzou, J. & D. Penrith, p.163. The Commandos returned to Diego Suarez, but the company of 5 KAR remained as the island's garrison, TNA DEFE 2/319, *Operations in Madagascar*, pp.538–9.
49. Grafftey-Smith, p.39.
50. Lord Rennell of Rodd, pp.212–3.
51. TNA HS 3/22 Cipher Telegram from 121 Force to the War Office, 18.15 hours, 22 June 1942.
52. Smuts to Churchill 28 May and Eden to Churchill 29 May 1942, TNA PREM 3/265/6; TNA CAB 121/624, COS (42) 185th; J. Kemp, p.92.
53. *Naval Staff History, vol.III*, p.25; Simpson and Somerville, pp.418 and 427.
54. Woodburn Kirby, p.142; Danchev & Todman, p.285.
55. Grafftey-Smith, pp.48–9; Annet, pp.147–8 & 158.
56. Report by the Joint Planning Staff, 24 July 1942, TNA CAB 119/44; Nativel, p.52.
57. The troops personal weapons were Lebel 1915 pattern rifles, TNA WO 208/1519.
58. Grafftey-Smith, p.53.
59. In addition to the Beaufort lost on the Majunga raid another Beaufort of 37 Flight had gone down in French territory on 14 May. The crew survived, and were exchanged for captured French officers, Nesbit, p.44; Shores, p.288.
60. A. Banks, *Wings of the Dawning*, p.75.
61. Platt, "Operations of East Africa Command", pp.3716–7; *Naval Staff History*, vol.3, p.25; W. Dimoline, *Account of 22 E.A. Infantry Brigade*, p.1.
62. TNA CAB 121/623, Telegram from COS to SO Force F, 29 April 42.
63. TNA HS 3/23 HQ Report on Ironclad, p.9. SOE's Madagascar operation fell under the authority of the executive's East African Mission, whose headquarters were at Durban; TNA CAB 80/65 COS (42) 305 (0). Quite independently of Mayer's activities in Madagascar were those of France Antelme, who had used the *Lindi* to make a secret reconnaissance of Majunga in February. He had returned with a detailed report which indicated considerable effort was being undertaken to develop the airfield and to dig defensive trenches around

parts of the town. However, Antelme reported that at night there were no land patrols and just two armed native soldiers on guard in the port. There was every indication that, if the operation could be kept a secret, the landings at Majunga would be as easy and successful as those at Courrier Bay, "Report on my Raid in Majunga", 21 February 1942, in Antelme's Personal File SOE Records and Historical Department.

64. TNA HS 3/22 Progress Report No.7, pp.15–6 and Cipher No.0642, 29/06/42.
65. TNA DEFE 2/319, *Operations in Madagascar*, p.538; Shores, p.287.
66. Gandar Dower, p.38; Croft-Cooke, pp.83 and 111–12. These two accounts of the incident differ considerably; C. Shores, p.288.
67. The South African actions in support of *Stream-Line-Jane* were named Operation *Esmé*. The capture of Nosy Bé was *Esmé B*, WD 304 A4, 7th Infantry Brigade Instruction No.1; *Naval Staff History, vol. III*, p.27; A. Bintliff, *Nossi Bé*, pp.1–3.
68. Buckley, p.200.
69. Breldford, p.83; Page, p.119; Dimoline, p.1.
70. Osborne, p.244.
71. Platt, "Operations of East Africa Command", pp.3716–7.

Chapter 9: "Before the Last Battle"

1. Kennet and Tatman, pp.115–6; P. Kemp, *Red Dragon*, p.109; Gandar Dower, p.16.
2. *Union War History*, vol.126, 1699, Account of Sergeant Lawrie.
3. UWH 126, 1700.
4. *Naval Staff History, vol. III, War With Japan*, p.26; The Swordfish were from No.810 and No.829 Squadrons, in addition to twelve Martlets of No.881 Squadron and six Fulmars of No.806 Squadron, C. Shores, p.288.
5. P. Kemp, *The Red Dragon*, p.110.
6. J. Kemp, p.93. Modern maps show Datsepe as Katsepe.
7. Gandar Dower, p.23.
8. P. Kemp, *The Red Dragon*, pp.110–11.
9. Buckley, p.194; Gandar Dower, pp.27–9 and 34.
10. *Combined Operations*, p.104.
11. Neillands, p.126.
12. Gandar Dower, p.34; P. Kemp, *Red Dragon*, p.111.
13. UWH 126, 1701.
14. *Naval Staff History, vol. III*, p.26.
15. Croft-Cooke, pp.167–8; Grafftey-Smith, p.54.
16. Platt, "Operations of East Africa Command", p.3718; Lord Rennell of Rodd, pp.217–8.
17. Guillemet's full title was "*Commandant Supérieur des Troupes du Groupe de l'Afrique Orientale*", TNA WO 208/1519.
18. Aron, p.389.
19. Grafftey-Smith, pp.57–8; C. Messenger, *The Commandos*, p.137. See also C. Buckley, *Five Ventures*, p.194 and Platt "Operations of East Africa Command", p.3717. The operation was code-named *Tamper*, *Naval Staff History, vol. III*, p.27.
20. Considerable difficulty was experienced in landing all the motor transport for the 22nd Brigade, which was not fully achieved until 29 September. *Naval Staff History*, vol. III, p.27.
21. Platt "Operations of East Africa Command", p.3716.
22. SOE Cabinet Reports, HQ File 50, "The Operations in Madagascar".
23. Dimoline, p.9; UWH 126, 170; Page, pp.119–20.

24. Dimoline, p.10.
25. Page, pp.119–20; UWH 126, 1700–1.
26. Gandar Dower, p.37; Nativel, p.56.
27. Grafftey-Smith, p.57.
28. UWH 126, 1702.
29. Shores, p.298.
30. Annet to Secrétariat d'Etat aux Colonies, 28/9/42, S.H.A.T. 2P12 d5.
31. E. Nativel, p.54.
32. Gandar Dower, pp.41–2.
33. WD 307 E5-10, Account of A. Purvis, No.4 Troop, 'A' Squadron; 1st Armoured Car Commando; "Diary of events of part played by No.1 Fighting Group in the Operations *Stream-Line-Jane*", TNA WO 169/7020. The term 'askari' referred to East African native troops, regardless of either their nationality or for whom they were fighting.
34. WD (SAAF) Air 27 Box 30 (A2), pp.5–7; Shores, p.289.
35. UWH, 126, pp.1704–5 and 6.
36. Account of Sergeant Laurie, UWH, 126, p.1710; Navitel, p.56; Dimoline, p.16.
37. Corporal Smit of the Armoured Car Commando wrote that it was only the "rank bad fire" of the enemy that allowed the vehicles to escape unscathed from a very exposed position, WD 307 E5-10.
38. TNA WO 169/7020.
39. This was No.28 Battery, Moyse-Bartlett, *The King's African Rifles*, p.588.
40. WD AIR 27, vol. 30, pp.13–14; Shores, p.291.
41. Dimoline, p.18.
42. UWH 126, 1708.
43. GETCOL, SEACOL AND VOLCOL together were named Operation *Esmé A*, WD 304 A4; Account of Corporal Smit, W.D. 307 E5-12.
44. Croft-Cooke, p.99.
45. Gandar Dower, p.46.
46. WD 302, First City Regiment, *Esmé* Operations – 10 September to 20 September 1942.
47. Buckley, p.201.
48. F. Boyle, *A Brief Survey of Operations*; UWH 126.
49. WD vol. 302, First City Regiment, *Esmé* Operations – 10 Sept. to 20 Sept. 1942.
50. A. Bintliff, *Nossi Bé: The Attack and After*, p.7.
51. Page, p.123.
52. UWH, vol.126, p.1611.
53. UWH, vol.126, p.1612.

Chapter 10: "Death to the Traitors of Vichy"

1. Emerton, p30.
2. *Naval Staff History*, vol. III, p.27.
3. Sturtivant, *The Swordfish Story*, p.119.
4. The exchange of messages went as follows:
   Birmingham: "Do not fire. Order troops to remain in barracks. Envoy is being sent."
   Chef du Région: "Do not send personnel for we have orders to defend the town."
   Birmingham: "Unless you consent to receive our envoy under white flag within half an hour, I shall be forced to commence bombardment to cover landing of troops."
   Chef du Région: "We require extension of time limit."

Birmingham: "I am sending envoy in boat with white flag. If you open fire I shall at once bombard." Gandar Dower, p.61.

5. Hammerton, p.2245; Buckley, p.202.
6. Emerton, p.29.
7. P. Calvert, *Rings on my Sleeve*, p.27.
8. Gandar Dower, p.65.
9. Mullally, p.388; Gandar Dower, p.66.
10. J. Kemp, p.91.
11. P. Kemp, *The Red Dragon*, p.113.
12. Buckley, p.203.
13. Hammerton, p.2246; Gandar Dower, p.44.
14. Page, p.123.
15. S.H.A.T. 8H 105 d1, telegram from Guillemet to l'Etat-Major des Colonies.
16. Moyse-Bartlett, p.592; Report of B.J. Stubbins, TNA WO 169/7034.
17. Simpson Jones Documents, Department of Documents Imperial War Museum.
18. Hammerton, p.2246.
19. Grafftey-Smith, p.59.
20. Thomas, *The French Empire at War*, pp.147–9.
21. TNA PREM 3/265/10, Eden to Churchill, 29 August 1942.
22. Grafftey-Smith, pp.63–5.
23. *The Times*, 29 October 1942.
24. M. Hickey, *The Unforgettable Army*, p.72.
25. Buckley, p.205; J. & D. Penrith, *Madagascar*, p.145; UWH, vol.126, pp.1642–3. The occupation of Tulear was Operation *Rose*. The other naval vessels involved in this operation were HMS *Inconstant*, HMNS *Vangalen*, and HMAS *Napier*, Platt "Operations of East Africa Command", p.3728; *Naval Staff History*, vol. III, p.28; The Vichy coaster, *Maréchal Galliéni*, was intercepted as it left Tulear and was taken to Durban, WD 301, *7 S.A. Infantry Brigade Intelligence Summary No.7*.
26. Gandar Dower, p.39.
27. Gandar Dower, p.38.
28. WD 307 E5-10, Account of A. Purvis; Gandar Dower, p.38.
29. *The Times*, 12 October 1942.
30. WD 307 E5-10, Account of A. Purvis.
31. Page, p.124; WD 307, E5-10, Account of D. Smit.
32. Account of D. Smit.
33. Report of 'D' Company, 1/6 K.A.R, TNA WO 169/7034.
34. WD AIR 27, vol. 30.
35. HMSO *Fleet Air Arm*, p.115.
36. TNA DEFE 2/230.
37. Platt, "Operations of East Africa Command", p.3719.
38. Moyse-Bartlett, pp.600–1.
39. WD 307 E5-10, Account of A. Purves.
40. E. Nativel, "*La 'Guérilla'*", p.56.
41. Hytier, p.350.
42. Shores, p.295.
43. Moyse–Bartlett, p.604.
44. Report of B.J. Stubbins, 1/6 KAR, 28/29 October TNA WO 169/7034.
45. Moyse–Bartlett, p.603.

46. Gandar Dower, p.92.
47. UWH, vol.126, pp.1642–4, *Detachment of 88 Field Coy. Attached to 'A' Company Pretoria Rifles*.
48. Moyse-Bartlett, p.607; Annet, *Aux heures troublées*, p.206; Details of the surrender terms can be found in Lord Rennel of Rodd, p.218.
49. Grafftey-Smith, p.56.
50. R. James, Vol. VI, p.6696.
51. C. Williams, pp.188–9. Lord Rennell, *British Military Administration*, pp.233–7; R. Osborne, *World War II in Colonial Africa*, p.270.
52. Lord Rennell, p.237. According to Thomas, *French Empire at War*, p.152, Legentilhomme's title was "High Commissioner of French Possessions in the Indian Ocean"; L. Woodward, *British Foreign Policy in the Second World War*, p.329.
53. Thomas, *The Historical Journal*, 39, 4, p.1072.
54. Moyse-Bartlett, p.608.
55. Dimoline, Appendix 'A'.
56. Hammerton, p.2246.
57. Gandar Dower, pp.107–8.
58. Buckley, p.207.
59. Moyse-Bartlett, p.608.
60. Between them, 16 Squadron SAAF and 1433 Flight conducted operational flights on every day of the campaign, undertaking a total of 230 sorties, Dimoline, Appendix "A".
61. Jackson, p.151.
62. Aron, p.387.
63. Buckley, p.207.
64. Mulally, p.389. 'Sickle cell syndrome', present in some African genes, produces immunity to malaria.
65. UWH 126, 1723 & 1726.
66. Page, pp.130–1; Breldford, p.87.
67. Page, pp.131–2.
68. The entire battalion was disarmed and some 300 stood trial. Sentences of between three and fifteen years were handed out. The CO, Colonel Yates, was sent back to Britain. A. Jackson, "The Madagascar Mutiny of the First Battalion the Mauritius Regiment, December 1943" *Journal of the Society for Army Historical Research*, No.323, Autumn 2002, pp.232–50; G Sauzier, *Les événements qui ont marché l'arrivée du bataillon Mauricien à Diego Suarez en 1943*.
69. The seaplanes landed in the Bay de Gaullois and were tended by the Marine Craft Unit of No.26 Squadron based at Chameleon Camp, which is about 1.7 miles S.W. of Antsiranana, Testimony of R. Walter.

Chapter 11: "Incalculable Consequences"

1. Aron, p.420.
2. W. Stevenson, *A Man Called Intrepid*, p.319.
3. Jackson, pp.55–6.
4. Churchill, *Hinge of Fate*, p.212.
5. Gandar Dower, Preface; Festing's report is in TNA ADM 199/937.
6. Harrison, p.367; Grafftey-Smith, p.70; TNA FO 371/36203 & 36204. Testimony of A.L. Brown, p.244.

7. Graphite absorbs neutrons and allows atomic experiments to be controlled, E. Fermi, *The Chain-Reacting Pile*: Report on the Los Alamos Conference 15–24 April 1943.

8. P. Allen, *Madagascar*, p.45; Lush, p.145.

9. Of these losses, 175 were the result of German U-boat action, with the Germans using the Japanese naval base at Penang, Slader, p.169.

10. Mayotte was the base for four Catalinas and HMS *Albatross*, which acted as a seaplane tender. This force operated in conjunction with two destroyers against enemy submarines in the Mozambique Channel, *Naval Staff History*, vol. III, p.10; Testimony of J. Howell.

11. H. Probert, *The Forgotten Air Force*, pp.142, 196 & 199; J. Slader, *The Fourth Service*, p.169. The aircraft were from 259 and 265 squadrons, see N. Franks, *Search, Find and Kill*, pp.260–1; A. Hendrie, *Flying Cats*, p.85; P. Kemp, *U-Boats Destroyed*, p.142.

12. Thomas, *The Historical Journal*, 39, 4, p.1050.

13. De Gaulle, p.356.

14. Kersaudy, pp.192–3.

15. Thomas, *The Historical Journal*, p.1066.

16. TNA PREM 3/265/11.

17. Grafftey-Smith, p.55; I. Ousby, *Occupation. The Ordeal of France 1940–1944*, p.309; Moulins, *Magazine 39–45*, No.214, p.26; Darrieus & Quéguiner, p.284.

18. Tute, pp.206–7.

19. TNA ADM 1/14315.

20. Personal file of Percy Henry Mayer, TNA HS 9/1011/7; Harrison, p.367.

21. Fisher Papers, Vol. 73, ff.342 & 348.

22. M. Glover, *That Astonishing Infantry*, p.195.

23. J. Kemp, pp.96–8.

24. TNA CAB 79/21, COS (42) 171st (8).

25. Osborne, p.244.

26. J. and D. Penrith, p.25.

27. Turner, Gordon-Cummings & Betzler, pp.115–6.

28. J. Butler, *Grand Strategy*, vol. III, pp.486–7; Harrison, p.354.

29. Turner, Gordon-Cumings & Betzler, p.117; Buckley, p.166.

30. Butler, *ibid*, pp.484–5 and 491.

31. P. Kemp, *The Red Dragon*, p.98.

32. Interestingly, in native rural areas of South Africa the rumour was spread that if the Japanese invaded South Africa the blacks would be liberated from "white slavery", Jackson, p.54.

33. De Gaulle, p.333; S.M.H. TTD 772.

34. A. Wessels, "South Africa and the War Against Japan", pp.9–10.

35. J. Van der Poel, *Selections from the Smuts Papers*, Volume VI, p.364.

36. TNA CAB 121/623, JP (42) 435, 23 April 1942.

37. TNA CAB 81/107, J.I.C. (42) 152; CAB 81/108, JI.C (42) 160 (0).

38. Harrison, p.358. Woodburn Kirby, p.58; Butler, p.491.

39. G. Weinberg, *A World at Arms*, p.307.

40. H. P. Wilmott, *The Barrier and the Javelin; Japanese and Allied Pacific Strategies, February to June 1942* (Annapolis 1983), cited in Simpson & Somerville, p.354.

41. Turner, Gordon-Cummings & Betzler, pp.141–2.

42. It is now known that Hitler had not planned to seize the French fleet, see Spears, *Assignment to Catastrophe*, p.576.

43. Stevenson, p.309; Paxton, p.313.

44. Churchill, *Hinge of Fate*, p.212; *The Times*, 12 May 1942.

45. Churchill told Wavell that "only in China can the Japanese obtain a major decision this year", *Hinge of Fate*, pp.163–4.
46. Quoted in Jackson, p.31.
47. *Naval Staff History*, vol.III, p.28; Danchev & Todman, p.254.
48. Thomas, *The Historical Journal*, 39, 4, p.1054.
49. Overy, pp.136–7.
50. Gilbert, *Road to Victory*, p.81.
51. Dinan, pp.216 & 232–3.
52. Thomas, *French Empire at War*, pp.153–4.
53. B. Liddell Hart, *History of the Second World War*, p.248.
54. Hytier, p.348.
55. Y. Buffetout, "Opération Ironclad, L'invasion de Madagascar", *Marines & Forces navales*, No.66, Avril/Mai 2000, p.52.
56. P. Auphan, *The French Navy in World War II*, p.204.

Bibliography

Primary Sources

Unpublished Documents

Museum of the Queen's Lancashire Regiment, Fulwood Barracks, Preston: Memoirs of Major R.J. Manners, 2nd Battalion South Lancashire Regiment, *My War Years*.

Museum of the Queen's Own Highlanders, Fort George, Inverness: Memoirs of Lieutenant Ronald Morton, 6th Battalion Seaforth Highlanders.

Fleet Air Arm Museum, Yeovilton:
Squadron Diaries of Nos.881 and 888 Naval Air Squadrons.

The Franklin D. Roosevelt Library, New York:
The Roosevelt papers (NLR–MR–FDRWSC–1942).

The King's Royal Hussars Museum, Peninsula Barracks, Winchester:
The Royal Hussars Journal, 1990, "Madagascar and the Special Service Squadrons".

Liddell Hart Centre for Military Archives, King's College London:
Collected Papers of Colonel S.C. Aston:
Field Security Orders – IRONCLAD;
Report on the Interrogation of German and Italian prisoners, 16 June 1942.
W.A. Dimoline, *An Account of 22 E.A. Infantry Brigade, 10 September–6 November 1942*.

Lambeth Palace Library, London:
The collected papers of:
Bishop Lang, Vol. 184;
Bishop Fisher, Vols. 67 & 73.

Department of Documents at the Imperial War Museum, London:
Calvert, P., *Rings on my Sleeve* (unpublished memoir).
Emerton, H.W., *Unfeignedly Thankful* (unpublished memoir, 1988).
Helm, D.O., (unpublished memoir).
Knight, W.S., *Some Memories of the Second World War* (unpublished memoir).
Legg, H., *The Turn of the Tide* (unpublished memoir).
Patterson, J.H. (unpublished memoir).
Simpson Jones; Collection of documents and letters relating to his military service.

Documents held at the Château de Vincennes, Paris:

Service historique de l'armée de terre
S.H.A.T. 1 P 34 – dossier 6; *Etude sur la défense de Madagascar March 1941.*
  2 P 12 – dossier 5; *Madagascar – Situation, défense, attack anglais.*
  8 H 82 – dossier 3; *Secretariat d'état aux Colonies.*
    – dossier 4; *Bataille de Diégo-Suarez.*
  8 H 83 – dossier 6; *Situation des effectifs aux Colonies à la date du 1er Avril 1942, 11 June 42.*
  8 H 105 – dossier 1; *L'attaque de Diégo par les Forces Britanniques au cours des 5,6 et 7 mai 1942.*

Service historique de la Marine
S.H.M. TTD 772, Marine à Madagascar, Operations à Diégo-Suarez.

Documents held at the Department of Defence, Documentation Centre, Pretoria, South Africa:
Union War History vol. 126, NAREP, MAD 1.
A. Bintliff, *Nossi Bé: The Attack and After* (unpublished memoir).

War Diaries of the following units:

Reference no.	Dates covered (1942)	Unit
WD AIR 23/6587		Narrative of SAAF
WD AIR 27	Sept–November	16 Squadron. SAAF
WD 301 A5/A6	June–October	7 SA Infantry Bde HQ
WD 302 C16	September	First City Regiment
WD 302 B10	September	6 Field Regiment, SAA
WD 303 A3/A4	Sept–October	"A" Sqdn., 1st ACC
WD 303 B8	September	1st Pretoria Highlanders
WD 304 A4	September	Pretoria Regiment
WD 305 A4	September	88th Field Company SAEC
WD 307 E5	October	First City Regiment
WD AIR 23/6587		Narrative of SAAF Operations in Madagascar, Preparatory Period: '*Lunatic*' and '*Sugarcane*' Operations.

Documents held in The National Archives (TNA), Kew, London:

Admiralty Records
ADM 1/14315   DSC for Lieutenant Booker RNVR/SOE.
ADM 199/3527   East Indies Station War Diaries.
ADM 199/937   Operation *Ironclad* diaries and reports.
ADM 202/363   Report of Captain Price Royal Marines
ADM 202/395   Orders for Diversionary Operation off Ambodi-Vahibe
ADM 202/397   121 Force Operational Instructions
ADM 203/60   Operation IRONCLAD – A lecture, by Lt.-Commander G.G. Butler
ADM 202/307   Royal Marines, War Diaries

ADM 203/355	Administrative Preparations for Operation IRONCLAD.
ADM 203 394–397	Force 121, Instructions, intelligence notes, assessments and War Diary.
ADM 199/1277	Madagascar: Capture and Policy.
ADM 207/11, 26/37	Fleet Air Arm Squadron Diaries of No.810 Squadron; No.827 Squadron, and No.880 Squadron.
ADM 223/550 & 551	Operations IRONCLAD and BONUS.
ADM 14315	Reconnaissance work in preparation for Allied Occupation of Madagascar.

Cabinet Office Records

CAB 79 & 80 COS (40), (41), (42).	Chiefs of Staff Committee papers.
CAB 81/107 JIS	1 March 1942–30 April 1942.
CAB 81/167	War Cabinet, Joint Intelligence Sub-Committee.
CAB 81/127B	Proposals by Col. Stanley, Operation IRONCLAD, Note on cover.
CAB 84 JP (40), (41), (42).	Joint Planning Staff reports.
CAB 84/43	Madagascar, Draft Report by the Joint Planning Staff.
CAB 102/650	W. Mackenzie, *History of the Special Operations Executive*.
CAB 106/674	Report by GOC 121 Force.
CAB 106/749	Report by Capt. R. W. Roberts (Master SS *Oransay*).
CAB 120/535–38	Minister of Defence Secretariat.
CAB 121/622	Plans for the capture of Madagascar – Volume I (19 November 1940–4 April 1942).
CAB 121/623	Plans for the capture of Madagascar – Volume II (7 April 1942 to 20 July 1942).

Ministry of Defence Records

| DEFE 2/230 | Intelligence Report on the Madagascar Operation. |
| DEFE 2/319 | Operations in Madagascar, No.5 Commando. |

War Office Records

WO 106/3624	Operation *Ironclad* Order of Battle.
WO 170/30	War Diary, 2nd Btn East Lancashire Regiment.
WO 208/928, 929, 1493 & 1519	Intelligence Reports.
WO 208/929	Japan, possible attack on North West Australia.
WO 208/1518	M.I.3; Summary of Intelligence Reports on MADAGASCAR received between 31 December 1941 and 21 March 1942.
WO 208/1620	Summary of cables to Admiralty from Force F.
WO 373/29	Honours and Awards.

Foreign Office Records

FO 371/31897 & 31907	Proposed operation against Madagascar, and eventual administration of the territory.
FO 371/36203 & 36204	Economic situation in Madagascar.
FO 954/18A	Operation *Ironclad*.

Prime Minister's Office Records

PREM 3/120/7	Meetings with Foreign Secretary and Prime Minister.
PREM 3/265/1	Gen. de Gaulle and the Free French occupation of Madagascar.
PREM 3/265/6	Policy in Madagascar after *Ironclad*.
PREM 3/265/10 & 11	Transfer of Madagascar to Free French.

Special Operations Executive Records

HS 3/21 & 3/22	Operation *Ironclad* SOE support.
HS 3/23	Reports on Operation IRONCLAD.
HS 9/1011/7	Personal File of Percy Henry Mayer.

Air Ministry Records

AIR 8/1135	Operation "Ironclad".
AIR 23/6587	South African Air Force, narrative of operations in Madagascar.
AIR 27/2387	No.806 Squadron Record Book.

War Diaries of the following Army units

PRO reference	Dates covered (1942)	Unit
WO 174/19	March–November	9th Field Regiment RA.
WO 174/21	March–October	19th Field Battery.
WO 174/22	March–November	20th Field Battery.
WO 174/23	May–November	28/76 Field Battery.
WO 174/24	March–June	455th Indp. Light Battery Det.
WO 174/27	August	145th LAA Troop.
WO 174/30	March–December	2nd East Lancs. Regt.
WO 174/31	March–December	2nd South Lancs. Regt.
WO 174/32	March–July	2nd Northamptonshire Regt.
WO 174/33	March–December	1st Royal Scots Fusiliers.
WO 174/44	March–June	2nd Royal Scots Fusiliers.
WO 174/45	March–June	6th Seaforth Highlanders.
WO 174/46	April–December	2nd Royal Welch Fusiliers.
WO 169/7029	Sept–November	1st King's African Rifles.
WO 169/7033	Sept–November	5th King's African Rifles
WO 169/7034	Sept–November	6th King's African Rifles

Memiors, Diaries, etc

Annet, A. *Aux heures troublées de l'Afrique française, 1939–43* (Paris, 1952).

Churchill, W. *The Second World War*, vol. IV, *The Hinge of Fate*. (London, 1951).

Croft-Cooke, R. *The Blood-Red Island* (London, 1953).

Danchev, A. and Todman, D. (editors), *War Diaries 1939–1945, Field Marshal Lord Alanbrooke* (London, 2002).

De Gaulle, C. *War Memoirs, Volume One, The Call to Honour, 1940–1942*. Translated by J. Griffin (London, 1955).

Dilks, D. (ed.) *The Diaries of Sir Alexander Cadogan 1939–1945* (London, 1971).

Gandar Dower, K.C. *Into Madagascar* (London, 1943).

Grafftey-Smith, L. *Hands to Play* (London, 1975).

Harvey, J. (ed.) *The War Diaries of Oliver Harvey 1942–1945* (London, 1978).

James, A. *No Easy Choices: A Personal Account of Life on the Carrier H.M.S. Illustrious 1940–1943* (Upton on Severn, 1994).

James, R.R., (ed.) *Winston S. Churchill, His Complete Speeches 1897–1963*, Volume VI, 1935–1942 (New York, 1974).

Kimball, W. (ed.) *Churchill & Roosevelt, The Complete Correspondence*, vol. I. (London, 1984).

Lush, M., *A Life of Service, The Memoirs of Maurice Lush 1896–1990* (Privately published in 1992).

Sauzier, G. *Les événements qui ont marché l'arrivée du bataillon Mauricien à Diégo Suarez en 1943*, (Mauritius, 1998).

Simpson, M. (ed.) with Somerville, J. *The Somerville Papers: Selections from the Private and Official Correspondence of Admiral of the Fleet Sir James Somerville* (Aldershot, 1995).

Spears, E. *Assignment to Catastrophe* (London, 1956).

Stockman, J. *Seaforth Highlanders 1939–45: A Fighting Soldier Remembers* (Somerton, 1987).

Van der Poel, J. (ed.) *Selections from the Smuts Papers*, Vol.VI, December 1934–August 1945, (Cambridge, 1973).

Newspapers, reports and other contemporaneous documents

Crockford's Clerical Directory, London, 1941.

Evening Standard: 14, 18, 23, 24 March 1942; 21 April 1942; 5, 6, 7, 8, 11, 13 15 May 1942.

Platt, W., "Operations of East Africa Command, 12th July, 1941 to 8th January, 1943", *Report on the Los Alamos Conference*, 15–24 April 1943.

Supplement to *The London Gazette*, 17 July, 1946.

Syfret, E.N. "The Despatch of Rear-Admiral E. N. Syfret", Supplement to *The London Gazette*, 4 March 1948.

The Daily Express, 11 June 1942.

The Daily Mail, 28 May 1942.

The Daily Telegraph, 6, 8,19 & 25 May & 12 September 1942.

The Times, May through to December 1942.

The Pioneer: First British Newspaper In Madagascar, Wednesday May 20 1942.

War Illustrated, 2 April 1942; 29 May 1942; 12 June 1942; 2 October 1942.

The War In Pictures: Third Year, Oldhams Press, London, 1942.

Thursfield, H.G. (ed). *Brassey's Naval Annual 1948*, "Fuehrer Conferences on Naval Affairs", London, 1948.

Secondary Sources

Official reports and histories

Admiralty Historical Section, C.B. 3303 (3), *Naval Staff History, Second World War, War with Japan*, Volume III, 1956.

Battle Summaries No.16. Naval Operations at the capture of Diego Suarez (Operation "*Ironclad*") May 1942.

Cabinet Office Historical Section, TNA ADM 239/213 *History of the Special Operations Executive*, Vol. II, pp.498–500. TNA CAB 102/650.

Garnett, D. *Political Warfare Activities Carried Out by the Departments E.H. and S.O.1. and P.W.E.* TNA CAB 102/610. 1947.

Lemoine, H. *Inventaire des archives de Madagascar et ses dépendances* (Château de Vincennes, 1995).

Notes from Theatres of War, No.9, Madagascar 1942. TNA WO 106/3611.
S.O.E. Reports to the Cabinet, "The Operations in Madagascar" and "An Account of S.O.E Operations in Madagascar". HQ File 50, TNA HS 8/242.

HMSO Publications
Buckley, C., *Five Ventures: Iraq-Syria-Persia-Madagascar-Dodecanese* (London, 1954).
Butler, J.R.M., *History of the Second World War: Grand Strategy, Volume III*, Part II (London, 1964).
Combined Operations Command, *Combined Operations, 1940–1942* (London, 1943).
Fleet Air Arm – The Admiralty Account of Naval Air Operations (London, 2001).
Joslen, H.F. *Orders of Battle. Second World War 1939–1945*, vols.I & II (London 1960).
Hinsley, F.H. *British Intelligence in the Second World War: Volume Two, Its Influence on Strategy and Operations* (London, 1981) and *Volume Four, Security and Counter-Intelligence* (London, 1990).
M. Howard, *British Intelligence in the Second World War: Volume Five, Strategic Deception* (London, 1990).
Ministry of Information, *The Royal Marines: The Admiralty Account of Their Achievement, 1939–1943* (London, 1944).
Rodd, Lord Rennell of, *British Military Administration of Occupied Territories in Africa, during the years 1941–1947* (London, 1948).
Roskill, W. *The War at Sea, 1939–1945: Volume Two, The Period of Balance* (London, 1956).
Ships of the Royal Navy, Statement of Losses During the Second World War, 3rd *September 1939 to 2nd September 1945*.
Woodburn Kirby, S. *History of the Second World War. The War Against Japan: Volume II, India's Most Dangerous Hour* (London, 1958).
Woodward, L. *British Foreign Policy in the Second World War*, vol. I. (London, 1962), vol. II (London, 1971).

Articles
Buffetout, Y., "Opération Ironclad. L'invasion de Madagascar". *Marines & Forces navales*, No.66, Avril/Mai 2000, pp.50–7.
Clayton, J., "The South African Air Force in the Madagascar Campaign". *The South African Military History Society Military History Journal*, Vol.9, No.2.
Evetts, M.J., "Return to Madagascar, May 1992". *The Journal of the Royal Highland Fusiliers*, Winter 1992.
Fletcher, D., "The Flying Tank". *Military Illustrated Magazine*, September 1996.
Harrison, E., "British Subversion in French East Africa, 1941–42: SOE's Todd Mission", *English Historical Review*, vol. CXIV, No.456, April 1999.
Moulins, J., "Diego-Suarez, 5–8 mai 1942, Opération Ironclad", *Magazine 39–45*, No.212, Mai 2004 and No.214, Juillet 2004.
Jackson, A., "The Madagascar Mutiny of the First Battalion The Mauritius Regiment, December 1943". *Journal of the Society for Army Historical Research*, No.323, Autumn 2002.
Nesbit, R., "The Majunga Raid". *Aeroplane Monthly*, March & April 1995.
Nativel, E., "La 'Guérilla' des troupes Vichystes à Madagascar en 1942", *Revue Historique Des Armées*, No.210, March 1998.
Pepin-Lehalleur, J. "'Ironclad' – Les Britanniques S'emparent de Diégo-Suarez", *Historia Magazine 2ᵉ Guerre Mondiale*, No.39.

Stockman, J., "Madagascar 1942" *British Army Review*, No.82 April 1986 & No.83, August 1986.

Thomas, M., "Imperial Backwater or Strategic Outpost? The British Takeover of Vichy Madagascar 1942". *The Historical Journal*, 39, 4 (1966).

Voller, R., "The Assault on Madagascar, 5 May 1942". *The Bulldozer*, No.9, Autumn 2003.

Wessels, A., "South Africa and the War against Japan 1941–1945" *The South African Military History Society Military History Journal*, Vol.10, No.3.

Studies

A Book of Thanks to the South African Women's Auxiliary Service (A private publication, South Africa, 1980).

Allen, P., *Madagascar: Conflicts of Authority in the Great Island* (Oxford, 1995).

Aron, R., *The Vichy Regime 1940–44*. Translated by H. Hare (London, 1958).

Auphan, P. and Mordal, J., *The French Navy in World War Two* (Annapolis, 1952).

Bagnavco, E., *Submarines of World War Two* (London, 1973).

Banks, A., *Wings of the Dawning: The Battle for the Indian Ocean 1939–1945* (Malvern, 1996).

Bell, P.M.H., *France and Britain 1940–1994, The Long Separation* (Harlow, 1997).

Boyd, C. & Yoshida, A., *The Japanese Submarine Force and World War II* (Shrewsbury, 1996).

Bradt, H., *Madagascar, The Bradt Travel Guide* (Chalfont St Peter, 1999).

Breitman, R., *The Architect of Genocide: Himmler and the Final Solution* (Brandeis, Boston, 1992).

Breldford, W. V., *The Story of the Northern Rhodesia Regiment* (Bromley, 1990).

Bright, J. (ed.), *The 9th Queen's Royal Lancers 1936–1945: The Story of an Armoured Regiment in Battle* (Aldershot, 1951).

Brown J.A., *Eagles Strike. The campaigns of the South African Air Force in Egypt, Cyrenaica, Libya, Tunisia, Tripolitania and Madagascar* (Cape Town, 1974).

Brown, M., *A History of Madagascar* (Cambridge, 1995).

Bryant, A., *The Turn of the Tide, 1939–43* (London, 1957).

————., *Triumph in the West, 1943–1946* (London, 1959).

Clark, S., *The Man who is France, The Story of Charles de Gaulle* (London, 1960).

Darrieus, H. and Quéguiner, J., *Historique de la Marine française 1922–1942* (Saint-Malo, 1996).

Dawidowicz, L.S., *The War against the Jews, 1933–45* (London, 1975).

De Courcy, J., *Behind the Battle* (London, 1942).

Dinan, D., *The Politics of Persuasion; British Policy and French African Neutrality 1940–1942* (London, 1988).

Durtnell, C.S., *The Fifth British Division, 1939–1945* (London, 1959).

Ehrengardt, C.J. and Shores, C., *L'aviation de Vichy au Combat, les Campaignes Oubliées*, Vol.1 (Paris, 1983).

Farmer, A., *Anti-Semitism and the Holocaust* (Abingdon, 1998).

Fergusson, B., *The Watery Maze* (Holt, Rinehart and Winston, Austin, 1961).

Franks, N., *Search, Find and Kill* (London, 1995).

Gates, E.M., *End of the Affair, The Collapse of the Anglo-French Alliance, 1939–40* (London, 1981).

Gilbert, M., *History of the Second World War* (London, 1989).

————., *Road to Victory, Winston S. Churchill 1941–1945* (London, 1986).

Glover, M., *That Astonishing Infantry. The History of the Royal Welch Fusiliers 1689–1989* (London, 1989).

Goldhagen, D.J., *Hitler's Willing Executioners. Ordinary Germans and the Holocaust* (London, 1996).

Hammerton, J.A. (ed.), *The Second Great War* (London, 1946).

Hendrie, A. *Flying Cats. The Catalina Aircraft in World War II* (Shrewsbury, 1988).

Hickey, M., *The Unforgettable Army. Slim's XIVth Army in Burma* (Tunbridge Wells, 1992).

Hytier, A.D., *Two Years of French Foreign Policy, Vichy 1940–1942* (Conneticut, 1958).

Jackson, A., *War and Empire in Mauritius and the Indian Ocean* (London, 2001).

_____., "The Madagascar Mutiny of the First Battalion The Mauritius

James, W.M., *The British Navies in the Second World War* (London. 1946).

Jervois, W.J., *The History of the Northampton Regiment 1934–1948* (Northampton, 1953).

Keegan, J., *The Second World War* (London, 1989).

Kemp, J.C., *The Royal Scots Fusiliers 1919–1959* (Glasgow, 1963).

Kemp, P., *U-Boats Destroyed* (London, 1999).

_____., *Underwater Warriors: The Fighting History of Midget Submarines* (London, 2000).

Kemp, P.K., *The Red Dragon, The Story of the Royal Welch Fusiliers, 1919–1945* (Aldershot, 1960).

Kennett, B.B. and Tatman, J.A., *Craftsmen of the Army, The Story of The Royal Electrical and Mechanical Engineers* (Chatham, 1970).

Kersaudy, F., *Churchill and de Gaulle* (London, 1981).

Keyes, The Lord, *Amphibious Warfare and Combined Operations* (Cambridge, 1943).

Kimball, W., *Forged in War. Churchill, Roosevelt and the Second World War* (London, 1997).

Ladd, J.D., *Commandos and Rangers of World War II* (London, 1978).

_____., *By Sea By Land, The Authorised History of the Royal Marine Commandos, 1919–1997* (London, 1998).

Lamb, R., *Churchill as War Leader. Right or Wrong?* (London, 1991).

Leasor, J., *War at the Top* (London, 1959).

Lee, D., *Beachhead Assault: The Story of the Royal Naval Commandos in World War II* (London, 2004).

Liddell–Hart, B.H., *History of the Second World War* (London, 1970).

MacDermott, B., *Ships Without Names: The Story of the Royal Navy's Tank Landing Ships of World War Two* (London, 1992).

Macksey, K., *Commando Strike. The Story of Amphibious Raiding in World War II* (London, 1985).

Marder, A., *Operation Menace* (London, 1976).

Marder, A. Jacobsen, M. and Horsfield, J., *Old Friends New Enemies, The Royal Navy and the Imperial Japanese Navy, Vol. II: The Pacific War, 1942–1945* (Oxford, 1990).

Marrus, M.R., *The Holocaust in History* (London, 1989).

Messenger, C., *The Commandos 1940–1946* (London, 1985).

Mockler, A., *Our Enemies the French* (London, 1976).

Moyse-Bartlett, H., *The King's African Rifles. A Study in the Military History of East and Central Africa, 1890–1945* (Aldershot, 1956).

Mullaly, B.R., *Regimental History of the South Lancashire Regiment* (Bristol, 1952).

Neillands, R., *The Raiders, The Army Commandos 1940–1946* (London, 1990).

Néré, J., *The Foreign Policy of France from 1914 to 1945.* Translated by Translance (London, 1975).

Neville, P., *The Holocaust* (Cambridge, 1999).

Osborne, R., *World War II in Colonial Africa: The Death Knell of Colonialism* (Indianapolis, 2001).

Ousby, I., *Occupation. The Ordeal of France, 1940–1944* (London, 1997).

Overy, R., *Why the Allies Won* (London, 1995).

Page, M., *A History of the King's African Rifles and East African forces* (London,1998).

Paxton, R.O., *Vichy France: Old Guard and New Order 1940–1944* (New York, 1982).

Pendlebury, J.W., *History of the East Lancashire Regiment in the War 1939–45* (Manchester, 1953).

Penrith, J. And Penrith, D., *Madagascar, Mayotte & Comoros* (Oxford, 2000).

Ponting, C., *Churchill* (London, 1994).

Probert, H.., *The Forgotten Air Force, The Royal Air Force in the War Against Japan* (London, 1995).

Rigge, S., *World War II: War in the Outposts* (Alexandria, Virginia, 1980).

Robertson, K.G., (ed.), *War, Resistance and Intelligence* (Barnsley, 1999).

Rohwer J., *Axis Submarine Success of World War Two, German, Italian and Japanese Successes, 1939–45* (Greenhill, London, 1998).

Roskill, S.M., *War at Sea. H.M.S. Warspite* (London, 1974).

Shores, C., *Dust Clouds in the Middle East: The Air War for East Africa, Iraq, Syria, Iran and Madagascar, 1940–42* (London, 1996).

Slader, J., *The Fourth Service: Merchantmen at War 1935–45* (London, 1994).

Steenkamp, W. and Potgieter, H., *Aircraft of the South African Air Force* (London,1981).

Stevenson, W., *A Man Called Intrepid: The Secret War 1939–1945* (London, 1976).

Sturtivant, R., *The Swordfish Story* (London, 1993).

Sturtivant, R. and Ballance, T., *The Squadrons of the Fleet Air Arm* (London,1994).

Suret-Canale, J., *French Colonialism in Tropical Africa 1900–1945*, Translated by T. Gottheiner (London, 1971).

Sym, J., *Seaforth Highlanders* (Aldershot, 1962).

Thomas, M., *The French Empire at War 1940–45* (Manchester, 1998).

Thomas, R.T., *Britain and Vichy. The Dilemma of Anglo-French relations 1940–42* (London, 1979).

Thompson, J., *The Royal Marines: From Sea Soldiers to a Special Force* (London, 2000).

Turner, L., Gordon-Cummings, H.R., and Betzler, J., *War in the Southern Oceans 1939–45* (Cape Town, 1961).

Tute, W., *The Reluctant Enemies: The story of the last war between Britain and France 1940–1942* (London, 1990).

Waites, N. (ed.), *Troubled Neighbours: Franco-British Relations in the Twentieth Century* (London, 1971).

Ward, G.K. and Gibson, E., *Courage Remembered* (London, 1995).

Warner, G., *Iraq and Syria* (London, 1974).

Warner, P, & Seno, S., *The Coffin Boats: Japanese Midget Submarine Operations In the Second World War* (London, 1986).

Webster, P., *Pétain's Crime: The Full Story of French Collaboration in the Holocaust* (London, 2001).

Weinberg, G.L., *A World at Arms. A Global History of World War II* (Cambridge, 1994).

Williams, C., *The Last Great Frenchman* (London, 1993).

Wheatley, D., *The Deception Planners: My Secret War* (Hutchinson, London, 1980).

Williams, J., *The Guns of Dakar, September 1940* (London, 1976).

Wilmot, H.P., *The Great Crusade; A New Complete History of The Second World War* (London, 1989).

Index